Reaching Out to
Religious Youth

REACHING OUT TO RELIGIOUS YOUTH

A Guide to Services, Programs, and Collections

L. Kay Carman, Editor

Carol S. Reich, Assistant Editor

Libraries Unlimited Professional Guides for Young Adult
Librarians Series
C. Allen Nichols and Mary Anne Nichols, Series Editors

A Member of the Greenwood Publishing Group

Westport, Connecticut • London

Library of Congress Cataloging-in-Publication Data

Reaching out to religious youth : a guide to services, programs, and collections / L. Kay
    Carman, editor ; Carol S. Reich, assistant editor.
        p. cm. — (Libraries Unlimited professional guides for young adult librarians series)
        Includes bibliographical references and index.
        ISBN 0–313–32041–1 (alk. paper)
        1. Libraries—United States—Special collections—Religious literature. 2. Young adults'
    libraries—Activity programs—United States. 3. Public libraries—Services to
    teenagers—United States. 4. Religious literature—Bibliography. 5. Young adult
    literature—Bibliography. I. Carman, L. Kay. II. Reich, Carol S. III. Libraries Unlimited
    professional guides for young adult librarians.
    Z688.R4R43   2004
    027.62'6—dc22   2003069495

British Library Cataloguing in Publication Data is available.

Library of Congress Catalog Card Number: 2003069495
ISBN: 0–313–32041–1
ISSN: 1532–5571

First published in 2004

Libraries Unlimited, 88 Post Road West, Westport, CT 06881
A Member of the Greenwood Publishing Group, Inc.
www.lu.com

Printed in the United States of America

The paper used in this book complies with the
Permanent Paper Standard issued by the National
Information Standards Organization (Z39.48–1984).

10   9   8   7   6   5   4   3   2   1

CONTENTS

SERIES FOREWORD

We firmly believe in young adult library services and advocate for teens whenever we can. We are proud of our association with Libraries Unlimited and Greenwood Publishing Group and grateful for their acknowledgment of the need for additional resources for teen-serving librarians. We intend for this series to fill those needs, providing useful and practical handbooks for library staff. Readers will find some theory and philosophical musings, but for the most part, this series will focus on real-life library issues with answers and suggestions for front-line librarians.

Our passion for young adult librarian services continues to reach new peaks. As we travel to present workshops on the various facets of working with teens in public libraries, we are encouraged by the desire of librarians everywhere to learn what they can do in their libraries to make teens welcome. This is a positive sign since too often libraries choose to ignore this underserved group of patrons. We hope you find this series to be a useful tool in fostering your own enthusiasm for teens.

Mary Anne Nichols
C. Allen Nichols
Series Editors

PREFACE

To Bigotry No Sanction, To Persecution No Assistance

Congress shall make no law respecting an establishment of religion,
or prohibiting the free exercise thereof; or abridging the freedom of
speech, or of the press; or the right of the people peaceably to assemble, and to petition the Government for a redress of grievances.
(*Encyclopedia Americana*, 2002, v. 7, p. 669)

The First Amendment to the Constitution of the United States speaks to
me, the individual citizen, and for me, giving me the right to worship in
the manner I choose, or not to worship at all. It also gives me permission,
as a citizen, to insist that people of all religions be allowed to freely worship under the protection of my government. I consider this to be one of
the most fundamental freedoms in the world.

But with this freedom comes responsibility. The First Amendment
allows me to speak out for my friend who is not of my religion, without
fear of reprisal from my government, and it also gives me the responsibility to do so. It gives me the ability to confront and disarm those in current political power who attempt to impose their version of religion on
the people of my country, and it also imposes upon me the necessity to do

so. This first clause of the Constitution's First Amendment comes to me, and to every American citizen, laden with great liberty and great obligation.

In August of 1790, as President George Washington traveled through the nation seeking support for the adoption of the Bill of Rights, he exchanged letters with Moses Seixas, warden of the Hebrew congregation in Newport, Rhode Island. The letters read, in part:

To the President of the United States of America

Deprived as we heretofore have been on the invaluable rights of free Citizens, we now with a deep sense of gratitude to the Almighty...behold a Government...which to bigotry gives no sanction, to persecution no assistance—but generously affording to all Liberty of conscience, and immunities of Citizenship—deeming every one...equal parts of the great government machine...

For all these Blessings of civil and religious liberty which we enjoy under an equal benign administration, we desire to send up our thanks to the Ancient of Days, the great preserver of men...

Moses Seixas, Warden

George Washington, in his reply, echoed Seixas's words and, in doing so, gave credence and legitimacy to the hopes of that congregation for recognition as full citizens under the Constitution.

It is now no more that toleration is spoken of, as if it was by the indulgence of one class of people, that another enjoyed the exercise of their inherent natural rights. For happily the Government of the United States, which gives to bigotry no sanction, to persecution no assistance requires only that they who live under its protection should demean themselves as good citizens, in giving it on all occasions their effectual support.

May the Children of the stock of Abraham, who dwell in this land, continue to merit and enjoy the good will of the other Inhabitants, while everyone shall sit in safety...and there shall be none to make him afraid. May the father of all mercies scatter light and not darkness in our paths, and make us all in our several vocations useful here, and in his own due time and way everlastingly happy.

G. Washington (see Fisher, pp. 7–8)

The words of Moses Seixas and George Washington ring in my mind as I sit at my desk reading review journals, choosing the books and materials my public library will offer to its patrons. My hope is that, in the execution of my everyday tasks, I will give "to bigotry no sanction, to persecution no assistance."

Sue Plaisance

WORKS CONSULTED

Fisher, Leonard E. *To Bigotry No Sanction.* New York, NY: Holiday House, 1998.
"Text of the Constitution of the United States." *Encyclopedia Americana*, v. 7, pp. 665–671. Danbury, CT: Grolier Incorporated, 2002.

INTRODUCTION

The teenage years can be very introspective, and religion can be a large part of a teen's life. It is important that teens find a respectful reception at their local library and a collection that includes materials of interest; that they feel both welcome and that the library has something to interest them. It is also important that teens and others in the community have access to materials that inform them of beliefs other than their own, elucidating differences and similarities, and hopefully leading to an increased tolerance and respect among community members.

Although religion is often thought of as a private matter, it has its public aspects as well, including library service. Public libraries are charged to serve all facets of their communities, and it is important that they be prepared to serve the needs of the religious communities in their area.

This publication provides an overview of potential library service to teens of the major religious groups found in the United States. The chapters fall into two broad categories, Christian and non-Christian faiths, and are then ordered based upon the number of U.S. adherents for each religion: Protestant, Evangelical, Catholic, Latter-day Saint, Orthodox Christianity, Seventh-day Adventist, Jewish, Muslim, Buddhist, and Hindu. The first two chapters feature Protestants and Evangelicals separately. While rooted in the same traditions, there are enough differences between the two that they merit separate treatment.

The essays provide background information on the history and doctrine of these faiths and discuss the formative experiences faced by teens, as well as common misconceptions and stereotypes. They address what teens might be looking for in their local library with regard to their own religion, and they describe some potential programming and service ideas. They also provide guidance regarding selection criteria, the types of materials available for purchase, and their publishers. Bibliographies of suggested materials are included. The materials and suggestions found in the chapters provide a basis for library staff to begin their collection development and service, but none of the lists are exhaustive; it is expected that each library would do well to engage in a dialogue with their religious community and be responsive to their expressed requests and interests beyond the suggestions offered.

The authors of these essays drew primarily on their experiences as librarians as the basis for their chapter content. When possible, a librarian was selected to write a chapter concerning his or her personal faith. It was not always possible, however, to find this preferred combination. In one instance, the chapter on Orthodox Christianity, the authors are not librarians. The chapter on Islam was written by a woman who is not a Muslim, and the author of the chapters on Seventh-day Adventists, Buddhism, and Hinduism is not a member of any of the three religions discussed. In these cases, chapter content was vetted by a practicing member of the faith or a person in authority in the religious organization.

It was not within the scope of this publication to address library service to every religious group. For those readers whose local communities include religions not specifically addressed, the various suggestions, both for making contact with religious groups found in the chapters (*i.e.* the yellow pages, home schooling organizations, local ministry groups, etc.) and for collecting materials pertinent to local faiths, hold valid and may be successfully adapted for working with a wide variety of local religious groups.

Active marketing to religious groups may make some public librarians uncomfortable, but Mike Wessells provides a sensible perspective in his chapter on Evangelical Christians that is pertinent to all the religious groups covered in this book:

> Is library advocacy to one specific religious subgroup a blatant disregard for the neutrality of the public library? No, it is an example of targeted marketing, in the same way that publishing booklists for a specific subsection of the collection does not imply favoritism for that part of the collection. If Christian teens feel that "there is noth-

ing in the library for me" while other teens do not feel this way, surely this calls for attention to redress the balance. This is very different from endorsing one set of values as superior to another....With many evangelical Christians, separation of church and state is a sensitive issue. Feeling increasingly squeezed out of the public marketplace of ideas, they will point out that the phrase "separation of church and state" appears nowhere in the Constitution, but instead in a letter of Thomas Jefferson's imported into numerous court decisions. The First Amendment only prohibits governmental bodies, including publicly funded libraries, from favoring one set of religious beliefs over another. It does not prohibit religious expression in public places altogether.

So whether you are helping a teen find information on Jewish holidays, assisting Latter-day Saint or Evangelical Christian teens in finding a young adult novel with characters from their religious group, or helping an Orthodox Christian teen plan a youth ministry project, we hope this book provides useful information and serves as a catalyst in establishing or enhancing public library service to religious youth.

Carol Reich
Assistant Editor

1

PROTESTANTISM

Jenna and Stephen Miller

Protestantism—A group of Christian denominations

Beginnings:

The Protestant Reformation (early 1500s) divided Christianity into Protestants and Roman Catholics.

The Reformation began in 1517 when Martin Luther (a German monk) protested against practices of the Roman Catholic Church.

Beliefs and practices:

Protestants believe in Trinity (Father, Son, Holy Spirit); believe in Christ as Savior of mankind.

The Holy Bible (Old and New Testaments) is considered to be the word of God.

Demographics:

Approximately 165 million Protestants in the United States.

Includes several thousand denominations and sects that can differ slightly or greatly from one another.

(continued)

(continued)

Information point:

Christianity About.com. URL: http://christianity.about.com (accessed March 2004) Updated frequently; good starting point for Christian information and links.

Depending on your own religious affiliation, you may wonder why there are two chapters in this book about American Protestant Christians: "Protestantism" and "Evangelical Christianity." It is true that the term "Protestantism" generally encompasses all Christian churches that separated from Rome during the Reformation (and beyond), as well as the many Christian denominations that have splintered from other Protestant churches. European movements initiated by church leaders during the sixteenth century first earned the label "Protestant" for their rejection of certain doctrines and positions of the Roman Catholic Church, most notably the issues of papal authority, and which sources could be relied upon for divine revelation.

The basic beliefs of all Protestant churches are an emphasis on the Christian Bible as the revealed word of God, salvation by faith, and the universal priesthood of believers, where laity is equally able (along with clergy) to discern God's will, pray, minister, and evangelize. Considering the focus placed on the individual by these beliefs, it is no wonder that Protestantism has evolved historically into an extremely varied faith, with literally thousands of denominations (worldwide, there are over 33,000, according to the *World Christian Encyclopedia*). Protestantism is, indeed, a collective term, rather than one that refers to a specific church or organization. When their numbers are calculated together, Protestants comprise the largest religious grouping in the United States, with fifty-six percent of the total population in 2000, according to a Gallup poll of April 2001 (U.S. Census Bureau, *Statistical Abstract of the United States,* 2002, table 64).

Evangelicalism encompasses one portion of the American Protestant churches. It is also a term that signifies different things to different people. However, since the Evangelical Christian Publishers Association (ECPA) dominates so much of the Christian book market, and so many library patrons looking for "Christian" materials would designate themselves as evangelical Christian, you will see more information particular to evangelicalism in a separate chapter.

This chapter focuses on the historical American Protestant churches, sometimes referred to as "mainline" or "mainstream": Lutheranism, Presbyterian/Reformed, Episcopalian, and Methodists/Wesleyan. Keep in mind that although these groups may be labeled "mainstream," primarily because they have been large groups in this country for a long time, they represent a wide variety of current practices, doctrines, and political or moral views. Indeed, there are so many separate "synods," "conferences," or individual parishes that operate from common historical routes that it is impossible to singularly categorize Protestantism as one entity.

In the next section, we discuss a brief history of these four groups, mentioning some distinctive practices or doctrines. Since it is not our intent to provide you with a theological work or book about religious history, but rather a guide to serving Protestant young adult library patrons, we refer you to the following sources for in-depth descriptions of the various Protestant denominations: Mead's *Handbook of Denominations in the United States* and Dillenberger and Welch's *Protestant Christianity,* particularly their chapter entitled "What is Protestantism?" Additionally, more information regarding the basic approaches to the worship service and identifying doctrines within these denominations can be found in *How to be a Perfect Stranger: A Guide to Etiquette in Other People's Religious Ceremonies.*

HISTORY AND CORE BELIEFS AND VALUES

The following Protestant denominations are listed in chronological order according to their historical foundings:

Lutheran

Lutheranism is one of the oldest Protestant movements, dating back to early sixteenth-century Germany and to the Catholic priest Martin Luther's reforms of conditions in the Roman Church. It is the largest Protestant denomination in the United States. In the early seventeenth century, Lutherans, mostly from Germany and Scandinavia, migrated to the United States. They have since comprised a large portion of the population in some areas, particularly in the Midwest. Over time, groupings called "synods" or "conferences" have formed or merged to yield the groups of today. The two largest national groups are the Evangelical Lutheran Church in America (ELCA) and the Lutheran Church, Missouri Synod (LCMS), which together comprise at least ninety percent of Lutheran membership in this country. Most Lutheran synods practice a liturgical form of worship and look to the Bible, as well as to Luther's extensive spiritual writings, for doctrine. There can be clear differences of opinion among synods about contemporary political and moral issues (*e.g.,* homosexual clergy and abortion), as well as about church practices and teachings (*e.g.,* contemporary worship formats, female clergy, and communion practices).

Presbyterian and Reformed (the Calvinist traditions)

The Presbyterian Church is another of the oldest Protestant denominations, tracing its history to the French Reformer John Calvin, a contemporary of Martin Luther. It came to the United States chiefly through British and Scots-Irish settlers beginning in the seventeenth century. The largest denominations today are the Presbyterian Church in America and the Presbyterian Church (USA). Other churches are the Associate Reformed Presbyterian, the Bible Presbyterian, the Cumberland Presbyterian, the Evangelical Presbyterian, the Orthodox Presbyterian, the Reformed Presbyterian Church of North America, and the Second Cumberland Presbyterian Church in the United States.

The Reformed churches also specifically follow Calvinist tradition, having originated in sixteenth-century Switzerland with the teachings of Zwingli, Calvin, and Melanchthon, prominent Christian reformers. Related groups originated in the Netherlands, Belgium, and other European countries. Dutch immigrants in particular brought the Reformed tradition to America. Contemporary Reformed groups are the Christian Reformed Church in North America, the Hungarian Reformed Church in America, the Netherlands Reformed Congregations, the Protestant Reformed Churches in America, the Reformed Church in America, and the Reformed Church in the United States.

Episcopal/Anglican

The Episcopal/Anglican churches in America trace their roots to the Anglican Church of England, which originated during the reign of Henry VIII. The Protestant Episcopal Church, the name first used in America, took root primarily with British settlers in the American South. Over time, several groups broke from the original American Episcopal church over doctrinal issues. The largest groups existing today are the African Orthodox Church, the Anglican Orthodox Church, the Episcopal Church, and the Reformed Episcopal Church. Episcopal/Anglican worship services are generally high liturgical; African American Episcopal churches have a looser structure and a greater emphasis on gospel music. Today, even among churches in the largest group, the Episcopal Church, there is sometimes wide diversity in members' views on doctrine and contemporary moral and political issues.

Methodist and Wesleyan

The Methodist movement was inspired by teachings of the English Anglican priest John Wesley and came to the United States via British settlers in the latter part of the eighteenth century. Today there are twenty-three Methodist denominations practicing in the United States. Some groups are part of African American church traditions that began in the late eighteenth century over charges of racial discrimination against Blacks in Methodist congregations. The first official such denomination was established in 1816 as the African Methodist Episcopal Church. Today the primary African American Methodist denominations are African Methodist Episcopal (AME), African Methodist Episcopal Zion, Christian Methodist Episcopal, and the Union American Methodist Episcopal.

Other Methodist denominations can vary in their practices and level of conservatism. The groups include the Congregational Methodist Church: the Evangelical Methodist Church; the Free Methodist Church of North America: the Primitive Methodist Church, U.S.A; the Reformed Methodist Union Episcopal Church; the Southern Methodist Church; and the United Methodist Church, which is the largest. There is also the separate Wesleyan Church that, because of its strong abolitionist stance, broke from the American Methodist church in the nineteenth century.

FORMATIVE EXPERIENCES

All of the denominations covered in this chapter include in their teachings a confirmation experience for adolescents (and sometimes pre-adolescents). For these teens, the experience is an affirmation of their baptism within the church, and usually includes special instruction with a culminating ceremony often celebrated as part of a Sunday worship service. Confirmation is a rite of passage for teens to become adult members of the parish. Given the analytical skills and desire for spiritual exploration that occur in adolescent development, the churches consider confirmation a time for teens to make a serious, conscious choice to practice their faith. Some denominations draw from historical teaching texts, in addition to Scripture, to provide doctrinal instruction for confirmation candidates. For instance, in the past the Lutheran denominations almost always used Martin Luther's *Small Catechism* to teach church foundations to confirmands, but books like this are now used less often as part of the confirmation curriculum or are excerpted.

MISCONCEPTIONS AND STEREOTYPES

People can easily become entrenched in their own religious background and, with the variety of religious groups, opinions, and expressions in their country, it is no wonder that most people don't grasp the breadth and variety that is to be found in American Protestantism, even if they themselves are members of a Protestant church. Certainly, American concepts rooted in Protestantism, like the image of the stern, critical Puritan and the idea of the Protestant work ethic, continue to linger as part of the nation's self-definition, though they may have little connection with any particular current church body. Some in this country may carry the false notion that mainstream Christians are less serious about their faith than evangelical Christians, or especially than fundamentalists. Considering that many Protestants consider themselves evangelical Christians, and no less reverent, spiritual, or faithful than their Christian peers in other groups, the distinctions in the terms can become irrelevant. Some people are suspicious of, and uncomfortable with, the liturgical churches (especially Anglican/Episcopalian and some Lutheran groups) that often put more focus on sacraments and ritual. Even categorizing mainstream Protestants as "mainstream" contributes to the misleading idea that all of these churches participate in the mainstream of society, as if they were all middle-class and average. In truth, because of their large numbers and diversity, mainstream Protestant groups include people from many walks of life and backgrounds.

WHAT ARE PROTESTANT TEENS LOOKING FOR AT THE LIBRARY?

Just as with the general public, Protestant teenagers will likely have a variety of backgrounds and reading preferences, so not every book included will appeal to every teenager seeking material related to their faith.

Both authors were raised as Lutherans and have visited many other Protestant worship services. We have been part of interdenominational Bible study and community groups. However, to get a better grip on current young adult attitudes, we surveyed youth groups from four denominations about their reading tastes and conducted a discussion with one youth group. Generally, these teens knew about materials labeled as "Christian" but also read other genres. They did not feel influenced by their parents or peers to read only Christian materials. The teens read a wide variety of materials from both Christian and secular publishing markets.

Sometimes members of these denominations have a long family tradition of belonging to the denomination. These denominations all have a long history in the United States, as well as roots in European religious movements. Therefore, some of their religious practices are not only spiritually significant but are also part of the basic fabric of their family culture and history. In any church there are likely to be teens that are fully committed to their faith, those who hate church and are forced by their parents to participate, and those who fall between the two extremes. When considering how to serve young Christians in your library, keep in mind the wide variety of how teens involve their Christian faith in their lives, as well as the diversity of churches and their doctrines within Protestantism. There is no "one size fits all."

When it comes to materials concerning faith, there is a huge disconnect between most public libraries and the Christian families who are their patrons. Few teens or their families look to the public library to supply the kind of books they need to nourish their faith or that will allow them to incorporate their faith into their reading life. The vast majority of public libraries are either unfamiliar with the full breadth of contemporary Christian materials, or they are wary of including distinctly religious materials in their collections because of a strong stand on the separation of church and state. Almost exclusively, people of faith expect to buy religious materials from their church, Christian bookstores, or Christian catalog vendors like the Christian Book Distributors (CBD). Since churches encourage a strong spirit of community, materials may be borrowed from friends or a church lending library. Most Christians, however benevolently they feel about their library, do not expect it to have the Christian materials they want. The more we can connect with them and fulfill their requests, the more they will trust us to supply these materials.

Librarians who would like to succeed at providing more Christian materials for young adults need to communicate with various local Protestant parishes and/or significant community groups, moving beyond traditional methods of collection management and collection promotion by talking with people in the community. Important information about demand for materials will be gained, and new materials can be publicized to the people who most desire them.

Just as in the secular publishing market, younger teens are more likely to read series than are older teens. They have probably been exposed to short devotionals, Christian living books, and possibly magazines like *Brio* and *Breakaway* (both published by Focus on the Family). Older teens may also select more complex Christian classics, literary fiction, adult fantasy, and nonfiction. Teens from both groups are likely to own their own Bible, sometimes a special student or teen Bible edition, which is usually a standard Bible translation (like the New International Version [NIV], the New King James Version [NKJV], or the Living Bible) that is specially formatted for young people. These editions often include sidebar devotions or study notes that are directed toward young adults.

The Christian publishing world often experiences similar trends to the secular publishing world. Currently, one parallel is the adaptation and remarketing of a successful adult title for teenagers. Two examples are Lee Strobel's *The Case for Christ* and Bruce Wilkinson's *The Prayer of Jabez*. Secular publishing houses have been establishing religious/Christian divisions, or are publishing special lines of inspirational materials for teens. Some Christian publishers are owned by secular publishing groups; for example, Zondervan was recently purchased by HarperCollins. Selecting books by evangelical Christian publishers (of the Evangelical Christian Publishers Association, or ECPA) is not as essential to mainstream Protestant teens as it is to evangelical Christian teens. In fact, many mainstream Protestants are not interested in these publications, considering them too "black and white" or simplistic.

Regarding multimedia materials, keep in mind the significance of popular music in a teen's life. Contemporary Christian music has become a huge industry, with genres that parallel secular music. Specific artists and titles are not included in this chapter, but we do list two magazines for teens that focus on music and provide reviews. Annual awards are given to Christian music as well, which may assist in selection. The Dove Awards Web site is at http://www.doveawards.com (accessed March 2004).

BUILDING YOUR COLLECTION

As librarians, we like to be fair. We want to include everyone, and sometimes we end up promoting a universalistic attitude that offends people who are serious about their faith. Many Christians don't want recommendations of materials that are purportedly "Christian" but are only generically "spiritual," or are from another faith altogether. Materials are sometimes cataloged with a subject heading of "Christianity" or "Christian life" because they happen to include a religious theme or character. However, Christians may not feel that these materials portray the Christian faith accurately or respectfully. Mainstream Protestant teens are more likely than evangelical Christians or fundamentalists to accept materials published by secular publishers, particularly if they do not contain material that is offensive to their Christian values. They are also more likely to enjoy reading books about other religious traditions, including Roman Catholicism and world religions.

The teen years are a natural time of spiritual exploration and questioning and many young adults wish to explore their spirituality within the framework of their Christian beliefs. There are, however, few contemporary novels that reflect their life experiences. Secular young adult novels, in particular, commonly portray Christian characters with cynicism. Christians, and particularly clergy, in the secular market's young adult books are generally characterized as shallow, closed-minded, or hypocritical. Common portrayals are the predatory clergy, the hypocritical traveling preacher, or the closed-minded, book-banning school-board member. Teen characters in secular novels are rarely shown doing the normal things that many Christian teens do in real life: praying, attending youth group meetings, talking with friends about values and beliefs, or being involved in church activities.

Often a gap exists between the literary quality of the general secular young adult (YA) fiction market and the Christian YA fiction market. The Christian fiction market, and especially fiction for teens, is still relatively new, with most popular books for young adults being series, romances, historical sagas, and fast-paced adventure stories. The literary quality is similar to most secular books of the same genre, although the variety and quality of Christian materials continues to improve with time.

Reviews: Where Can I Find Them?

Reviews of Christian fiction are published regularly in *Library Journal* and *Booklist*. Special sections of certain issues of *Publishers Weekly* are devoted to religious publishing, including reviews of religious materials and current trends and topics in the industry. *School Library Journal, Publishers Weekly,* and *VOYA* all publish reviews of some new Christian materials for teens. Each issue of *CBA Marketplace*, the trade magazine of the Christian Booksellers' Association, and *Christian Retailing*, the "trade magazine of Christian retailing," includes reviews of Christian fiction and nonfiction, roughly divided by age. *Christian Library Journal*, previously published in print but now available only online, can be viewed by purchasing individual issues or by an inexpensive annual subscription.

Coverage of Christian materials is still inconsistent in library review journals, and sometimes reviewers of Christian materials take issue with the content of the materials because they themselves do not agree with the lifestyle or values, or find the characters "closed minded." Few libraries subscribe to selection aids specific to a Christian market. A brief comparison on First-

Search's Union List Web database shows holdings of *CBA Marketplace* at twenty to thirty libraries while a similar search of the library review journal *Booklist* indicates ownership at over 3,800 libraries. Christian materials are still a niche market in the broad scheme of selection work. However, as more people in our communities become interested in seeing Christian materials in the library, it becomes worthwhile to invest in tools that will help meet the demand. Though they are not review sources, it is important to mention Barbara Walker's *Developing Christian Fiction Collections for Children and Adults* and John Mort's *Christian Fiction* as bibliographic sources for librarians hoping to build up their collection of Christian materials.

Librarians naturally have to consider quality when ordering materials for their community. We rate a book's quality by traditional collection development standards, such as the number of starred reviews it has received. Considering that many Christian fiction titles have not been reviewed, however, we should broaden our criteria for selection. We must also consider customer demand. Public libraries are intended to offer materials that the community wants and needs. Libraries with significant demand for Christian titles should thoughtfully consider providing the materials their community requests, whether or not the books are well reviewed or have been reviewed at all.

Christian Review Publications

CBA Marketplace, formerly *Bookstore Journal*
P.O. Box 62000
Colorado Springs, CO 80962–2000
(800) 252–1950
URL: http://www.cbaonline.org (accessed March 2004)

The Christian Library Journal
P.O. Box 1309
Florence, OR 97439
E-mail: nlhesch@harborside.com (editor Hesch prefers e-mail correspondence to phone calls)
URL: http://www.christianlibraryj.org (accessed March 2004)
Includes 300 reviews of Christian books and media per issue.

Christian Retailing: The Trade Magazine of Religious Retailing,
    formerly *Christian Bookseller*
Strang Communications
600 Rinehart Road
Lake Mary, FL 32746

(407) 333–0600
URL: http://www.christianretailing.com (accessed March 2004)

Lutheran Libraries, journal of the Lutheran Church Library Association
122 W. Franklin Ave.
Minneapolis, MN 55404
(612) 870–3623

Plugged In
Focus on the Family
P.O. Box 15379
Colorado Springs, CO 80995
(800) 232–6459
URL: http://www.pluggedinonline.com (accessed April 2004)
Reviews films, popular music, and television from an evangelical
    perspective.

Christian Magazines That Include Reviews

Christianity Today
465 Gundersen Drive
Carol Stream, IL 60188–2498
(800) 999–1704
URL: http://www.christianitytoday.com (accessed March 2004)

Cornerstone
939 W. Wilson
Chicago, IL 60640
(773) 561–2450
URL: http://www.cornerstonemag.com (accessed March 2004)

Current Thoughts and Trends
NavPress
P.O. Box 469085
Escondido, CA 92046–9627
(760) 781–5219
URL: http://www.navpress.com/magazines/CTT/(accessed April
    2004)

True Tunes News
1710 Gen. George Patton Dr., #103
Brentwood, TN 37027
(615) 263–6300
URL: http://truetunes.com (accessed March 2004)
Reviews music and other current media from a Christian perspective.

Listservs

CHRISTLIT Sponsored by Bethel College, St. Paul, Minnesota. The listserv is "an open, moderated discussion list featuring the interrelations between Christianity and Literature." URL: http://listarc.bethel.edu/cgi-bin/wa?SUBED1= christlit&A=1 (accessed April 2004)

YALSA-BK Sponsored by the Young Adult Library Services Association (YALSA), a division of the American Library Association. Discussions of young adult literature with occasional discussions of Christian literature. URL: http://www.ala.org/yalsa/professional/yalsalists.html (accessed April 2004)

Indexes

Christian Periodical Index (CPI) Published three times a year, and produced by the Association of Christian Librarians, CPI provides access to English language articles and reviews written from an evangelical Christian perspective or of interest to the evangelical community. Coverage includes over one hundred selected publications.

TYPES OF BOOKS AVAILABLE
Fiction

As previously mentioned, many fiction genres offered by Christian publishers are similar to those issued to the general market. The most popular Christian fiction titles are usually offered as a series: romances, adventures, suspense-thrillers, mysteries, and historical sagas. As the market grows, more serious literary fiction is also being published, though that market is still small.

Modern Christian fiction does not usually focus on a particular denomination. Certain broad assumptions of Protestant faith do apply, including reliance upon Scripture as authority, and the acknowledgement that faith, redemption, and a relationship with Christ as Savior are crucial to a person's life.

There are several categories of religious fiction that may appeal to Protestant young adults. First, there are books issued by Christian publishing houses most obviously incorporating Christian faith. As stated previously, these may be popular with more conservative Protestant teen readers, but may not be as appealing to more liberal Protestants.

Second, there are books by professing Christians that are published by secular publishing houses. These sometimes include references to faith or to God but the characters' faith may have little to do with the story. Katherine Paterson and Madeline L'Engle, two famous authors in this category, have spoken about the ways that their Christian viewpoint and personal experiences of faith influence their writing. When the matters of faith included in the book are clouded or complex, or when the writer's personal faith is unorthodox, some patrons may be uncomfortable calling the material "Christian." Some of L'Engle's works present these issues; one example is her renowned book, *A Wrinkle in Time,* which includes a scene in which the characters mention the people in history who have been influences for good. Jesus is presented on the same level as Buddha and Einstein. Mainstream Protestants would probably view this book as a secular or "inspirational" book; they might read it, but they would not call it "Christian." More conservative elements would question L'Engle's religious orthodoxy. Other books in this second category, like the *Space Trilogy* by C.S. Lewis, are generally recognized as orthodox by mainstream Protestants. Evangelical vendors like Christian Book Distributors include these books in their catalogs. Christian vendors and bookstores are also increasingly stocking and marketing not only "Christian classics" like Lewis's *Chronicles of Narnia,* but also "family friendly" items, like L.M. Montgomery's *Anne of Green Gables,* that are issued by secular publishers.

Also of interest to Protestant teen readers are literary classics, such as books written by Austen, Bronte, Hardy, Hawthorne, Crane, Taylor Caldwell, and Lloyd C. Douglas. Although these books may not carry an overtly Christian message, the stories are rooted in Christian values, and they generally do not offend mainstream Protestant readers.

Finally, there are novels with spiritual themes that are written by people who do not profess to be practicing Christians. These books are often labeled "Inspirational Fiction," and they are often grouped with Christian fiction titles in the professional literature. It is books in this category that librarians need to be careful about recommending to patrons as "Christian." As stated earlier, sometimes these novels include negative, disrespectful, or stereotypical portrayals of serious Christians, and characters represented in this way may offend people who take their faith seriously.

In this chapter, we include materials primarily from the first category—items offered by Christian publishers. A few classics that are available through secular publishers are also mentioned.

Nonfiction, Magazines, Audio-Visual, and Web Sites

There is a broad spectrum of nonfiction topics available. The most popular materials for teens are devotionals, biographies of faith heroes, books that give insight into Christian living, and Bible translations.

There are many good magazines for Christian teenagers. Listed in the bibliography are those that are produced specifically by the mainstream Protestant denominations mentioned in this chapter, as well as non-denominational publications that would appeal to Protestant teens.

Audio recordings and video recordings, including DVDs, are also marketed for Christian teens. *Adventures in Odyssey* and *Radio Theater,* two radio dramas produced by Focus on the Family, dominate the audio recording market. Video recordings and DVDs are mostly classic family and historical films, as well as a few modern theatrical releases like *Left Behind* and a smattering of instructional recordings. Christian vendors like Christian Book Distributors often feature family movies like *Anne of Green Gables* or *The Robe,* even though the films were not produced for the Christian market.

Official Web sites of the various Protestant denominations have been included, when available. Some of these groups offer teen pages; others offer sections for people who work with teens. Also listed are some inter-denominational Christian Web sites for teens.

Historical Context: The Tradition of Christian Fiction

From the Reformation to the seventeenth century, young people of the Protestant faiths had almost no literature published specifically for their age group. Most families had a copy of the Bible at home, and there were tracts and pamphlets aimed at inspiring young girls and boys toward right living. Other tracts were designed to inform people of the "evils" of Papism (the schism of the Reformation still being fresh in the minds of former Catholics) and to educate the public in the new catechism of the Protestant church. These publications ranged in length from single broadsheets to more than one hundred pages.

The publication of John Bunyan's allegorical novel, *The Pilgrim's Progress,* in the mid-1600s, garnered an audience of young and old alike. This lyrical, powerful work, still readable today, illustrates the seductive powers of earthly pleasures, the weakness of man, the strength of God, and the redemptive power of Jesus Christ. The quest of the main character, Christian, was staple reading in households for hundreds of years. A full description of the influence of this seminal work can be found in Ruth K. MacDonald's book, *Christian's Children.*

The nineteenth century saw a great increase in Christian literature, especially fiction. Sermon novels, based on popular sermon topics of the day, entertained as well as provided education to both children and adults regarding Christian morals and virtues. Harriet Beecher Stowe's *Uncle Tom's Cabin* is the best known. An annotated list of sermon novels can be found in Leo O'Connor's book, *The Protestant Sensibility in the American Novel.*

Also appearing in the nineteenth century were three authors who influenced later Christian writers: Martha Finley, Louisa May Alcott, and George MacDonald. Though their books may have been read by mainstream audiences, their influence on later Christian works was important. They were, as well, an important reflection of the sensibilities of the times.

Finley, a Presbyterian, wrote the popular Elsie Dinsmore books featuring a young girl "whose faith and obedience to God's commandments uphold her in the great troubles she often faces" (Letterman, p. 35). The *Elsie* series, as well as another series by Finley about preteen Mildred Keith, have been recently adapted and reprinted and are enjoying a new popularity among younger teen girls. Elements of the *Elsie* books can be seen in the writings of such twentieth-century authors as Maude Hart Lovelace and Laura Ingalls Wilder.

Louisa May Alcott was brought up in a household where *Pilgrim's Progress* was read. This book was a great influence on her seminal work, *Little Women,* which has been seen as an allegory for Pilgrim's search (MacDonald, p. 68).

At about the same time, George MacDonald, a Scottish Anglican minister, began writing books for young adults. In *Phantastes, The Golden Key,* and *Lilith,* MacDonald wrote allegories of faith, fear, and atonement using the literary styles of fantasy and fairy tale to explore the tenets of Christian faith. Influenced by *Pilgrim's Progress* and German fairytales, MacDonald combined the deductive elements in Pilgrim's search and the pervading presence of God in the German folktales to create an imaginary depiction of Christian beliefs about the end of the world.

In the late 1800s and early 1900s, the social gospel movement became popular among American Protestant churches. A natural progression of the concepts fashioned in the sermon novels, this movement encouraged Christians to solve social problems within the framework of their faith. The social gospel movement provided Christian literature with one of its most popular novels, Charles M. Sheldon's *In His Steps.* With its premise of church members promising to always ask the question "What would Jesus do?" before making a decision, *In His Steps* was the precursor to the modern WWJD (What Would Jesus Do?) movement.

George Alfred (G. A.) Henty began a trend of writing realistic adventure novels with a decidedly Christian overview for young boys. Extremely popular during their initial publication, Henty's books have enjoyed a resurgence in readership with republication. The writing of realistic historical fiction began in earnest in the latter part of the nineteenth century with the publication of Lew Wallace's *Ben Hur.*

The Scottish writer George MacDonald was the single largest influence on C. S. Lewis, author of the extremely popular and critically acclaimed *Chronicles of Narnia* and *Space Trilogy* series. Lewis wrote of MacDonald, "I know hardly any other writer who seems to be closer, or more continually close, to the Spirit of Christ Himself. Hence his Christ-like union of tenderness and severity. Nowhere else outside the New Testament have I found terror and comfort so intertwined" (Lewis, preface pp. xxx–xxxi). Lewis' own novels, first published in the 1940s and 1950s, are considered classics by both Christians and non-Christians. They are thick with Christian parallels, with Christ thinly veiled as Aslan the lion. Young adults can enjoy the *Narnia* chronicles, approachable from an early age but meaningful throughout life, and also the *Space Trilogy,* a more complex and mature series.

Modern Christian fiction continued in the social gospel and Henty tradition of providing straightforward, realistic settings or contemporary situations to tell its story. The 1960s saw increasing publication of many books for young adults. One of them, Elizabeth Speare's *The Bronze Bow,* is an historical novel of a young man's contact with Jesus Christ and his apostles, and earned Speare the 1962 Newbery award. Even as Speare's book credentialed Christian fiction as having important literary value, the culture of the times saw the genre moving away from having been the mainstream to becoming an almost underground movement. Books that may have been read by all readers, regardless of whether they attended church or not, became important mostly to those families that stressed the values of their faith. Even though the content and the message of the books had not changed, society had, and so did publisher's attitudes toward what would sell.

Interestingly, at this same time there was an explosion in Christian music. Just as there was a parallel in the publishing world with an underground Christian market, so there was in rock music an underground movement of music with Christian themes and values. The underground spirit of revival in these books and music particularly appealed to young adults. Both of these small seeds of Christian art have fully blossomed in today's lively arena of Christian literature and music.

PUBLISHERS

Most publishers listed below require a credit application for the establishment of an account. The application may be returned to the publisher by mail or fax; a few companies will set up an account by phone. Once an account is established, most accept orders by mail, fax, phone, or Web.

Popular Christian teen titles can often be obtained through vendors like Baker & Taylor, Book Wholesalers (BWI), or Ingram. Vendors seldom supply the full catalog offered by Christian publishers, especially small press titles, so ordering directly from publishers will allow the greatest access to Protestant Christian materials. Libraries are generally given a discount when ordering directly from the publisher, but the percentage often depends on the dollar amount of the order. Most of these publishers regularly do business with public libraries, but some carry only a few library accounts, while others employ a public libraries sales representative. They all are interested in selling you their materials, however, and it is worthwhile to talk with them about their offerings.

> Abingdon Press, publishing imprint of the United Methodist Publishing House
> 201 Eighth Ave. S.
> Nashville, TN 37202
> (800) 251–3320; fax (800) 836–7802
> URL: http://www.abingdonpress.com (accessed March 2004)

> Albury Publishing, parent company Bethany House
> P.O. Box 470406
> Tulsa, OK 74147–0406
> (800) 304–5327
> URL: http://www.alburypublishing.com (accessed March 2004)
> Key title: *Jesus Freaks* books

> Augsburg Fortress, publishing company of the Evangelical Lutheran Church in America
> 100 S. 5th Street, #700
> Minneapolis, MN 55402–1222
> (800) 328–4648; fax (800) 722–7766
> URL: http://www.augsburgfortress.org (accessed March 2004)

> Barbour Publishing, Inc.
> P.O. Box 719
> Uhrichsville, OH 44683
> (800) 847–8270; fax (800) 220–5948
> URL: http://www.barbourbooks.com (accessed March 2004)

> Beacon Hill Press, Division of Nazarene Publishing House
> P.O. Box 419527
> Kansas City, MO 64141

(800) 877–0700; fax (800) 849–9827

URL: http://www.nph.com (accessed April 2004)

Bethany House Publishers

11400 Hampshire Avenue South

Minneapolis, MN 55438

(800) 328–6109; fax (952) 829–2503

URL: http://www.bethanyhouse.com (accessed March 2004)

Key authors: Shirley Brinkerhoff, Gilbert Morris, Janette Oke, Patricia Rushford

Key series: *Cedar River Daydreams, High Hurdles, Jenny McGrady, Nikki Sheridan, Unmistakably Cooper Ellis*

Broadman & Holman Publishers

127 9th Avenue North

Nashville, TN 37234

(800) 251–3225

URL: http://www.broadmanholman.com (accessed March 2004)

Concordia Publishing House, the official publishing arm of the Lutheran Church, Missouri Synod

3558 South Jefferson Avenue

St. Louis, MO 63118

Ordering/customer service: (800) 325–3040

URL: http://www.cph.org (accessed March 2004)

Online catalog includes teens under "Family" materials.

Eerdman's

255 Jefferson S.E.

Grand Rapids, MI 49503

(800) 253–7521; fax (616) 459–6540

URL: http://www.eerdmans.com (accessed March 2004)

Fleming H. Revell, division of Baker Book House

P.O. Box 6287

Grand Rapids, MI 49516–6287

(800) 877–2665; fax (800) 398–3111

URL: http://www.bakerbooks.com (accessed March 2004)

Focus on the Family, partners with other publishers to produce materials.

P.O. Box 15379

Colorado Springs, CO 80995

(800) 232–6459

Resource sales line, organizational discounts and bulk orders: (800) 932–9123; public library sales representative, extension 5656

URL: http://www.family.org (accessed March 2004)

Key series: *Adventures in Odyssey* radio drama series (also on audio book); *Radio Theater* radio drama series; *Brio Girls* series; *Sierra Jensen* by Robin Jones Gunn

Key nonfiction authors/series: *Dare 2 Dig Deeper* teen series; *Life on the Edge* by James Dobson, video recordings and books; *Mind Over Media* series, video recordings and books

Good News Publishers/Crossway Books
1300 Crescent Street
Wheaton, IL 60187
(800) 543–1659; fax (630) 682–4785
URL: http://gnpcb.org (accessed April 2004)
Key authors: Stephen Bly, Frank Peretti

Group Publishing, Inc.
P.O. Box 485
Loveland, CO 80529
(800) 635–0404; fax (970) 679–4392
URL: http://www.grouppublishing.com (accessed March 2004)

Harvest House
1075 Arrowsmith
Eugene, OR 97402–9197
(800) 547–8979; fax (888) 501–6012
URL: http://www.harvesthousepubl.com (accessed March 2004)

Honor Books
P.O. Box 55388
Tulsa, OK 74155
(800) 708–5550; fax (800) 430–0726
URL: http://www.cookministries.com/books/honor/ (accessed April 2004)

Howard Publishing
3117 North 7th St.
West Monroe, LA 71291
(800) 858–4109; fax (318) 397–1882
URL: http://www.howardpublishing.com (accessed March 2004)

Intervarsity Press
P.O. Box 1400
Downers Grove, IL 60515
(800) 843–9487; fax (630) 734–4200
URL: http://www.gospelcom.net/ivpress (accessed March 2004)

Lost Classics Book Company
254 E. Stuart Avenue
Lake Wales, FL 33853–5720
(888) 611–2665
URL: http://www.lostclassicsbooks.com (accessed April 2004)
Key author: G. K. Henty

Moody Press
820 N. LaSalle Blvd.
Chicago, IL 60610
(800) 678–6928; fax (800) 678–3329
URL: http://www.moodypress.org (accessed March 2004)
Key authors: *Bonnets and Bugles* series by Gilbert Morris

Multnomah, an imprint of Questar Pubs., Inc.
P.O. Box 1720
Sisters, OR 97759
(800) 929–0910; fax (541) 549–2044
URL: http://www.multnomahbooks.com (accessed March 2004)
Key series: *Diary of a Teenage Girl; O'Malley*

Preston-Speed Publications
51 Ridge Road
Mill Hall, PA 17751–8859
(570) 726–7844
URL: http://www.prestonspeed.com (accessed March 2004)
Key author: G. K. Henty

Shaw Books, imprint of Waterbrook Press (Random House)
Random House Customer Service
400 Hahn Road
Westminster, MD 21157
(800) 733–3000; fax (800) 659–2436
URL: http://www.randomhouse.com/waterbrook/shaw/ (accessed
   March 2004)

Soli Deo Gloria
P.O. Box 451
Morgan, PA 15064
(888) 266–5734
URL: http://www.SDGbooks.com (accessed March 2004)

Thomas Nelson
P.O. Box 141000
Nashville, TN 37214–1000

Encourages online ordering rather than phone inquiries.
URL: http://www.thomasnelson.com (accessed March 2004)

Tommy Nelson, division of Thomas Nelson
P.O. Box 141000
Nashville, TN 37214
Encourages online ordering rather than phone inquiries.
URL: http://www.tommynelson.com (accessed March 2004)
Key series: *Veritas Project* by Peretti, *ICB Bible, Todaysgirls.com*

Tyndale House Publishers
P.O. Box 80
Wheaton, IL 60189–0080
(800) 323–9400
URL: http://www.tyndale.com (accessed March 2004)
Key series and authors: *Left Behind: The Kids* by Tim LaHaye and
    Jerry Jenkins; *Forbidden Doors* by Bill Myers

Upper Room Books
1908 Grand Avenue/P.O. Box 340004
Nashville, TN 37203–0004
(615) 340–7200
URL: http://www.upperroom.org (accessed March 2004)

WaterBrook Press, division of Random House, Inc.
5446 N. Academy, Suite 200
Colorado Springs, CO 80918
(800) 726–0600
URL: http://www.randomhouse.com/waterbrook/(accessed April
    2004)

Zondervan, division of HarperCollins
5249 Corporate Grove
Grand Rapids, MI 49512
(800) 727–1309
URL: http://www.zondervan.com (accessed March 2004)
Key work: *NIV Bible* translation

LIBRARY SERVICES AND PROGRAMS

If you are unfamiliar with the major church groups in your service area,
take a closer look at your community. Talk with church and youth group
leaders to improve your connection to the people in their congregations.

Ask what kind of materials they wish you carried. Let them know what you *do* have; they probably will be pleasantly surprised. Offer tours and orientations to the library for local youth groups or other church groups. Let them use your community meeting room. Send them your general-interest program announcements for their community bulletin board. Sometimes confirmation classes or youth groups require service hours, so connect with youth group leaders and local Christian teen organizations to make use of their volunteer power.

SELECTED TITLES

Fiction

Series

Christian series, like their counterparts in the secular publishing world, can be erratic. This list includes only series titles that are currently active or in print. It is only a sampling of the most popular series available. With frequent changes in series runs, this list may quickly become outdated.

For Younger Teens

The Cooper Kids Adventure Series by Frank Peretti, Thomas Nelson. Supernatural suspense stories in which an archaeologist and his two children have adventures in exotic locales.

Elizabeth Gail by Hilda Stahl, Tyndale House. Mystery and relationship series involving Elizabeth Gail, who learns Christian values from her adopted family.

Horsefeathers by Dandi Daley MacKall, Concordia. Eighth-grader Scoop solves mysteries and trains horses with her aunt and grandfather at the Horsefeathers Stable.

Left Behind: The Kids by Tim LaHaye and Jerry Jenkins, Tyndale. A teen version of the popular adult series that takes place during and after The Rapture, when believers are taken up to heaven and the rest of humanity are left to survive.

Mars Diaries by Sigmund Brouwer, Tyndale. Science-fiction series set in an experimental community on Mars features fourteen-year-old virtual reality expert.

Riverboat Adventures by Lois Walfrid Johnson, Bethany. Adventure stories involving life on the Mississippi River in pre–Civil War times.

Seven Sleepers by Gilbert Morris, Moody Press. Science fiction series about a group of teens who awaken after a fifty-year sleep to encounter evil priests, Atlantis, and their own doubts about their faith.

Todaysgirls.com by various authors, Tommy Nelson. Realistic stories about six high-school girls who create a Web site where they discuss their faith and popular culture.

Trailblazer Books by Dave and Neta Jackson, Bethany. Historical adventure stories that involve Christian heroes of the past.

Young Underground by Robert Elmer, Bethany. World War II adventure series set in Nazi-occupied Denmark.

For Older Teens

Brio Girls by Jane Vogel, Focus on the Family/Bethany. Real-life stories about high-school girls and their relationships with boys, school, and God.

Diary of a Teenage Girl by Melody Carlson, Multnomah. Caitlin O'Connor keeps a diary in which she records daily events as well as her struggles to understand herself and God's plan for her future.

Forbidden Doors by Bill Myers, Tyndale. The adventures of Scott and Rebecca Williams and their dealings with spiritual warfare.

Jennie McGrady by Patricia Rushford, Bethany. Jennie McGrady is a high-school girl who also has excellent detective skills. Lots of mystery and danger, as well as messages of faith, friendship, and trust in God's protection.

Left Behind graphic novels, Tyndale. A graphic novelization of the teen version of the popular adult series. See *Left Behind: The Kids* above.

Passport to Danger by Mary Reeves Bell, Bethany. Adventures of an Austrian teen whose search for a spy uncovers dark secrets, important history, and treachery.

Sierra Jensen by Robin Jones Gunn, Bethany. Fun, upbeat series about an unconventional sixteen-year-old who explores school, friends, guys, family, and her faith.

Soul Survivor by Tim LaHaye and Bob DeMoss, W Publishing Group. Real-life, modern, cutting-edge stories about maintaining your faith in a corrupt world.

Springsong by various authors, Bethany. Each book in the series has a different author and features a different main character. The stories are about relationship issues and challenging circumstances, and are similar to some Lurlene McDaniel books.

Veritas Project by Frank Peretti, Thomas Nelson. Elijah and Elisha Springfield and their parents, undercover investigators, are sent to find the truth behind unusual and supernatural events. Similar in tone to Peretti's *Cooper Kids Adventure*.

Adult Series with Teen Appeal

Bonnets and Bugles by Gilbert Morris, Bethany House. Civil war dramas about faith and relationships.

Dragon King Trilogy by Stephen Lawhead, Zondervan. Fantasy series about a boy who is on a quest to discover the one true God.

Gresham Chronicles by Lawana Blackwell, Bethany House. English drama about a woman whose change of life and fortune force her to make decisions about faith and family.

Joshua books by Joseph Girzone, Macmillan. A retelling of the story of Christ through Joshua, a young man who moves into a small town in New York State.

Left Behind series by Tim LaHaye and Jerry Jenkins, Tyndale. The popular adult series that takes place during and after The Rapture, when believers are taken up to heaven and the rest of humanity are left to survive in the world without the Holy Spirit.

The Mitford Years series by Jan Karon, Penguin. Stories of the interwoven lives of the townspeople of fictional Mitford, North Carolina, as seen through the eyes of Father Tim, their Episcopalian priest and friend.

O'Malley series by Dee Henderson, Multnomah. Kate O'Malley is a hostage negotiator involved in life-and-death situations.

Tales of London by Lawana Blackwell, Bethany. Set in Victorian England, devoted workers do their best to offer lonely orphans a good life.

Women of the West by Janette Oke, Bethany House. Stories of pioneer women and their tests of faith.

Novels

Blackstock, Terri. *The Gifted Sophomores*. Nashville, TN: Thomas Nelson/Word, 2002. ISBN 0849943426 (pbk.). Blessed with supernatural gifts, three teens learn life-changing lessons about unity and the tangible power of the Holy Spirit.

Daoust, Jerry. *Waking Up Bees: Stories of Living Life's Questions*. Winona, MN: Christian Brothers Publications, 1999. ISBN 0884895270. Short stories about life issues.

Jenkins, Jerry. *Rookie*. Sisters, OR: Multnomah Books, 1997. ISBN 157673045X (pbk.). Story of a boy who has a real talent for playing baseball.

Marshall, Catherine. *Christy*. New York, NY: Avon, 1967. ISBN 0380001411. A young woman chooses to teach in an Appalachian mission school where she encounters unique mountain customs, poignant human needs, humor, and adventure.

Myers, Bill. *Eli*. Grand Rapids, MI: Zondervan, 2000. ISBN 0310218039 (pbk.). What would it be like if Jesus had been born thirty years ago rather than two thousand?

——— and Angela Hunt. *Then Comes Marriage: A Novella*. Grand Rapids, MI: Zondervan, 2001. ISBN 0310230160. A young married couple's first major fight, separation, and reconciliation, told alternately through each partner's eyes.

———. *When the Last Leaf Falls: A Novella*. Grand Rapids, MI: Zondervan, 2001. ISBN 0310230918. A pastor and his family confront lapses of faith when they discover that their teenage daughter has cancer.

Peretti, Frank. *This Present Darkness* and *Piercing the Darkness*. Wheaton, IL: Crossway Books, 2000. ISBN 1581342144. Ashton, a typical small town, has drawn powerful demonic beings to it. Angelic forces rally as Christians prepare for spiritual warfare.

Rivers, Francine. *The Atonement Child*. Wheaton, IL: Tyndale, 1997. ISBN 0842300414 (pbk.). When tragedy strikes Dynah, a devout Christian with a bright future, she and her family must come to terms with God's provision and goodness, and what it means to live out the truth, even when the cost is high.

Stokes, Penelope. *The Blue Bottle Club*. Nashville, TN: W Pub. Group, 1999. ISBN 0849937809. Four young women friends write down future hopes and desires and place the papers in a blue bottle. Reporter Brendan Delaney discovers the bottle sixty-five years later and searches for the elderly women.

Wangerin, Walter. *Paul: A Novel*. Grand Rapids, MI: Zondervan, 2000. ISBN 0310218926. A fictionalized account of the life of the Apostle Paul from the point of view of various people in his life.

Authors of Classics

Henty, George Alfred. This popular nineteenth-century author has found a new readership, particularly among boys who desire adventure stories within the framework of Christian beliefs. Most of Henty's books are being republished by Preston-Speed Publications and the Lost Classics Book Company. Some of his titles are *St. George for England: A Tale of Cressy and Poitiers* and *Winning His Spurs: A Story of the Crusades*.

Lewis, C.S. *The Space Trilogy*. Scribner. Lewis' acclaimed Trilogy, beginning with *Out of the Silent Planet* and continuing with *Perelandra* and *That Hideous Strength*. Dr. Ransom's allegorical adventures to other planets.

MacDonald, George. MacDonald is an enduring figure in fantasy literature, as well as in realistic fiction. C.S. Lewis acknowledged that MacDonald was one of his greatest influences. Look for *Golden Key, Knowing the Heart of God, Lilith, Marquis Secret,* and *Phantastes: A Faerie Romance for Men and Women*.

Marshall, Catherine. *A Man Called Peter*. Chosen Books, 2002, 1998. A biography of the author's Presbyterian minister husband who became the chaplain of the United States Senate.

Sheldon, Charles M. *In His Steps*. Fleming H. Revell, 1993 (reprint). Members of a church promise to always ask the question "What would Jesus do?" before making a decision.

Ten Boom, Corrie. *The Hiding Place*. New York, NY: Bantam, 1971. Classic story of courage in Nazi-occupied The Netherlands.

Wilkinson, David. *The Cross and the Switchblade*. New York, NY: Jove, 1962. The true story of the beginning of David Wilkerson's ministry to the gangs of New York City and the conversion of Nicky Cruz, a notorious gang leader.

Nonfiction

Christian Living

Arterburn, Stephen. *Every Young Man's Battle: Strategies for Victory in the Real World of Sexual Temptation*. Colorado Springs, CO: WaterBrook Press, 2002. ISBN 1578565375. Biblical strategies for young men to maintain sexual purity.

Budziszewski, J. *How To Stay Christian In College: An Interactive Guide to Keeping the Faith*. Colorado Springs, CO: NavPress, 1999. ISBN 1576830616. A guide to keeping the faith in a new environment.

Clark, Jeramy. *I Gave Dating a Chance*. Colorado Springs, CO: WaterBrook Press, 2000. ISBN 1578563291. A response, promoting godly dating, to Joshua Harris' *I Kissed Dating Goodbye*.

Harris, Joshua. *I Kissed Dating Goodbye*. Sisters, OR: Multnomah, 1997. ISBN 1576730360. Calls young adults away from playing the dating game, and into purposeful singleness.

Johnson, Kevin. *Bust Loose: Become the Wild New Person You Are in Jesus*. Minneapolis, MN: Bethany, 2002. ISBN 0764224360 (pbk.).

———. *Get God: Make Friends with the King of the Universe*. Minneapolis, MN: Bethany, 2000. ISBN 1556616368 (pbk.).

————. *Get Smart: Unscramble Mind-Boggling Questions of Your Faith.* Minneapolis, MN: Bethany House, 2002. ISBN 0764224352 (pbk.).

————. *Pray Hard: Talk to God with Total Confidence.* Minneapolis, MN: Bethany House, 2001. ISBN 1556616392 (pbk.). A personal manual on prayer.

————. *Stick Tight: Glue Yourself to Godly Friends.* Minneapolis, MN: Bethany House, 2001. ISBN 0764224344 (pbk.). Twenty-five anecdotes depict real-life situations for teenagers and their friends, followed by questions and relevant Bible verses.

————. *Wise Up: Stand Clear of the Unsmartness of Sin.* Minneapolis, MN: Bethany House, 2000. ISBN 1556616376 (pbk.).

Langteux, James Alexander. *God.net.* Sisters, OR: Multnomah, 2001. ISBN 1576739902. Shows readers how to rely on the safety net of God's Word, depend on the network of fellow believers and become better fishers of men.

Maxwell, John C. *Leading from the Lockers.* Nashville, TN: Tommy Nelson, 2001. ISBN 0849977223. Offers young readers the tools they need to develop leadership before reaching high school and college.

Strobel, Lee. *Case for Christ: A Journalist's Personal Investigation of the Evidence for Jesus* (student edition). Grand Rapids, MI: Zondervan, 2001. ISBN 0310234840 (pbk.). An investigative journalist retraces his journey from skepticism to faith.

The Student's A to Z Guide to Bible Application. Wheaton, IL: Tyndale House, 1996. ISBN 0842359389. Discusses biblical principles students need to tackle the issues and problems they face daily.

Wilkinson, Bruce. *The Prayer of Jabez for Teens.* Sisters, OR: Multnomah, 2001. ISBN 1576738159. A discussion of the prayer of the obscure Bible hero mentioned in 1 Chronicles 4:10.

Devotionals

Boshers, Bo with Kim Anderson. *Doing Life with God: Real Stories Written by High School Students.* Loveland, CO: Group Pub. Inc, 2000. ISBN 0764422278 (v. 1), ISBN 0764422286 (v. 2).

DC Talk. *Live Like a Jesus Freak: Spend Today as if It Were Your Last.* Tulsa, OK: Albury Pub., 2001. ISBN 1577782089.

Johnson, Kevin. *Cross Train: Blast Through the Bible from Front to Back.* Minneapolis, MN: Bethany House, 2001. ISBN 1556616384 (pbk.).

————. *See Jesus: Peer Into the Life and Mind of Your Master.* Minneapolis, MN: Bethany House, 2001. ISBN 0764224336 (pbk.). Presents the life of Jesus from a teenage perspective.

Key, Dana, compiler. *WWJD [What Would Jesus Do] Interactive Devotional: Top CCM (Contemporary Christian Music) Artists Answer One Tough Question.* Grand Rapids, MI: Zondervan, 1997. ISBN 0310222346.

Polich, Laurie. *Dive into Living Water: 50 Devotions for Teens on the Gospel of John.* Nashville, TN: Dimensions for Living, 2001. ISBN 0687052238 (pbk.).

Schmitt, Betsy, ed. *The One Year Jesus Devotional Bible.* Wheaton, IL: Tyndale House, 2002. ISBN 0842370358 (pbk.).

Shellenberger, Susie. *Girl Talk With God.* Nashville, TN: Word Pub., 2001. ISBN 084994290X.

St. James, Rebecca. *40 Days with God: A Devotional Journey.* Cincinnati, OH: Standard Publishing, 2001. ISBN 0784712743.

Stand Your Ground: Devotions for Teens by Teens. St. Louis, MO: Concordia, 2001. ISBN 0570052912.

Tenney, Tommy. *God Chasers for Teens.* Shippensburg, PA: Destiny Image, 2002. ISBN 0768421535.

Voice of the Martyrs. *Extreme Devotion.* Nashville, TN: W Pub. Group, 2002. ISBN 0849917395 (pbk.).

Biographies

DC Talk. *Jesus Freaks: Stories of Revolutionaries Who Changed Their World: Fearing God Not Man, Vol. II.* Minneapolis, MN: Bethany, 2002. ISBN 0764227467 (pbk.).

——— and Voice of the Martyrs. *Jesus Freaks: Stories of Those Who Stood for Jesus: The Ultimate Jesus Freaks.* Tulsa, OK: Albury Pub., 1999. ISBN 1577780728.

Heroes of the Faith series. Various authors. Uhrichsville, OH: Barbour Publishing, 2001, 1995. 38 v. Biographies of missionaries, evangelists, and explorers who brought the word of God to the world.

Peretti, Frank. *The Wounded Spirit.* Nashville, TN: Word, 2000. ISBN 0849916739. Peretti discusses his personal journey through pain, disfigurement, and abuse, offering hope for those struggling with emotional wounds.

Bibles and Bible Reference

Extreme Teen Bible: The Holy Bible, New Century Version. Nashville, TN: Thomas Nelson, 2001.

ICB (International Children's Bible), teen cover. Nashville, TN: Tommy Nelson, 2001.

Littleton, Mark and Jeanette Gardner Littleton. *What's in the Bible for Teens.* Lansing, IL: Starburst Pub., 2000. ISBN 1892016052 (pbk.).

Peterson, Eugene H. *The Message: The Bible in Contemporary Language.* Colorado Springs, CO: NavPress, 2002. ISBN 1576832899 (hardcover), ISBN 1576832740 (pbk.).

Richards, Larry and Sue Poorman Richards. *Teen Study Bible New International Version.* Grand Rapids, MI: Zondervan, 1998. ISBN 0310900964.

Student's Life Application Bible: New Living Translation. Wheaton, IL: Tyndale House, 1997. ISBN 0842333258.

Wilkinson, Bruce. *Youthwalk Devotional Bible.* Grand Rapids, MI: Zondervan, 1997. ISBN 0310900875.

Yancey, Philip and Tim Stafford. *The Student Bible: Updated New American Standard Bible.* Grand Rapids, MI: Zondervan, 1999. ISBN 0310931487.

Magazines

Breakaway. Focus on the Family, since 1990. Monthly circulation of 105,000. For teen boys. URL: http://www.family.org/teenguys/breakmag (accessed March 2004).

Brio. Focus on the Family, since 1990. Monthly circulation of 210,000. For teen girls. URL: http://www.briomag.com (accessed March 2004).

Contemporary Christian Music (CCM). CCM Communications, since 1978. Monthly circulation of 80,000. Seeks to promote spiritual growth by using contemporary Christian music as a "window" into issues of life and faith. URL: http://www.ccmmagazine.com (accessed March 2004).

Cornerstone. Jesus People, USA. Erratic schedule, circulation of 37,000. Issues of faith and culture, reviews of current books and media. URL: http://www.cornerstonemag.com (accessed March 2004).

Devo'Zine. The Upper Room, a ministry of the United Methodist Church. Bi-monthly circulation of 85,000. Contains meditations, scriptures, prayers and articles for teens. URL: http://www.upperroom.org/devozine (accessed March 2004).

Guideposts for Teens. Guideposts Associates, Inc., since 1998. Bi-monthly circulation of 160,530. Contains true stories about real people and religious faith as told by teens.

Inteen. Urban Ministries, Inc., since 1971. Presents a Christian perspective on social, economic, and ethical issues African American teenagers face.

True Tunes Music Magazine. Online magazine that covers music and culture, from both the secular and Christian markets, from a Christian perspective. URL: http://www.truetunesnews.com (accessed March 2004).

Audio Books

Adventures in Odyssey. Focus on the Family.
LaHaye, Tim and Jerry Jenkins. *Left Behind: The Kids* series. Recorded Books.
Radio Theater. Focus on the Family.

Web Sites

Interdenominational groups
Campus Life. URL: http://www.christianitytoday.com/teens/ (accessed March 2004).
YoungLife. URL: http://www.younglife.org (accessed March 2004).
AME (African Methodist Episcopal). Home page for the church body. URL: http://www.amecnet.org (accessed March 2004).
AME Zion (African Methodist Episcopal Zion). Home page for the church body, includes links to colleges. URL: http://www.theamezionchurch.org (accessed March 2004).

Episcopalian
Home page for the church body. URL: http://ecusa.anglican.org (accessed March 2004).
Home page for youth ministries. URL: http://www.episcopalchurch.org/myp (accessed March 2004).

Lutheran
Listing of various Lutheran church bodies, including those without Web sites or teen ministries. URL: http://www.valpo.edu/lutheran/LutheranChurchBodies.html (March 2004).
Youth Encounter. Serves all Christian denominations, incorporated by Lutherans in Minnesota in 1965. URL: http://www.youthencounter.com (accessed March 2004).

LCMS (Lutheran Church, Missouri Synod) Teen Page. URL: http://www.lcms. org/pages/internal.asp?navid=2093 (accessed April 2004).

ELCA (Evangelical Lutheran Church in America) Youth Page. URL: http://www. elca.org/youth.html (accessed March 2004).

Wisconsin Evangelical Lutheran Synod. URL: http://www.wels.net (accessed March 2004); Teen e-zine, *Living Bold.* URL: http://www.wels.net/sab/ frm-cyd.html (accessed April 2004).

Methodist

United Methodist Youth Organization. Primarily for youth leaders but some information for teens (scholarships, etc.). URL: http://www.umyouth.org (accessed March 2004).

Chrysalis. Retreat ministry for teens and young adults. URL: http://www.upper room.org/chrysalis (accessed March 2004).

Presbyterian/ Reformed Tradition

Cumberland Presbyterian Youth. URL: http://members.aol.com/mleslie598/ youth.html (accessed March 2004).

Presbyterian Youth of America. URL: http://www.pya.net (accessed March 2004).

Presbyterian Youth Connection. Includes an online catalog with resources published within the denomination and a "Youth and Youth Ministries" section with some teen materials. URL: http://pyc.pcusa.org (accessed March 2004).

Reformed Presbyterian Church Youth Ministries. URL: http://hometown. aol.com/ rpyouth (accessed March 2004).

WORKS CONSULTED

Barrett, David B., ed. *World Christian Encyclopedia: A Comparative Survey of Churches and Religions in the Modern World.* New York, NY: Oxford University Press, 2001.

Baxter, Kathleen. "On Selecting Christian Books." *School Library Journal* (March 1985): 118.

Beall, Carol. "Beyond Christy: New Demands for YA Christian Fiction." *School Library Journal* (September 1995): 130–131.

Caroll, Colleen. *The New Faithful: Why Young Adults are Embracing Christian Orthodoxy.* Chicago, IL: Loyola Press, 2002.

DeLong, Janice and Rachel Schwedt. *Contemporary Christian Authors: Lives and Works.* London: The Scarecrow Press, 2000.

Dillenberger, John and Claude Welch. *Protestant Christianity.* Prentice Hall, 1988.

Dole, Patricia Pearl. *Children's Books About Religion.* Englewood, CO: Libraries Unlimited, Inc., 1999.

Greenlee, A. A. "The Lure of Series Books: Does it Affect Appreciation for Recommended Literature?" *The Reading Teacher* (November 1996): v. 50, no. 3.

Hein, R. *George MacDonald: Victorian Mythmaker.* Nashville, TN: Starsong, 1993.

Katz, Bill and Linda Sternberg Katz. *Magazines for Young People.* New Providence, NJ: R.R. Bowker, 1991.

Letterman, K. *Biblical Counsel: Resources for Renewal.* Keezletown, VA: Letterman Associates, 1994.

Lewis, C. S. *George MacDonald: An Anthology*. New York, NY: Macmillan, 1974.

MacDonald, Ruth K. *Christian's Children: The Influence of John Bunyan's 'The Pilgrim's Progress' on American Children's Literature*. New York, NY: Peter Lang, 1989.

Magida, Arthur J., ed. *How to be a Perfect Stranger: A Guide to Other People's Religious Ceremonies, volume 1*. Woodstock, VT: Jewish Lights Publishing, 1996.

Matlins, Stuart M. and Arthur J. Magida, eds. *How to be a Perfect Stranger: A Guide to Other People's Religious Ceremonies, volume 2*. Woodstock, VT: Skylight Paths Publishing, 1999.

Mead, Frank S. and Samuel S. Hill. *Handbook of Denominations in the United States*, 11th ed.. Nashville, TN: Abingdon Press, 2001.

Mort, John A. *Christian Fiction: A Guide to the Genre*. Greenwood Village, CO: Libraries Unlimited, 2002.

Norris, Alice. "Should We Buy Religious Fiction?" *School Library Journal* (January 1993): 42.

O'Connor, Leo F. *The Protestant Sensibility in the American Novel: An Annotated Bibliography*. New York, NY: Garland, 1992.

Roberts, Denise. "A Market Coming Alive: Christian Press Literature." *VOYA (Voice of Youth Advocates)* (February 1997): 315–320.

Smith, Christian. *Christian America? What Evangelicals Really Want*. Berkeley, CA: University of California Press, 2000.

Statistical Abstract of the United States: The National Data Book. Washington, D.C.: U.S. Government Printing Office, 2002.

Ulrich's Periodicals Directory. New Providence, NJ: Bowker, 2002.

Walker, Barbara J. *Developing Christian Fiction Collections for Children and Adults: Selection Criteria and a Core Collection*. New York, NY: Neal-Schuman, 1997.

Wright, Robert Glenn. *The Social Christian Novel*. New York, NY: Greenwood Press, 1989.

2

◇ ◇ ◇

EVANGELICAL CHRISTIANITY

Michael Wessells

Evangelical Christianity—cross-denominational movement within Christianity, mainly associated with Protestantism

Beginnings:

American evangelicalism began to form during Great Awakening of eighteenth century. New evangelical movement linked to Billy Graham emerged after World War II.

Beliefs and practices:

One God exists eternally in three persons: Father, Son, and Holy Spirit. Some evangelical Christians, however, believe that God exists in only one person. The Bible is the inspired, infallible, authoritative Word of God.

Demographics:

May be as many as forty-five million evangelical Christians in the United States. Difficult to establish number because those who self-identify as Evangelical may also be members of other religious organizations.

As many as forty percent of all Americans describe themselves as "born-again."

(continued)

(continued)

Information points:

National Association of Evangelicals. URL: http://www.nae.net (accessed March 2004).

See also http://www.upci.org (accessed March 2004), *United Pentecostal Church International,* for example of non-Trinitarian belief.

As a librarian, I grab every chance to pitch library services. When a teen at my church youth group asked where she could try out a CD from Christian rappers DC Talk, I told her, "We have it down at the city library." She looked at me as if I had just arrived on a shuttle from Mars. "Christian music at the library? You've got to be kidding—there's nothing in the library for me."

A few months later we hosted a public meeting on our Internet Access Policy. Teens from a local church youth group, as well as numerous parents of Christian teens, protested against the open access we allow and the offensive images that can result from it.

Both stories illustrate how libraries can lose out among evangelical Christian teens; often we are seen as repositories for evil materials and devoid of supportive ones. And no wonder—until recently, many public and school libraries did not:

- Systematically collect materials specifically aimed at evangelical Christian teens.
- Market library services directly to these teens.
- Understand the language, priorities, and concerns specific to them.
- Move beyond society's stereotypical image of evangelical Christians as Bible-thumping fundamentalists opposed to open access to library materials.
- Explore ways to serve this significant portion of our communities.

Thankfully, over the last decade, these tendencies have been positively affected by several trends. Many standard library review periodicals, for example *Publishers Weekly* and *Booklist,* now include materials designed for evangelical Christians, rendering collection development easier. Internet access has provided selectors with a bonanza of collection development opportunities, including more convenient access to materials with appeal to evangelical Christians.

Evangelical Christianity is a cross-denominational movement that is mainly associated with Protestantism and has undergone several iterations throughout history. Because it is a movement, it is not tied directly with any denomination, but specific churches within denominations, or even sometimes individuals within particular churches, consider themselves evangelical Christian.

The defining characteristic is a focus on individual salvation, a transformation of one's relationship to God in an instantaneous conversion experience. Preaching is often focused on altar calls, a routine part of many evangelical worship services. Congregants are invited to come forward and achieve or renew the conversion experience. The preaching is a climactic and often lengthy portion of the service, directive and hortatory in nature.

Prayer is more individual, spontaneous, and emotional than liturgical and contemplative.

To evangelical Christians, faith is a highly personal and individual decision, and therefore the movement is very diverse.

It is important to keep in mind that there is a distinction between "evangelical" and "fundamentalist," though the terms may be used interchangeably by our culture. Many evangelical Christians do not consider themselves fundamentalists, and vice versa. The most useful way to distinguish the two is in how they view themselves. Generally, evangelical Christians live within the prevailing culture and use their example and influence to encourage that culture to be transformed by the Gospel of Jesus Christ. Fundamentalists are more traditional and conservative Christians. They may resist and even react against aspects of the surrounding culture, taking a substantially more separatist approach. Fundamentalists, as their title would imply, tend to be more prescriptive. Their approach to libraries is more likely to heavily stress strict limitations on what family members may read or view and to include more aggressive steps to protect loved ones from exposure to materials that might be considered harmful.

The evangelical Christian is "a conservative traditionalist Christian whose Christianity is the bedrock of decision making and the basis of self-understanding."[1] This is a person who when asked, "Who are you?" does not answer, "I'm an American," or "I'm a dentist," or "I'm a person of color," but, "I'm a Christian." Every moral decision or action is made in the light of a concept encapsulated in the slogan WWJD (What Would Jesus Do?). Codes of behavior are based on acting differently from the way the rest of humanity, "the world," acts. Maintaining this separation, being "*in* the world," but not sharing the general attitude "*of* the world," is essential. Some evangelical Christians can easily maintain this equilibrium within themselves, using only personal examples to encourage non-

Christians to modify their own behavior. Others need to have varying degrees of control over their surroundings to maintain their balance. They will then seek to have surrounding institutions, such as libraries, conform to overtly Christian codes of morality, as defined by evangelical Christians, or at least to codes more congenial to Christian lifestyles.

One characteristic of the language of evangelical Christians is the self-defining use of the word "Christian" in a way that seems to imply that only those who accept evangelical understandings of Christianity are included. This is a troubling usage to many, for whom "Christianity" applies also to mainline Protestants, Roman Catholics, and Greek Orthodox. While hard lines are often taken between denominations about how essential a given doctrine may be to salvation, it is only the most fundamentalist believers who would deny that any of the above denominations are "Christian." That said, it is true that when evangelical Christians use the word "Christian," they are nearly always referring to evangelical Christians.

Except where the text states otherwise, the comments in this chapter apply to both evangelical and fundamentalist Christians.

HISTORY

Christianity grew out of Judaism. As the Christian Church became institutionalized and was absorbed into the ruling Roman Empire, it also garnered the power to impose an orthodox way of understanding, and could relegate to the outer fringes, or exterminate, those few heretics who adopted variant views. This orthodoxy developed in the West into Roman Catholicism, in the East into Eastern Orthodoxy. In the early sixteenth century, with the invention of the printing press and lay translations of the Bible, movements of protest against orthodoxy and papal authority arose. This movement was called the Reformation. Martin Luther, a Roman Catholic monk, was one of the first individuals to break away from the Church, but many others followed. The churches that grew out of the reformation movement are called Protestant because they protested against the edicts and papal authority of Rome.

Luther and other Protestant reformers used the word "evangelical," derived from the Greek word meaning "good news," to describe their emphasis on salvation, Biblical authority, and the equality of all believers before God. But it wasn't until the eighteenth century that evangelicalism became a full-blown movement.

At that time, the term "evangelical" took on added meanings, describing a specific approach to conversion and preaching that evolved out of the Methodist Movement. John Wesley and George Whitefield, founders of the Methodist Church in England, were two of the first evangelical preachers, but many others followed. Brought to America, the fervently emotional, deeply individualistic Christianity of the Wesleys took hold in what is called the First Great Awakening in the 1720s and 1730s. The fiery evangelism of such great preachers as Jonathan Edwards, a Calvinist, imbued this style of Christianity with many of the characteristics it still displays—the centrality of preaching, the emotional messages and strong emphasis on individual relationships with a God who must be pleased by proper conduct, the presence of ecstatic behavior and loud responses by the congregation, altar calls, emphasis on salvation, and baptisms by immersion. Evangelical Christianity became a broad, cross-denominational movement embraced by some, but not all, Protestant churches and denominations.

The formative era of American folk religion in the seventeenth and eighteenth centuries was replicated in a Second Great Awakening in the early nineteenth century. Baptists, Congregationalists, Dutch Reformed, Methodists, Presbyterians, and many smaller groups came together to form the Evangelical United Front, which grew to be the most powerful religious group in the United States. Evangelical Christians became involved in many social reforms, such as the abolition and temperance movements.

As numerous evangelical denominations defined themselves by differences with fellow Christians, the movement as a whole flourished by defining the surrounding culture as "sinful." One of the prime vehicles that differentiated evangelicals from other Protestants was the "revival," wherein emotional calls for complete conversion combined with shouting and singing to draw people to the new Faith.

As the pace of change in the outside world quickened at the turn of the twentieth century, the calls to repentance became more strident and the call for resistance to "modernism" further split evangelical ranks. The most conservative groups became known as "fundamentalists." Differences between conservative and liberal factions brought an end to the Evangelical United Front, and by the end of the century evangelical Christianity was fading.

However, the twentieth century witnessed another wave in the evangelical movement that continues to this day. Billy Graham was a spearhead of this resurgence; the Youth for Christ movement, which was founded in the 1940s, added to the momentum.

In more recent years, evangelical Christianity has taken on many forms and permeated media ranging from television, with such popular and diverse "televangelists" as Pat Robertson, Jimmy Swaggert, and Franklin

Graham (Billy Graham's son), to the publishing industry, where the Evangelical Christian Publishers Association (ECPA) holds tremendous clout and Christian fiction tops best-seller lists, to the Internet, where evangelical resources ranging from Web sites to cyber churches abound.

James Dobson and Focus on the Family also rose in popularity during the latter half of the twentieth century.

Needless to say, today evangelical Christians are a very diverse and widespread group.

CORE BELIEFS AND VALUES

Evangelical Christians from different denominations hold different views on specific doctrines, but they share certain values and beliefs. Chief among these is the understanding that every aspect of one's life is subject to the iron disciplines of God's calling. Whatever a believer is doing at any given time—working, dating, playing, reading—is done under the earnest watchfulness of God and should conform to his expectations. Any pursuit carried on inside or outside of church should be carefully edited so as not to include a sinful act or an act that might tempt oneself or one's companions to sin. This constant editing is a time-consuming activity and is made easier by simply avoiding certain activities altogether when such activities might lead to sin. Among activities to be avoided by many or most evangelicals are smoking, drinking alcoholic beverages, engaging in extramarital or premarital sex, cursing or swearing, wearing provocative clothing, taking drugs, and reading or viewing certain materials.

While personal standards in these areas may vary, the universal standard for evangelical Christians is the Bible. Here God himself sets the rules, and evangelicals regularly memorize and quote Bible verses as a shorthand way of communicating about what these expectations are agreed to be. In fact, evangelical Christians immerse themselves in the Bible so that everyday activities can be conformed to God's expectations with a minimum of re-examination. The wheel need not be reinvented— the Bible tells us so.

Evangelical Christians take very seriously their Biblical definition as "a peculiar people, zealous to good works" (Titus 2:14; King James Version), set aside from other people. Evangelical denominations carefully define themselves in terms of their separation from the world at large and other Christian denominations in particular.

Baptist denominations have a very different belief about the activity of the Holy Spirit than Pentecostal denominations that believe in "speaking in tongues." Even Pentecostals are split between those who believe in a

Godhead made up of Father, Son, and Holy Spirit and those who believe in Jesus only. Almost every possible variation on orthodox Christian doctrines will find some denomination holding it as a basic tenet.

A large number of the major evangelical Christian denominations belong to the National Association of Evangelicals (NAE), whose Web site (http://www.nae.net, accessed March 2004) provides links to the various denominational Web sites for the interested reader,[2] with two exceptions: the more fundamentalist Southern Baptist Convention (http://www.sbc.net, accessed March 2004), which at nearly sixteen million members is the second largest denomination in the United States (behind the Roman Catholic Church), and the next largest denomination within evangelical Christianity, the Church of God in Christ (http://www.cogic.org, accessed March 2004), the largest Pentecostal denomination. Other large denominations include the Assemblies of God and several variations of the Baptist Church, each with membership in excess of two million. Some of the largest evangelical churches are independent of any denomination but may belong to a loosely formed group of mutually supportive independent evangelical churches.

Even the larger denominations split readily into several like-named subgroups, illustrating the tendency of evangelical Christians to position themselves in terms of differences. The one common emphasis is that denoted by the name—evangelism—the direct and unabashed sharing of the Gospel. An evangelical Christian is the one most likely to ask a total stranger: "Do you know Jesus as your personal Savior?" One hardly expects that behavior from the typical mainline Protestant.

Another core belief common to nearly all evangelical Christians is the authority of the Holy Bible as the inspired word of God and the final authority on any subject. God may communicate through direction given during personal prayer, or through public utterance in a Pentecostal meeting, but he will never contradict his word in the Bible. Different interpretations of Scripture may abound but there is general agreement that the Bible is authoritative. When a Christian teen states, "the Bible says...," it is much like a librarian stating, "our library policy is...." In both cases, the effect is, "We're through debating; here's the answer."

Evangelical Christians also emphasize God's continuing action in the world, asking for God to intervene in the daily events of life. His active interest in, and direction of, the affairs of each individual requires the Christian to be constantly attentive to God's presence. This is comforting in times of trial, but produces anxiety in times when one is doing something wrong and wishes God were looking the other way, or when one needs God but cannot sense his presence. Wrestling with the pros and cons of God's continuing presence in one's personal space is a source of creative tension among evangelical Christians, including teens.

If God is responsible for both major and minor events in the lives of individuals, surely God is responsible for the overall events of the universe. God's responsibility for the creation of everything, including life, is so essential to the understanding of an omnipotent God, that a threat to that belief undermines the entire belief structure. Some evangelical Christians sense an intrusion of the scientific world into the boundaries of their spiritual space and push back. For example, many evangelical Christians perceive that in the arenas of public education involving both "worldly" and "Christian" children, only the view of the former is given credence. Some evangelical Christians respond by seeking overt recognition in the public school of their spiritual values; others respond by choosing to homeschool their children, preferring to keep them out of the world lest they become "of the world." Yet others send their children to private Christian schools.

If God is a power for good, why are some people so lousy? Another common core belief of evangelical Christians is that of supernatural evil, the Devil and his demons, who work against the more powerful God and his angels. A direct trial of force led to the Devil's defeat, so he now works to hurt God through those whom God loves—his human creations. The cosmic battle between good and evil plays itself out on earth and each action we take has cosmic repercussions. If you understand this perspective, you can appreciate both the crusading fervor and inherent inability to compromise, characteristic of battles framed as crusades against evil.

Many of the intellectual freedom battles libraries face with evangelical Christians take this form. Perceived as especially dangerous, given the evil power of these dark forces, are books or films that intentionally or inadvertently promote witchcraft or the occult, which hold such a dangerous fascination for unwary Christian teens. An additional, though opposite, danger is the trivialization of demonic forces by folktales that make the Devil a harmless figure of fun, or by the confusion of invisible forces that are real (angels and demons) with invisible forces that are imaginary (fairies, Santa Claus, the Easter Bunny). Consequently, some Christian teens tell me they are not allowed to read mythology or fantasy, and some are not allowed to read fiction at all.

Another core belief emphasized in nearly all evangelical denominations is that God will not allow the current state of affairs to continue forever. At some undeterminable time, but soon, Jesus will return to Earth and God will call a halt to the world, overthrowing the Devil, judging human beings individually, and assigning them eternally to Heaven or Hell. The timing, the details, and the criteria for final judgment serve as some of the strongest boundary markers between evangelical Christian denominations; but the finality, the urgency, and the imminence of the Second Coming and Final Judgment are commonly agreed upon. The desire to bring other people into the spiritual sphere of safety before it is too late is what gives the name "evangelicals" to this segment of Christianity. One of the most popular current series of Christian fiction, the *Left Behind* series by LaHaye and Jenkins, puts one version of this scenario into science fiction story form.

In the face of this overwhelming variety, one may wonder how any generalizations can be made that will help librarians deal with evangelical Christian teens. Fortunately, there are several core beliefs common to evangelical Christians that in turn drive their approach to the library.

FORMATIVE EXPERIENCES

For evangelical Christians, the life-defining moment is the experience of salvation. This dramatic and intensely personal realization and acceptance that a loving God gave his only son in sacrifice, not just for mankind at large but for each individual in particular, is both a cathartic and life-changing event involving major celebration by fellow believers. Many even celebrate as a second birthday the date when they were "born again." One's life and one's actions are then changed to conform to those desired by God. This change is done as a "thank you" offering to God, but sometimes also as proof to oneself that one can somehow retrospectively deserve what one received solely by grace. The experience is the epitome of an intensely personalized relationship with God, which hopefully deepens as Christian life continues. God is regularly included in one's internal conversations about what to do next. Evangelical Christian teens, depending on their specific denomination, usually undergo baptism, confirmation, or profession of faith, which is usually preceded by catechism and/or Biblical studies.

The developmental tasks of an evangelical Christian teen include those of all teens, but with an added overlay in the spiritual dimension. Added to the normal anguish over relationships is a deep concern over the relationship with God ("Will He forgive me for what I've done?"). God may mirror, or substitute on occasion, for one's earthly parents. The common teen tendency to see things in black and white may be intensified by evangelical Christianity's dramatic view of good and evil. The expressive and ever-changing emotions of teens find a strong outlet in the free-flowing, hand-raising, emotional style of worship common to evangelical services.

Common in churches, as in most social groups, is the "clan leader," one who, because of personality or social placement, is looked on as a spiritual, moral, and social leader. Part of the success of any approach to Christian teens is winning over one of these group leaders, the ones whose choices set the tone of acceptability for the others. Often the leader of a church youth group, who is usually a little older than the teens, serves in this role, and it is common for such leaders to arise from within the teen group itself. To find and win over the leaders is a major goal for young adult (YA) librarians desiring to serve this group.

A key part of the self-definition of evangelical Christian teens is the call to "witness," to demonstrate to the world through word and deed the benefits of the Christian lifestyle, in hope that others will see the value of embracing Christianity. Outreach is a goal of Christians as well as librarians.

Evangelical Christian teens, like all teens, are finding out for themselves what values to hold most strongly and how to mold themselves into adults who can make a difference. Their relationships with important adults can help them affirm these decisions, and the librarian can be one of those adults. Like all teens, Christians need strong adult models and helpers, plus information that challenges, affirms, and deepens the Christian life. The question is, will they find all this at their library?[3]

MISCONCEPTIONS AND STEREOTYPES

Many Americans have a picture of evangelical Christians as Bible-thumping anti-intellectuals of limited understanding who are fanatically devoted to making everyone else live according to their rules. They are often equated with "the Christian Right," and while some evangelical Christians fall into this group, many do not. They are often seen as grimly humorless or conversely as overly emotional, but in any case, bent on making the world conform to their own images. In fact, evangelical Christians are an extremely varied lot and not really interested in taking over America as much as in transforming America, one person at a time. Sociologist Christian Smith of the University of North Carolina conducted in-depth interviews of hundreds of evangelical Christians in this country and found them to be much more tolerant and diverse than the stereotypes would hold.[4] He also found that self-styled spokesmen for fundamentalist Christianity were not typical representatives of evangelicalism.

LIBRARY SERVICES: CONNECTING WITH EVANGELICAL TEENS

As librarians working with evangelical Christian teens, we have two strikes against us. First, teens are the age group most reluctant to ask for help, and Christian teens are more so in an arena not explicitly Christian. Second, the mission of the library is to serve the entire population and all of its information needs, which makes us specifically a part of the secular world and therefore suspect. How do we establish credibility with Christian teens and yet still serve the needs of "the world"?

Do Ask, Do Tell: Being Approachable

In America today, one of the most effective means of advertising is through word-of-mouth. Establishing strong one-to-one relationships with Christian teens will foster the message to peer groups that "our librarian can be trusted." Prime candidates for such relationships are homeschooled teens, for whom the public librarian usually serves also as school librarian and is often the only teacher-figure external to the family or church. Many teens are being homeschooled for religious reasons, to remain separated from "the world." A librarian who knows the books, materials, and Internet sites most appropriate for Christian students is a treasure and one who will be rapidly shared with fellow Christian teens at church or youth group meetings.

Public librarians actively market the library to schools with visits and book talks designed to draw students to the library. As part of your marketing, consider appearing at Christian youth gatherings to promote your library. Most churches have a youth group; often a very large church will draw to its youth programs teens who are members of the smaller churches. Cultivate a relationship with the youth group leader of one of the larger evangelical churches in your service area and offer to present information on library services at a meeting. The best way to achieve this is to check the yellow pages. The larger churches generally place advertisements that identify at least the senior pastor and sometimes a youth pastor as well. If identified, the latter is your target. If not, call the church and ask for the youth pastor or youth leader. The local youth pastor or leader can be your entrée into many Christian organizations serving teens in your town. This is where your one-to-one relationships will pay off; groups that define themselves as separate from "the world" will be more likely to respond enthusiastically to visitors vetted by a group member or leader.

Many communities have a gathering of pastors from different evangelical churches, often going by a name such as "Ministerial Fellowship." A meeting of this group is an efficient target for a library presentation and may generate a list of contacts among church youth leaders.

If your community has a local Christian cable TV channel or radio station, the personnel are liable to be conversant with the many churches they serve. One call may put you directly in touch with the best means for contacting evangelical churches all in one setting.

Many communities have an active interdenominational program for teens that is a chapter of a national organization. Prominent examples are Young Life (http://www.younglife.org, accessed March 2004) or Youth for Christ (http://www.gospelcom.net/yfc/, accessed March 2004). If your local chapter is not listed in the telephone book, contact the national headquarters by e-mail and ask if a group is active in your area.

Is library advocacy to one specific religious subgroup a blatant disregard for the neutrality of the public library? No, it is an example of targeted marketing, in the same way that publishing booklists for a specific subsection of the collection does not imply favoritism for that part of the collection. If Christian teens feel that "there is nothing in the library for me" while other teens do not feel this way, surely this calls for attention to redress the balance. This is very different from endorsing one set of values as superior to another.

Librarians interacting with Christian teens or youth group leaders are advised to watch *your* and *their* language. Good communication skills are critical. Spiritual values are sensitive areas, and it is easy to unintentionally say or do something disrespectful to someone holding different values. Teens are working on the developmental task of defining themselves in terms of their beliefs and have quick ears when it comes to how people talk to them. They may quickly turn negative if they perceive approaches as disrespectful to their beliefs.

Simultaneously, librarians must be attentive to the specialized language of evangelical Christians. Any number of everyday words may have a specific meaning in the context of evangelical Christianity, for example, "world," "flesh," "tongues," and "deliverance." Other words may be heavily freighted with connotations, such as "evolution," or have meanings particular to evangelical Christian usage, such as, "traveling mercies" and "Spirit-filled."

To familiarize yourself with the language of evangelical Christians, scan publications such as Focus on the Family magazines. This will give you an idea of ways of thinking and usage of words common to this subgroup. Evangelical Christians make a conscious attempt to see the world differently, but at the same time partake of the common culture in ways that other, more strictly separatist groups, such as the Amish, do not.

Since the adjective "evangelical" denotes the desire to share the Gospel with others and invite them to join in, a side effect of establishing credibility and rapport with Christian teens may be an invitation to visit a church, join a Bible study, or "give your heart to Jesus." This crosses the line of professional service and may transgress your comfort level, depending on your own spirituality, but keep in mind that it is meant sincerely. As with any other well-meant but inappropriate invitation, a kind but firm response may be necessary. After all, your strong commitment to your own spiritual life is an affirmation of the value of theirs.

Teen Advisory Boards

Many YA librarians work with teens who help library staff plan and implement programs, select materials, and relate to the teens of the community. Including a Christian teen in your group can build your credibility with the Christian community and your success in integrating this group into your service program—but only if you pick the right teen. One youth group leader gave me this advice:

"It's a great temptation to pick a pastor's kid as your Christian representative. Avoid this temptation. Pastor's kids are not regularly representative of Christian teens at large. They have to hold strongly to the...particular denomination to which their family...is connected. Instead, pick a teen who is active in band or sports—who is already committed to making a success of a team composed of different beliefs."

Including a Christian teen on your advisory group will serve several purposes:

- including a major service population in your program planning
- building a one-on-one relationship to help serve as your entrée to promoting libraries to Christian youth
- giving you a trusted person on which to practice your "Evangelical Christian language" skills
- providing an early warning system for policy, programming, or collection decisions that may cause concern to evangelical Christians

Programming

Providing library programming to Christian teens is tricky business. After all, since you work in a library funded by tax dollars, whenever you gear programs toward any sectarian purpose, you may be accused of crossing the boundary separating church and state.

With many evangelical Christians, separation of church and state is a sensitive issue. Feeling increasingly squeezed out of the public market-place of ideas, they will point out that the phrase "separation of church and state" appears nowhere in the Constitution, but instead in a letter of Thomas Jefferson's imported into numerous court decisions.[5] The First Amendment only prohibits governmental bodies, including publicly funded libraries, from favoring one set of religious beliefs over another. It does not prohibit religious expression in public places altogether. In fact, court decisions may be redressing this imbalance, recently holding, for example, that public schools offering space for extracurricular activities must allow religious groups to meet on the same basis as other groups.

There are three important elements in relating your programming to evangelical Christian teens: equal access, adequate warning, and commu-nity partnering.

Equal access allows Christian teens or youth groups to make use of pub-licly available spaces such as meeting rooms, display cases, or bulletin boards on exactly the same basis as any other group, even for sectarian activities, as long as all religious groups have an equal opportunity to apply for such use. For example, one Timberland (Washington) Regional Library branch has had religious services in the meeting room on Sun-days. The key is that the policy be administered to give all religions an equal chance to book space and to favor no one religion over another. Mar-keting the availability of such spaces to Christian youth groups for their activities sends the message that the library is an inviting and acceptable place to hang out.

On the other hand, since the library serves the entire community against which the more prescriptive Christians define themselves, there is a strong likelihood that at some point a library program or story theme will deal with issues offensive to some Christians. Programs centering on Hal-loween, non-Christian symbols like Santa Claus, ghost stories, witchcraft, Harry Potter, non-Christian mythologies, creation stories from other reli-gions, evolution science or cosmology, or stories involving the Devil as a comic figure may be problematic for some Christians. A discreet warning to a leader about the sensitive nature of an upcoming program will send the message that you know and care about the concerns of Christian fam-ilies and helps establish a mutual trust. When making library visits to Christian schools or entertaining visiting classes, running your presen-tation past the teacher or principal may help you avoid an inadvertent gaffe in front of students. If you are planning to distribute bookmarks or annotated bibliographies, give copies to the teacher or principal before-hand.

Developing relationships with local Christian schools is only one example of community partnership opportunities. The possibilities for partnering are limited only by the time and energy you have to devote to cultivating them. The following examples have worked in various libraries.

Many Church youth programs require member teens to perform some kind of community service. Recruit Christian teens as volunteers to help with collection assessment and recommendations or program preparation. Placing a youth leader in such a position will show that the library is a place friendly to Christians. Use the opportunity to model librarianship as a profession choice.

Computer-savvy Christian teens or youth leaders can help you find Christian Web sites that may prove handy for reference service to Christian patrons—and they love to be asked.

Many areas have homeschool cooperatives that can be excellent venues for presenting library services to the homeschool community. Often state education departments, which may license homeschools, maintain a directory of such cooperatives.

Career days for Christian teens are sponsored by some larger churches to provide programs similar to those offered at the local high school. This is an opportunity to recruit volunteers or applicants for library page openings. It also may offer chances to address Christian teens' concerns about the kinds of materials libraries collect and create some dialogue about intellectual freedom. I have had occasion to counsel several teens who loved libraries and desired to enter the profession but were dubious about working in a library because they felt that the Internet, or another portion of the collection, was offensive to their beliefs. My general approach has been to suggest the opportunities for living as a Christian witness within the profession and to learn how libraries need to mirror and serve the entire community, including both Christians and non-Christians. This means welcoming a Christian presence in the workplace but also requires collecting for, and serving, all segments of the population.

Intellectual Freedom

Perhaps the area of greatest tension between libraries and evangelical Christians is intellectual freedom. The more prescriptive the Christian's belief, the greater the tension. Portions of your collection may come under attack for not reflecting Christian values because library selections must be made with the values of the entire community in mind. With the addition of the Internet to libraries, however, patrons potentially have access to thousands of sources unselected by any librarian. The availability of almost anything, no matter how offensive, seems to cry out for the imposition of some kind of moral order—and nothing advertises the void of order more clearly than this response of a library staff member to a patron complaint: "There's nothing I can do about it..."

There is something we can do about it. Nearly all libraries have written policies governing collection development and Internet access. These policies were developed for important reasons that are rooted in the role of a library in a democracy. Especially before, and certainly after, an intellectual freedom controversy, every presentation of library services should include the library's role, the value of open access, and how the library's collection development and access policies were formulated in light of this role.

In dealing with conflict, one strives to turn a negative interaction into a positive one. In intellectual freedom debates with evangelical Christians, librarians have two arenas for accomplishing this:

1. Neutrality protects the Bible too. Just as your critics have been offended by whatever materials are being challenged, so some are offended by the availability of explicitly sectarian religious materials in a tax-supported facility. In fact, some of the arguments used against certain offensive materials could be used against explicitly Christian materials: "They can look at that in the privacy of their own homes if they want to," or "There are book stores for that kind of thing—let them buy it if they want it," or "That kind of stuff is against my beliefs and I don't want my children exposed to it or accosted by people who have just been looking at it." The same rules of neutrality and open access that protect the presence of challenged material in the library protect the presence of the Bible and other Christian materials.

2. There is something in the library to offend everyone, and there is also something in the library to affirm everyone. Since the library reflects the entire range of interests of the community, one must expect all points of view to be covered in the collection. This criterion gives the option of shifting away from restricting the viewpoints of other community members to the focus of adding materials that reflect a point of view not currently represented. Or to put it in Christian terms, instead of concentrating on throwing the Devil out of the library, let's concentrate on putting more of Jesus in. Collection building is a much more positive role for librarians than gatekeeping.

Building a Collection for Evangelical Christian Teens

No amount of advocacy will have long-term effects unless our collections respond to my youth group member's cry, "There's nothing at the library for me!" In the past, a major reason for this was that materials were marketed directly to evangelical Christians through churches, small specialty shops, or direct mail, so very little of the material published for them found its way into standard review periodicals—and librarians didn't buy materials without reviews. The explosive growth of conservative Christianity in the past two decades has changed all this. Christian publishers are beginning to view libraries as another market, Internet access has revolutionized access to publishers and marketers, and teens are a growing population with money in their pockets.

Librarians are moving with the times. Periodicals such as *Booklist, Kliatt, Library Journal,* and *Horn Book* review materials from Christian publishers and occasionally include articles written from the evangelical Christian perspective. *Publishers Weekly* runs a regular column focusing on publications concerning religion as well as recent articles on teen religion and homeschooling. A Web-based review journal, *Christian Library Journal* (http://www.christianlibraryj.org, accessed March 2004), includes specific Christian criteria in its reviews.

Librarians are also expanding the boundaries of acquisitions procedure, often buying on the basis of customer request or projected demand, even in the absence of reviews. Barometers of popularity, such as the New York Times Bestseller List or *Billboard Magazine,* may drive acquisitions even in the face of negative or non-existent reviews.

The Internet has become the most revolutionary tool of all. Gone are the days when publishers' names and mailing addresses and stacks of catalogs were the librarian's only access to published materials. Catalogs are still wonderful, but Web sites pack so much more information into so little shelf space and are easily updated and linked to other sources in a seemingly endless chain. There is only one thing the Internet does not yet provide—the seasoned judgment of a knowledgeable librarian.

Start Outside the Library!

If you are serious about building a library collection for Christian teens, begin by doing research outside the library. As part of your campaign to build goodwill and support for the library among evangelical Christians, ask about recommended materials at every opportunity. It demonstrates your respect, communicates your commitment to these patrons, and may alert you to new material before your standard review tools find it. One librarian purchased a standard church collection plate and, when visiting youth groups, passed it around for purchase suggestions. Teens considered this quite a hoot and made a point of coming up with something to suggest.

It would be well worth a half day to visit a well-stocked Christian bookstore. You will quickly learn priority publications for Christians, major Christian publishers and their Web site URLs, names of Christian periodicals, and software packages. You will gain a new appreciation of the diversity of materials and viewpoints within this community. You will also increase your "evangelical Christian language" skills. Many Christian bookstores subscribe to the periodical *Christian Retailing*, which provides top twenty lists and publishing forecasts that will be valuable to you as a selector. Christian bookstores receive it free, or at nominal cost, and may be willing to loan it to you or let you use it in-house. It is available to those outside the retail trade by paid subscription (currently $75 per year) through http://www.christianretailing.com (accessed March 2004).

Another venue for good tips on collection development will be your local Christian radio or television station. Often they have a library of new video or audio materials as well as classics. Many times they will let you preview materials, which will allow you to be better informed in your selection decisions.

WHAT ARE EVANGELICAL CHRISTIAN TEENS LOOKING FOR AT THE LIBRARY?

In the chapter on mainline Protestantism, Jenna and Stephen Miller give an explanation of the differences and similarities in reading needs and habits of Protestant teens, emphasizing the special characteristics of evangelical Christians. I strongly recommend that the interested reader first consult that chapter, since, because of space limitations, I will try to minimize the amount of overlap in our coverage. Nearly all of the Christian classics, series, and individual titles they recommend are relevant to evangelical Christian teens. To increase the overall coverage, I will focus on materials not included in their chapter.

I cannot emphasize too strongly the value of the reader's advisory interview. Teens want materials that validate who they are and show them examples of who they can be. For strongly religious teens, this means finding role models within their spiritual belief system. When evangelicals say they are looking for Christian materials, they do not usually mean any materials in which a Christian character is included; they mean one in which the Christian character is portrayed in a positive fashion and where Christian values are clearly promoted. In a religious spectrum defined by its differences from other religions and often from other Christian sects, even this may not be enough of a distinction. Some may not choose to read any fiction; fantasy, even overtly Christian fantasy, such as C. S. Lewis's *Chronicles of Narnia,* may be off-limits. Generally, books including cursing, overt sexuality, and grim realism may raise red flags. This said, even devout Christian teens may wish to explore realms beyond their comfort zone or certainly beyond the comfort zone of their parents. All YA librarians are familiar with that phenomenon. The best response is clearly familiarity with the literature. Librarians should read enough of the literature aimed at Christian teens in order to help them make good decisions. For a number of us this may be tough, given the heavy didacticism of some of the literature, but there are definitely treasures to be uncovered.

Christian publishers and record labels learned quickly that Christian teens are still teens, and you can find Christian variations on major teen themes in literature as well as music trends. Rap, heavy metal, country, and rock music all have overtly Christian counterparts. Romance, science fiction, beauty advice, and series books for Christian teens can also be found.

BUILDING YOUR COLLECTION

The single most reliable selection criterion for Evangelical teens is the publisher. While mainstream publishers may put out books that appeal to Christians (Jan Karon's *Mitford Years* series) or may publish the occasional book by an evangelical/fundamentalist heavyweight author (Tim LaHaye writing for Warner), generally, and especially in series or genre books, they shy away from strong evangelical Christian protagonists. Classic literature also often appeals to Christian teens. For example, Hawthorne's *The Scarlet Letter* or various Thomas Hardy titles certainly reflect a Christian worldview and are not likely to offend Christian readers. On the other hand, publishers in the Christian book field can be counted on to provide reliably Christian slants.

Many publishers who specialize in Christian materials have a continuing or historical connection to a given denomination. Not all Christian publishers are interchangeable. There is a spectrum of publishers reflecting the differing boundaries between the Christian believers and the surrounding world. Publishers at one end of the spectrum, such as Bethany House, tend to reflect a Christianity that is a very matter-of-fact part of a character's everyday life. Some Bethany House authors, such as Janette Oke, while still distinctly Christian, have become almost mainstream.

Other publishing houses, such as Multnomah, reflect a more prescriptive outlook, respecting strong boundaries against the temptations of the world and suggesting a more separatist outlook. A recent example would be Joshua Harris's *I Kissed Dating Goodbye*, which propounds a radical Christian approach to gender relationships.

Yet another publisher, such as Focus on the Family, clearly draws sharp boundaries between the ways of a Christian and the ways of the world, but also seats the Christian family firmly in the middle of the same concerns all families face.

A large number of publishers targeting this market are members of the Evangelical Christian Publishers Association (http://www.ecpa.org, accessed March 2004).

SELECTED TITLES
Fiction

One publication of interest is Barbara J. Walker's *Developing Christian Fiction Collections for Children and Adults: Selection Criteria and a Core Collection* (Neal-Schuman, 1998), which is more comprehensive than I can be in this short essay. John Mort's *Christian Fiction* (Libraries Unlimited, 2002) takes a broader view of Christian fiction and includes titles that may not appeal to or may even offend evangelical Christians, but titles published by members of the ECPA are clearly identified by the symbol of a fish containing the letter "E" (for evangelical). Adult Christian fiction popular with teen readers are tagged "YA," and the guide contains a chapter of YA Christian fiction.

In addition, I endorse the Millers' comments and selections in their chapter. To their list of series, I would add:

For Middle Schoolers

Accidental Detectives (Sigmund Brouwer, Bethany)
Adventures of the Northwoods (Lois Wilfrid Johnson, Bethany)
Bloodhounds, Inc. (Bill Myers, Bethany)
Hidden Diary (Sandra Byrd, Bethany)
Mandie (Lois Gladys Leppard, Bethany)
Parker Twins (Jeanette Windle, Legacy Press)
Ponytail Girls (Jeanette Windle, Legacy Press)
Wakara of Eagle Lodge (Linda Shands, Revell/Baker)
X-Country Adventures (Bob Schaller, Baker)
Young Women of Faith: Lily (Nancy Rue, Zonderkidz/Zondervan)

For High Schoolers

Extreme (for Jesus) Fiction Series (Mark Rempel, Nelson)
Jana's Journal (Jeanette Windle, Kreger)

Nonfiction

Clearly the Bible is the focus for a good portion of nonfiction aimed at this age group. The influence of MTV is shown in the teen Bible commentary *Extreme Journey: Get More Out of It,* by Extreme for Jesus (Nashville, TN: Thomas Nelson, 2001). One of the more attractive devotionals is the *Devotions for Young People* series by Martha Bolton published by Vine Publications, 2002. Each title in the series is centered on a book of the Bible and titles include *When You Walk Through Green Pastures, Stick to the Path* (Psalms), and *If the Tongue's Afire, Who Needs Salsa?* (James).

Recently published books that present a Christian slant on everyday teen concerns include *Stomping Out Depression* by Neil T. Anderson and Dave Park (Ventura, CA: Regal, 2001), *Looking Good from the Inside Out,* a beauty book for girls by Tammy Bennett (Grand Rapids, MI: Revell, 2002), *The Survival Guide for Christians on Campus,* a college prep book by Tony Campolo and William Willimon (West Monroe, LA: Howard Publishing, 2002), and *Bringing Up Good Parents and Other Jobs for Teenage Girls,* a family relationship guide by Nancy Rue (Ann Arbor, MI: Servant Publications, 2001).

Periodicals

Christian periodicals range from the fairly liberal *Christianity Today* to the denominational publications of the stricter fundamentalist sects, most easily located through the Web site of the denomination, many of which have pages specific to teens. More general evangelical periodicals that have broader appeal and are more versatile to librarians serving Christian teens include:

Breakaway and *Brio* (http://www.family.org, accessed March 2004). Published by Focus on the Family for young teen boys and girls respectively. Older teen girls (age sixteen and above) are served by *Brio and Beyond.*

Creation Illustrated (http://www.creationillustrated.com, accessed March 2004). Presents creationist, anti-evolution viewpoint of science.

HM The Hard Music Magazine (http://www.hmmagazine.com, accessed March 2004). Deals with Christian rock music and its producers and musicians.

Homeschooling Today (http://www.homeschooltoday.com, accessed March 2004). Addresses concerns of homeschooling families.

Practical Home-schooling (http://www.home-school.com, accessed March 2004). Addresses concerns of homeschooling families.

World Magazine (http://www.worldmag.com, accessed March 2004) is published as a Christian equivalent to *Time* or *Newsweek.*

In addition, the Evangelical Church Library Association Web site includes suggested core collections and periodicals for Christian school libraries (http://www.eclalibraries.org/magazine.htm, accessed March 2004), as well as links to several major evangelical publisher sites.

Christian Comic Books

The comic or graphic novel format has become increasingly popular among teens, and Christian publishers have not missed this fact. The major Web site for the format is International Christian Comics (http://members.aol.com/ChriCom/buybooks.html, accessed March 2004). It includes series comics, both teen and adult, and some comics in German, Spanish, and even Japanese. There is even a graphic novel version of the popular *Left Behind* series. Action/adventure in a highly stylized drawing mode is represented in the series *Archangels: The Saga,* published by Eternal Comics. Native American teens are featured in the *Dan Red Eagle* series by Lon Cowan. Another Christian adventure series is *Christian Crusader* by John Celesti. Cartoonist Ron Wheeler in his *Jeremiah* series, provides a more humorous take on teen life. The tone of the latter is indicated by some of the titles: *Help! I'm Late For School and I Can't Get Up* and *I Let My Words Be Sweet and Tender 'Cause I May Have To Eat 'Em.*

Music

Christian music crosses the same genre boundaries as popular music, and stardom is just as quickly attained and gone. While new groups will have arisen by the time you read this, there is still some staying power in certain stars that appeal to teens, such as Keith Green, who died before today's teens were born. Some of the current stars as of this writing are:

Christian Rap: DC Talk, Gospel Gangstaz, Primary Colorz
Christian Rock: Audio Adrenaline, Newsboys, Petra, Sonic Flood, Chris Taylor
Contemporary Christian: 4 Him, Michael Card, Steven Curtis Chapman, Points of Grace
Black Gospel: Kirk Franklin, T.D. Jakes, Ron Kenoly, Bebe and Cece Winans

Video

Videos are particularly appealing to teens who have grown up surrounded by visual media. The Millers list the best of the classics and Bible-related videos. Among the finest of the self-help videos is the series *Sex, Love, and Relationships: Straight Talk with Pam Stenzel,* issued by Gateway Films/Vision Video. Tied in with the expected abstinence and Bible-talk is some streetwise advice about sexually transmitted diseases and psychological effects of sexuality. Stenzel pulls no punches and works in stories of her own life, born as the product of a rape pregnancy that her mother elected to carry to term. The public health nurse to whom I am married has used this film series to great effect with teens and their parents.

Zondervan Publishers has issued a series called *Real Kids, Real Life, Real Faith, Real Deal,* a sort of video magazine involving interviews with various teens and their stories. Individual titles include *Castaways, Hardship and Healing,* and *Survivors.* The *Acquire the Fire Video Series for Teens* contains such titles as *How to Date God: Common Problems for Parents, Counselors, and Youth* (Pamplin).

Web Sites

The nesting habit of Web sites means that a single search may branch endlessly until one emerges days older from hours of following sites one to another. A good starting place is a Christian search engine such as http://www.Gospel.com (accessed March 2004) or the teen-friendly site at http://www.awesome.crossdaily.com (accessed March 2004). While I will list a few of the sites particularly useful for YA librarians, sites come and go with astonishing rapidity, so this list may be inaccurate when you read it. Productive searches may include specific doctrinal catchwords, such as "sanctification." More general searches can combine the terms "teen" or "teens" with clearly religious words like "gospel," "praise," and "worship" that are unlikely to be confused with the sort of worldly terms often combined with "teen" in more unsavory sites.

Denominational Web sites are very often linked to a host of supportive Web sites.

Adding "Christian" to a search term brings up a wealth of sources, for example, "Christian colleges" and "Christian music." Two additional arenas that many Christian teens are interested in are "Christian apologetics," which finds sites to help Christians defend the tenets of their faith, or "teenage short-term missions," listing a number of opportunities for mission work.

There are search engines directed at evangelical Christians, including the self-explanatory Biblestudytools.org and Gospelcom.net. There are also sites not explicitly Christian but that may be Christian-friendly, such as Screenit.com, which some Christian teens use to determine whether a given movie is one they should view.

CF Media. For Spanish speakers. URL: http://www.cfmedia.com/Navigation /Spanish.html (accessed March 2004).

Christian Answers Network. Available for teens in 28 languages. URL: http://www.christiananswers.net (accessed March 2004).

Christian Death Metal, Doom, Grind, etc. Music. URL: http://www.deadzine.com (accessed March 2004).

Christian Music Review Headquarters. URL: http://www.christianmusic.org/cmp/ cmrh (accessed March 2004).

CrossSearch.com. URL: http://www.crosssearch.com/Arts_and_Entertainment/ Performing_Arts/Music (accessed March 2004).

Links for Teens. URL: http://www.kids-teens.org/linksforteens.htm (accessed March 2004).

Praize. A search engine for Christian teens. URL: http://www.praize.com/ engine/People/Teens (accessed March 2004).

Suite 101.com. URL: http://www.suite101.com/welcome.cfm/Christian_ Teen_Preteen_Books (accessed March 2004).

DISTRIBUTORS AND DISCOUNTERS

Companies such as Baker & Taylor and Ingram may carry the vast majority of Christian book and audiovisual materials. Less well known are distributors that specialize in evangelical Christian materials. The Spring Arbor division of Ingram, for example, is a major distributor for Christian bookstores. While they do not distribute to libraries, they may provide useful information to selectors.

The leading discount distributor for individuals is Christian Book Distributors (http://www.christianbook.com, accessed March 2004; [800] 247–4784) who stock a wide variety of discounted book and audiovisual materials. Their catalogs can help selectors seeking a quick overview of materials aimed at evangelical Christian audiences; teen-interest pages are specified. They do not, however, establish accounts for libraries. All customer transactions are prepaid orders, regardless of customer status. Another option for closeouts, remainders, or discounted items is the Christian Book Clearinghouse (http://www.christianbookclearing-house.com, accessed March 2004).

Vision Video, a division of Gateway Films, offers a range of Christian video materials, many designed for teen audiences (http://www.vision-video.com, accessed March 2004; (800) 523–0226; Spanish speakers (888) 249–0359). While the initial order must be prepaid, they will establish an account for libraries and invoice subsequent orders. Many Christian book distributors carry films, but do some comparison shopping. For example, I found the series of *Real Kids, Real Life* listed from $8.99 to $20.00 per tape.

A number of independent Christian outlet and bookstores have joined together to form the Parable Group (http://www.parable.com, accessed March 2004). They offer service by mail, or you may consult their Web site for a directory of stores and outlets to see if there is a store near you. Most member Web sites contain specific pages for teen materials. Some individual outlets will establish accounts for libraries.

Larger chains of Christian bookstores have their own Web sites and directories, making it easy to discover a nearby outlet. Family Christian Stores, for example (http://www.familychristian.com, accessed March 2004), has over 300 stores in 39 states; you can find the one nearest you on their Web site by entering your zip code. While individual stores may establish discount programs for pastors, schools, or libraries, the chain as a whole does not invoice library orders. Their larger stores are good repositories, however, for title coverage that may not appear in library review sources.

Gospel music cassettes and compact discs are sometimes harder to find. Nearly all major distributors are contractually obligated to serve only retail outlets. Most of the above book distributors also carry some audiovisual materials. One music distributor willing to carry library accounts and work via purchase orders is Christian Sales (http://www.christiansales.com, accessed March 2004), but no discount is offered. Most of the Christian music labels are available in a single purchasing location and this distributor carries many titles in the cassette format. Beware, however, of the designation "Accomp.," which means that the item is background music designed for performance by a singer, much like a karaoke back-up tape. For more information on Christian Sales, call (615) 851–9114. Another starting point for exploring the realm of Christian music is the Gospel Music Association (http://www.Gospelmusic.org, accessed March 2004). Their Nashville location is a tip-off that this organization leans toward Southern Gospel. Information on black gospel may be found through the many links on http://www.blackgospel.com/links (accessed March 2004).

WORKS CONSULTED

Balmer, Randall. *Blessed Assurance: A History of Evangelicalism in America.* Boston, MA: Beacon Press, 1999. A short but pungent and insightful treatment.

Balmer, Randall. *Mine Eyes Have Seen the Glory: A Journey into the Evangelical Subculture in America.* Expanded ed. New York, NY: Oxford University Press,

1993. Companion to the PBS series; succeeds in personalizing the varieties of evangelical experience.

—— and Lauren F. Winner. *Protestantism in America.* New York, NY: Columbia University Press, 2002.

Cairns, Earle Edward. *Christianity Through the Centuries.* Third ed., revised and expanded. Grand Rapids, MI: Zondervan, 1996. A standard textbook written by an evangelical scholar with all the advantages and disadvantages of textbooks, but it is thorough, fair, and readable.

Carpenter, Joel A. *Revive Us Again: The Re-awakening of American Fundamentalism.* New York, NY: Oxford University Press, 1997. A more scholarly but still fascinating look at the recent upsurge of fundamentalist Christianity.

Marsden, George M. *Understanding Fundamentalism and Evangelicalism.* Grand Rapids, MI: Eerdmans, 1991. Series of very readable essays from a highly respected scholar.

Noll, Mark A. *American Evangelical Christianity: An Introduction.* London: Blackwell, 2000.

Smith, Christian. *Christian America? What Evangelicals Really Want.* Berkeley, CA: University of California Press, 2000. Summarizes, in a startlingly stereotype-breaking way, the findings of a massive study by Professor of Sociology Smith on the thoughts and opinions of American evangelicals. A more scholarly and quantified description is found in Smith's *American Evangelicalism: Embattled and Thriving.* Chicago, IL: University of Chicago Press, 1998.

Synan, Vinson. *The Holiness-Pentecostal Tradition: Charismatic Movements in the Twentieth Century.* Second ed. Grand Rapids, MI: Eerdmans, 1997. The classic study.

Trujillo, Michelle L. *Teens Talkin' Faith: A Christian Perspective.* Deerfield Beach, FL: Health Communications, 2001. The single best book to read on the topic.

NOTES

1. Michael Wessells, "Feeding the Hand that Bites You: Libraries and the Religious Right," oral presentations at numerous library conferences.

2. An excellent typological presentation of the spectrum of evangelical denominations is found in I. Gordon Melton, *The Encyclopedia of American Religions,* Wilmington, NC: McGrath, 1978, especially v. 1, chapter 7, "The Holiness Family"; chapter 8, "The Pentecostal Family"; chapter 10, "The Baptist Family"; and chapter 11, "The Independent Fundamentalist Family."

3. I most strongly recommend Michelle L. Trujillo, *Teens Talkin' Faith: A Christian Perspective,* Deerfield Beach, FL: Health Communications, 2001. This is a compilation of letters and life experiences of Christian teens, written by teens, with occasional commentary by counselor Trujillo. The book will acquaint you with the language and thought processes with which Christian teens face the same life situations as all other adolescents, and will help prepare you for talking with Christian teens, if you are not yet comfortable doing so.

4. Smith, Christian, *Christian America? What Evangelicals Really Want,* Berkeley, CA: University of California Press, 2000; and *American Evangelism: Embattled and Thriving,* Chicago, IL: University of Chicago Press, 1998.

5. For a fascinating discussion of the historical context, see Philip Hamburger, *Separation of Church and State,* Cambridge, MA: Harvard University Press, 2002.

3

◇ ◇ ◇

ROMAN CATHOLICISM

Rosanne Zajko

Roman Catholicism—denomination of Christianity

Beginnings:

Founding of the Church traced to first century Palestine, where Jesus Christ told apostles to spread the gospel and named St. Peter first vicar or pope.

Officially dates beginnings to the moment when Christ selected Peter as guardian of the keys of heaven.

Beliefs and practices:

Believe in Trinity: Father, Son Christ, and Holy Spirit.
Holy Bible comprised of Old and New Testaments, contains the word of God.
The pope is Jesus' representative on earth.

Demographics:

Approximately 65 million members in the United States.
Largest single religious body in the United States today.

Information point:

Catholic Internet Directory, extensive Web site with links throughout Internet. URL: http://www.catholic.net/RCC/Indices (accessed March 2004).

Roman Catholicism is a sacramental faith that believes Jesus is the Messiah, the Chosen One of God. Catholics believe that Jesus established the church and appointed the Apostles to teach all nations about God's love, forgiveness, and salvation through Jesus. Catholics adhere to the teachings of Jesus that are found in Sacred Scripture, to the traditions of the Church and to the teaching authority of the Church, and they endeavor to continue the work of the Apostles in their everyday lives. The Church is known as Roman Catholic because Rome is the city where the pope, the visible head of the Church and the Bishop of Rome, resides.

HISTORY

The Catholic Church, which has proclaimed the good news of salvation and redemption through Jesus for two thousand years, has its origins in the Jewish faith. Jesus' disciples followed Jewish traditions and worshiped at the temple even after Jesus' death, and they also incorporated a communal celebration of the breaking of bread in memory of Jesus into their worship at home. Eventually, Jesus' teachings reached people outside the Jewish faith and new communities of believers were formed. Until officially recognized by the Roman Emperor Constantine in A.D. 312, the early Christians were persecuted and martyred for their faith. The church became known as the catholic, or universal, church because it was open to all who believed in Jesus as the Messiah. As the faith spread from Jerusalem to new lands, the church adapted to local cultural customs. The Catholic Church today reflects that diversity and universality. The Roman Catholic Church is one of many rites, or expressions of worship, within the Catholic faith. Byzantine, Armenian, Coptic, Maronite, and others have their own traditions of worship but are united with the pope and with each other.

As the Church grew and adapted, Church leaders gathered in councils to discuss questions and to determine dogma, infallible teaching that was true to Jesus' teaching. In the early years, the Church in Rome, established by Peter, often intervened in settling doctrinal disputes. Because Jesus told Peter that he would be the rock upon which the church would be built, the Apostles, although equal with Peter, also deferred to him. Through this primacy of Peter, the Church of Rome became the final arbiter and leader among the many local churches. The Church continued to flourish, but eventually disputes arose that could not be settled, and in 1054 a schism developed between the Church of Rome and the Church of Constantinople. The latter separated from the Church of Rome, and became the Eastern Orthodox Church.

Another serious challenge to Church unity occurred in 1517 when the Augustinian monk Martin Luther attempted to reform the Church. Excommunicated for his beliefs, Luther and his followers broke away from the Church and, in response, the Council of Trent was held to address doctrine as well as the reforms Luther sought. The council's decisions regarding theology and reforms came too late to restore unity. Nonetheless, the council's reforms helped the Church recover from the break with Luther and others and gave the Church the identity, practices, and theology that guided it until the mid-twentieth century. The reforming spirit gave rise to the establishment of new religious orders and spreading of the faith through missionary activities in the Americas and Asia.

Before the American Revolution, Catholicism in America grew through Spanish missionary activity in California, and through the establishment of colonies, such as Maryland and Pennsylvania, that promoted religious tolerance. After the Revolution, Catholic immigrants began settling throughout the country, and by 1850 the Roman Catholic Church was the largest single denomination in the United States. This sudden dominance, paired with generalized resentment against immigrants, resulted in strong anti-Catholic sentiment. Members of the Know-Nothing Party wrongly accused Catholics of being loyal to Rome rather than to the democratic principles of America. Catholic churches in New York, Philadelphia, and elsewhere were burned. Continued immigration further established the Catholic Church in American life, and in response to the needs of the immigrants, the Church in America established educational and social welfare institutions, such as hospitals and orphanages, that still minister today to those in need.

The second Vatican Council, held from 1962 to 1965, revitalized the Church in America and throughout the world. Vatican II moved the Church from the sixteenth century into the twentieth century and was ecumenical in nature. Councils of the past had dealt with heresies or threats to Church unity. Pope John XXIII's call for a council took many by surprise because there was no theological dissent in the Church. Vatican II did not change doctrine but it did change other facets of the Church. Ecumenism, the presentation of doctrine and forms of worship that reflected modern thinking, and the place of the Church and the people of God in the modern world were among the teachings of the Council. Vatican II also called for increased participation in the mission of the Church by lay people. After Vatican II, there was concern that some of the changes were too radical, but with John Paul II, the first non-Italian pope since the sixteenth century, there has been more emphasis on the traditions of the Catholic faith.

CORE BELIEFS AND VALUES

When Catholics attend Mass, the communal worship commemorating Jesus' Last Supper, they pray the Nicene Creed, making a statement of their beliefs and summarizing what they believe about God. First formulated in A.D. 325, the Nicene Creed further defines the Apostle's Creed, which stated the tenets of what the early Christians believed about Jesus.

In the Nicene Creed, Catholics state their belief in God the Father, God the Son, and God the Holy Spirit. This belief in the Blessed Trinity does not mean that God, Jesus, and the Holy Spirit are three separate entities; rather, the Blessed Trinity emphasizes the nature of God as three divine Persons united in One God. God has revealed himself in several ways: through creation, through his relationship with the Jewish people, through the Bible, and through the life, death, and resurrection of Jesus Christ. In addition to these divine revelations, Catholics also believe that tradition, both divine and apostolic, and the teaching authority of the Church are the foundation upon which the Church, or the people of God, has been built.

Apostolic Tradition

Apostolic tradition is the handing down of the Catholic faith from the Apostles and the Holy Spirit through succeeding generations to the present day, and it provides a means of presenting Catholic beliefs within the contemporary culture. Tradition is never independent of Scripture, and it is with tradition in mind that Catholics read Scripture, God's revealed word, in context. The living tradition of the Apostles is still present in the Church today in their successors, the pope and the bishops. The bishops, through the Holy Spirit, continue to preserve the faith and continue to teach it. This teaching authority, or magisterium, is based on the tradition of the Apostles as teachers and preachers of the Word of God as revealed to them by Jesus. What the Apostles preached is the same "Good News" that the Church proclaims today: that Christ died for our sins, that he was buried, that he was raised on the third day.

Sacraments

The Apostles sought to bring Jesus' message of salvation to the world, not only through Jesus' words but also through his actions. Jesus himself and his actions were signs of God's love, and those signs and symbols are now present in the Church through the sacraments.

A sacrament is a sign of God's love, a liturgical celebration through which Catholics encounter God in a special way. It is within the sacramental life of the Church that the body of Christ, the Church itself, is united as a worshiping community. Theologian Joseph Martos defines sacraments as "doors to the experience of the sacred," and in passing through those sacramental doors Catholic youth form their religious identity.

Catholics celebrate seven sacraments: the sacraments of initiation or belonging, Baptism, Confirmation, and Eucharist; the sacraments of healing, Reconciliation and Anointing of the Sick; and the sacraments of service, Marriage and Holy Orders.

Baptism

The majority of Catholics are infants when Baptism, their first sacrament, is celebrated. In the sacrament of Baptism, children are welcomed or initiated into the Church community and the child is reborn into a life of faith. The symbols and actions of Baptism, the pouring of holy water, the anointing with oil, and the lighting of a candle, symbolize new life and the presence of the Holy Spirit. The holy water, the oil, and the candle are sacramentals, objects or external signs used by the Church that express faith. For example, in Baptism, the pouring of holy water over the child's head symbolizes life. The anointing with oil on the child's forehead and chest symbolizes that the child shares in the ministry of Jesus. (Jesus himself was anointed and is known as "The Anointed One.") The lighted candle, held by the parents or godparents, symbolizes Jesus, the Light of the World. The child's parents are responsible for seeking reception into the community of believers on behalf of the child and, along with the godparents, they bear the responsibility of instructing the child in the faith until the time of more formal instruction.

Occasionally, an adolescent who has not been baptized as an infant, either in the Catholic faith or another Christian religion, undergoes a spiritual conversion and joins the Catholic faith. In this instance, the adolescent will join the Rite of Christian Initiation of Adults (RCIA), a year-long program of religious instruction to prepare for reception into the Church community at the Easter vigil by receiving all three sacraments of initiation: Baptism, Confirmation, and Eucharist.

Reconciliation

Reconciliation, also known as Confession, is a sacrament of healing. The Church advises Catholics to receive this sacrament at least twice yearly, although more frequent attendance is encouraged.

After an examination of conscience, in which Catholics examine past actions and behaviors to determine if they have been living according to God's word, Catholics meet with a priest to confess their sins, to repent or express sorrow, and resolve to live better Christian lives and to re-establish a relationship with God. The priest's authority to forgive sins has its foundation in Jesus' instructions to his Apostles to forgive sins. Because sin not only affects the relationship with God, but with the entire Church community as well, sins are confessed to a priest who, as a representative of the Church, reminds us of God's forgiveness and the Church's support in the process of living the faith. Reconciliation with God is emphasized. Those receiving Reconciliation have the option of a private, anonymous confession, or a face-to-face confession that often offers an opportunity for pastoral counseling.

During the liturgical seasons of Advent, which prepares for Christ's birth at Christmas, and Lent, which prepares for Christ's death and resurrection at Easter, communal penance services with Scripture readings and prayer are available in addition to individual confessions.

Children are usually between the ages of seven and nine when they first receive Reconciliation. Reconciliation prepares children for their first Eucharist, also known as First Holy Communion.

Eucharist

The second sacrament of initiation into the community of believers is the Eucharist. Also known as Communion, the Eucharist is celebrated daily at Mass. There is no obligation to attend daily Mass, although many Catholics make an effort to do so.

Practicing Catholics attend Mass on Saturday evenings or Sundays. They gather as a community of believers to praise and worship God, to remember Jesus' sacrifice, and then be sent out to live and serve as Jesus did. The origins of the Mass are based on the Jewish Passover meal, the Seder, which Jesus celebrated the night before his death. In the Mass, Catholics celebrate their release from sin and death and the promise of a new life in Jesus. A new covenant with God, in which God is thanked and Jesus' death and resurrection are remembered, is established.

The Mass is composed of an Introductory Rite, the Liturgy of the Word, the Liturgy of the Eucharist, and the Closing Prayer. Scripture readings and communal prayers constitute the Liturgy of the Word, while the sacrament of the Eucharist is the primary focus of the Liturgy of the Eucharist. During the Liturgy of the Eucharist, the bread and wine are consecrated and made holy by the priest through the power of the Holy Spirit, and they literally become the body, the blood, the soul, and the divinity of Jesus. Catholics believe Jesus is present in the Scriptures and, as a matter of faith, believe that he is physically present in the Eucharist, the sharing of the bread and wine, his body and blood. The Eucharist is spiritual food that both nourishes the soul and offers the opportunity to be united with Jesus and united with each other by common beliefs with the Church community. After the Eucharist has been consecrated, the priest and appointed lay people, known as Eucharistic Ministers, distribute the Communion wafer and sacramental wine to those Catholics who wish to receive. A brief period of silent prayer, reflection or meditation occurs after receiving Communion and before the Closing Prayer.

First Holy Communion

The Church community and the family celebrate a child's first Communion with great joy. It occurs either as part of the weekly Sunday Mass or at a special First Communion Mass. Children usually receive their first Communion when they are between the ages of seven and ten, depending on the policy of the parish. Girls wear white dresses and veils, boys wear suits, or both may wear white robes. Reception of both Reconciliation and the Eucharist is made after a preparation period of one to three years. After making their first Reconciliation and First Communion, children continue their religious education and prepare for the third sacrament of initiation, Confirmation.

Confirmation

Confirmation strengthens the Baptismal gift of faith and the Holy Spirit received in infancy and also serves as a statement to the community that the children now accept the faith that their godparents accepted for them at Baptism. Confirmation is not a rite of passage, but it does signify the willingness to accept the adult responsibility of serving the community, the Church, and others. At this age, young Catholics begin serving the Church community as altar servers, musicians and singers, or as assistants in the parish education program. Confirmation is the connection between the personal Christian identity of Baptism with the identity of the larger Church community. Since Confirmation acknowledges a deeper understanding of the faith, most children who are confirmed are between the ages of twelve and sixteen.

Preparing for Confirmation entails continued religious instruction, including the study of saints as models of Christian living. Children will choose a Confirmation name, usually the name of a saint whose life embodies the values of life in Christ.

Additionally, many students will engage in a service project as a means of preparing them for their transition to adult members of the Church. The service projects can be performed either within the parish community or the community where the student lives. Some examples of service projects are assisting at soup kitchens, homeless shelters, nursing homes, or volunteering elsewhere in the community.

During Confirmation, which is celebrated within the Mass, the bishop of the diocese anoints the confirmation candidates with chrism (holy oil) and lays hands on them as a sign of being sealed with the gifts of the Holy Spirit. Just as at Baptism, when infants have godparents to accept the faith for them, the confirmation candidates have a sponsor who provides an example of living a faith-filled life.

Anointing of the Sick and Sacraments of Service

Catholics also celebrate several other sacraments. In times of serious illness, Catholics receive the Anointing of the Sick, a sacrament of spiritual healing.

The two sacraments of service, Marriage and Holy Orders, celebrate the married life and the vocation of the priesthood.

FORMATIVE EXPERIENCES

Parents are the child's first religious educators, but by the time children are three or four years of age a more formalized religious education program is begun. Most parishes provide Sunday school programs for preschool children while their parents attend Mass. Children in primary school attending Mass with their parents may also join a program known as "Liturgy of the Word for Children," in which children leave the assembled community during the Mass to hear the Scripture readings and have them explained and discussed on their level. They rejoin their parents and the community for the remainder of the Mass.

Children who attend parish elementary schools (sometimes called parochial schools) and diocesan high schools or who attend private Catholic elementary and high schools receive religious instruction and sacramental preparation as part of the school curriculum. Children who attend public schools receive their religious education through a parish program known as the Parish Religious Education Program (PREP) or the Parish School of Religion (PSR). Most parishes schedule the classes after school in the afternoon or the evening. Religious sisters (nuns), priests, or active members of the community teach classes. In the primary grades, religious instruction is centered on preparation for the two sacraments, Reconciliation and Eucharist, as well as continued instruction in the doctrine of the faith and Scripture.

Many parishes also offer an opportunity for young teens to socialize and to learn and reaffirm their faith outside of school through youth ministry programs. Youth group activities include prayers, retreats, games, and community service, all of which strengthen the Catholic identity, which is at risk in today's culture. Parishes also offer a competitive sports program known as the Catholic Youth Organization (CYO). Basketball, soccer, and volleyball teams compete against neighboring parish CYO teams.

MISCONCEPTIONS AND STEREOTYPES

Of all the misconceptions concerning the Catholic faith, perhaps none is so misunderstood as the doctrine of papal infallibility. The doctrine of infallibility guarantees that the pope and the bishops, under the guidance of the Holy Spirit, cannot err when teaching about faith and morals.

Another misconception is the place of Mary and the saints in Catholic theology and practice.

The Pope and Infallibility

The pope inherits his authority as the leader of the Catholic Church through the unbroken line of apostolic succession that began when Jesus chose Peter as the rock upon whom the church would be built. Peter, as the first pope or leader, was given the responsibility to teach the truths revealed by Jesus and Scripture. The current pope is a successor to Peter's authority and has the same responsibility unchanged through the centuries: to ensure that the Church remains faithful and true to the teachings of Christ. Jesus promised to send the Holy Spirit to guide the Church when he said, "But when he comes, the Spirit of truth, he will guide you to all truth" (John 16:13).

The belief that God will not permit a pope's humanity to lead the Church away from Christ's teaching is known as infallibility. During the early years of the Church, infallibility was used to respond to challenges or questions about beliefs. It wasn't until the nineteenth century that the doctrine of infallibility was formally stated, guaranteeing that the guidance of the Holy Spirit will keep the Church from promoting errors of faith or morals and will prevent the Church from turning away from God's truth.

Not every pronouncement of the pope is infallible. For a teaching to be infallible certain criteria must be met: 1) the teaching must concern faith or morals, usually already believed by all the Church, or is part of the tradition of the Church. 2) The teaching is addressed to the Catholic Church throughout the world rather than individual churches. 3) The teaching is stated explicitly and must be agreed to and believed by all Catholics as a matter of faith. Once a doctrine is taught infallibly, it cannot be changed.

There are two ways that the infallible teaching is formulated. The pope, on his own authority as official teacher and leader of the church, may speak infallibly, or infallible doctrine can be stated in consultation with the bishops during an Ecumenical Council.

Infallible doctrines are rare. There has been only one proclaimed in the last two centuries when, in 1950, the Church spoke infallibly on the Assumption of Mary, the Mother of Jesus. From its earliest days, the Church always believed that at her death Mary was assumed body and soul into heaven. This teaching, meeting the criteria, was pronounced infallible.

In addition to teaching infallibly, the pope also exercises the Church's magesterium, or teaching authority, in other ways. Papal letters (encyclicals) are letters for the entire Church that teach on a number of different subjects. When the pope issues encyclicals, he may not always be speaking infallibly, although some encyclicals may contain infallible teaching. These teachings illuminate the deposit of faith, doctrine that Catholics have held as true without an infallible pronouncement of the pope. Even when the encyclicals do not contain infallible teachings it does not mean that the teachings should be ignored. The pope is teaching authoritatively and the teaching is presumed true. Any non-infallible teaching has the possibility of error but, within the diversity of the Church, respectful and open discussion can result in clarifying the teaching.

A popular misconception is that the pope controls what Catholics believe and how they act. Within the doctrine of the Church there is some latitude as to what Catholics must assent to in their belief. For example, dogma, the deposit of faith and infallible teachings, requires assent, but belief in the recent apparitions of Mary at Medjugore in Yugoslavia do not require assent.

Mary, Saints, Devotions, and Sacramentals

Mary, as the Mother of Jesus, occupies a special place in the devotional practices of Catholics. Many Catholics honor Mary or other saints in a special way through prayers or novenas, a nine-day period of prayer. It is important to note that these devotions are in no way considered adoration or worship. Devotions can help increase praise and adoration of God as

Catholics reflect on the virtues of faith that were lived by Mary and the saints, but adoration and worship are reserved for God alone.

In addition to praying directly to God, Catholics also use a form of prayer known as intercessory prayer, in which Mary or the saints are asked to pray for us and with us to God—to intercede for us. Just as most Christians pray for others or ask others for their prayers in times of need, so do Catholics ask those who have gone before, the Community of Saints, to pray for them. The saints are models who serve as an example of Christian living. Catholics can enrich their prayer life through devotions and intercessory prayer as long as they lead us to Christ and do not overshadow him. Christ is always the center of all prayer so intercessory prayers to saints do not put the saints above Christ or equal to him.

Many objects when used properly in devotions or church rituals enhance prayer life. These objects, known as sacramentals, include the rosary, statues, holy water, ashes, and candles.

The rosary is a string of beads used by Catholics as a personal devotion and is most closely associated with Mary. The beads are used to keep count of prayers while meditating on the life of Jesus and Mary's role in helping Catholics draw closer to Christ. Like all sacramentals, the rosary is a reminder of God's presence and helps Catholics express their faith.

Another common expression of faith is the sign of the cross. Catholics touch their right fingertips to their forehead, their chest, and the left and right shoulder and pray "In the name of the Father, and of the Son, and of the Holy Spirit. Amen." When entering church, they dip their fingers into the holy water font and cross themselves. The gesture expresses what Catholics believe, and the holy water reminds Catholics of their baptism.

SENSITIVITIES IN WORKING WITH TEENS

Although Confirmation is not a "graduation," some teens see this as the end of their religious education. For others, however, their teenage years are the time to become more involved in the church as they seek to apply their faith to their everyday lives. Teens are moving away from teacher-based instruction about the basic facts of their faith to a process that involves personal questions and challenges about what they have learned. Religious instruction continues for students who have received Confirmation, either through the PREP, the PSR, or through the religious curriculum in the diocesan and private high schools.

Topics such as church history, morality, ethics, social justice, and chastity provide the setting for teens to form their Catholic identity in light of the contemporary culture presented by politics, mass media, and society. The development of their life of faith increasingly becomes their own responsibility rather than that of their parents. Their growing ability for critical analysis, coupled with questions or criticism, can also lead to doubt about practice or beliefs. In this instance, teens will need to have information or a qualified church member available to answer their questions.

The Center for Applied Research in the Apostolate (CARA), a non-profit organization that conducts social scientific studies about the Catholic Church, recently completed a survey among actively involved Catholic youth. In the survey of Catholic teens, three-quarters of whom attend public schools, they indicated that they have a deep commitment to the Church and its teachings.

WHAT ARE CATHOLIC TEENS LOOKING FOR AT THE LIBRARY?

Librarians working with young Catholics should be aware that adolescents' relationship with God often changes in response to their experiences. One of the most dominant aspects of their relationship with God is friendship and gratitude, nurtured through solitary or private prayer. God is seen as both Father and friend, the provider of life, family, and friends. Devotional reading is one need that public libraries can meet. Inspirational titles such as the *Chicken Soup* series or anthologies on teens and prayer help teens connect with the larger world around them.

The primary informational need of Catholic teens is materials on saints because students who are preparing for Confirmation research their lives and deeds. Biographies or biographical encyclopedias detailing the lives of the saints, as well as how they lived their faith, will be helpful for students as they go through the process of deciding which saint's name they will choose.

Catholic teens also look for information on Church history and the areas most likely studied include the Crusades, Martin Luther, the Reformation and the Counter-reformation, and Vatican II. Topics on ethics, morality, and social justice are other areas in which students will need information on a variety of viewpoints. Euthanasia, abortion, genetics, cloning, and other controversial subjects are often points of discussion as Catholic teens seek to understand the Church's stand on moral issues.

BUILDING YOUR COLLECTION

When choosing books that discuss Catholic doctrine and dogma, it is important to choose materials that are in keeping with the teachings of the

Church. Books that contain discussions and interpretations that are consistent with Catholic beliefs will have two statements on the verso of the title page indicating that the discussions and the interpretations are free from doctrinal error. These two statements are the *Nihil Obstat* and the *Imprimatur.* The Latin phrase, *Nihil Obstat,* meaning "Nothing stands in the way," is granted by a diocese's Reviewer of Books and indicates that there are no statements in the book that contradict Church teaching. After a second review, usually by the bishop, permission is granted for publication. This is the *Imprimatur,* meaning "Let it be printed." These statements are guarantees that the subject matter conforms to, and is consistent with, Church teachings, although the reviewer may or may not agree with the subject matter or presentation. As a result, even books that are approved may not always be in agreement if they concern subjects other than faith and morals, also known as the deposit of faith. These two areas are always consistent but other subjects are open for discussion. A variety of materials on the same or a similar subject will give teens an overall and balanced view of the topic. Textbooks always have *Nihil Obstat* and the *Imprimatur.* Other books that may display these two statements are books dealing with theology, canon law, Scripture, and Church history.

A further statement may be added to books if the author is a member of certain religious orders. That statement is *Imprimi Potest,* meaning, "It can be printed." This is the permission given to the author by the head of the religious order to publish the material.

Fiction books and some nonfiction, if they are not teaching faith and morals, do not require the *Nihil Obstat* and the *Imprimatur.*

LIBRARY SERVICES AND PROGRAMS

There are many opportunities for public librarians to work cooperatively with both Catholic school librarians and Catholic young adults, especially in those areas where patrons may not have access to a school library.

The most commonly offered services are bibliographies and reading lists. Bibliographies of saints offer a starting point for students researching them as part of their Confirmation preparation. Other bibliographies that Catholic teens find useful are inspirational books and religious or coming-of-age fiction with young adult characters facing moral dilemmas. These bibliographies can be distributed through parish youth groups or through Catholic schools. Bibliographies listing the library's holdings can be created for specific research assignments and forwarded to the school librarian or classroom teacher.

The public library's services can move beyond bibliographies to provide outreach services such as those offered by the Niles Library in suburban Chicago. Teachers who have completed a teacher form card may call the library and request that specific titles or books on certain subjects be checked out and sent to the school for a six-week loan period. The books are delivered to the schools via the library's homebound van or an interlibrary loan system.

Niles also collaborates with classroom teachers by sponsoring an Assignment Alert service. Teachers who notify the librarian of upcoming projects are eligible for a free dinner. Niles librarian Kate Wolicki requires no deadline on notification date. Teachers can phone, fax, or e-mail an Assignment Alert before an assignment is due or while the assignment is on-going. If the books need to be pulled and delivered by the van, however, the request is due two days before the books are delivered. Wolicki keeps the teachers' names on index cards and a winner is selected in mid-May. Wolicki believes the free dinner is responsible for the increase in the number of teacher Assignment Alerts since the inception of the service. In addition to preparing for the current information need, the Assignment Alert also helps the library plan for future needs. Wolicki said, "If I had a teacher or librarian tell me what was going to be new in the curriculum, I'd buy research and popular books in the area so kids with projects and with newly inspired interests would have books to fill their needs."

Wolicki connects with English department chairs about summer reading lists to guarantee that the library has multiple copies of the titles students are required to read.

Another example of services offered to Catholic youth are the programs offered by the Jervis Public Library in Rome, New York. Teen Services librarian Lisa Matte is actively involved with collaboration. The library and schools have worked together on programs—the library sponsoring speakers and the schools hosting. Because the schools' auditoriums are larger than the library's multipurpose room, library programs were able to reach a larger audience. Matte also offers library instruction by hosting visits from classes for guidance and personal reference services related to specific assignments. In-service programs are planned that will highlight what the library can do for teachers. And in an effort to get students into the library and learn to use technology, the library has been a partner on a Title III grant with a local Catholic elementary school.

Matte has also targeted church groups in an effort to promote the library. Students come to the library after church for a program styled on game shows. Matte has bibliographies prepared for distribution, and books are available that were chosen in response to a survey completed by group members several weeks prior to the event.

For public libraries that maintain Web sites, providing an online list of summer reading requirements is another beneficial service. The Boston Public Library provides online summer reading lists for schools dating back to 1998 on its Teen Lounge page (http://www.bpl.org/kids/summerlists/2003/index.htm, accessed March 2004). Providing Web bibliographies with online links of interest to Catholic teens supplements the library's print materials. Youth services librarians can also visit the schools for book talks and to promote the library's summer reading programs.

Libraries also offer opportunities for Catholic youth to volunteer time working in the community. Teens work as library pages and perform other duties as part of their community service requirement for Confirmation. They can also serve as youth advisors in developing services or programs for other Catholic teens.

PUBLISHERS

The publishers listed below accept orders through Web sites, by phone, or by catalog.

Ave Maria Press
P.O. Box 428
Notre Dame, IN 46556–0428
(800) 282–1865, ext. 1
URL: http://www.avemariapress.com (accessed March 2004)

Ligouri Publications
1 Liguori Drive
Liguori, MO 63057–9999
(800) 325–9521
URL: http://www.liguori.org (accessed March 2004)
Discounts available to libraries based on quantity and product type.

Our Sunday Visitor
200 Noll Plaza
Huntington, IN 46750
(800) 348–2440
URL: http://www.osvpublishing.com (accessed March 2004)

TAN Books & Publishers
P.O. Box 424
Rockford, IL 61105
(800) 437–5876
URL: http://www.tanbooks.com/index.php (accessed March 2004)

Twenty Third Publications
P.O. Box 180
Mystic, CT 06355–0180
(800) 321–0411
URL: http://www.twentythirdpublications.com (accessed March
    2004)

For a complete list of Catholic book publishers, contact:
Catholic Book Publishers Association Inc.
8404 Jamesport Dr.
Rockford, IL 61108
(815) 332–3245
URL: http://www.cbpa.org/index.html (accessed March 2004)

SELECTED TITLES

Many titles listed in the bibliography are available in Catholic bookstores.

Reference

Of the many Catholic reference titles available for collection development, teens will find most useful those that focus on church history and biographical reference for saints.

Glazier, Michael and Thomas J. Shelley, eds. *The Encyclopedia of American Catholic History.* Collegeville, MI: The Liturgical Press, 1997. ISBN 0814659195. A comprehensive view of the people, places, and events in American Catholic history, from its origins to the present day. Also includes related documents that provide background information.

New Catholic Encyclopedia. 2nd ed. Detroit, MI: Gale Group, 2002. ISBN 0787676942. $1,840.75. First new edition since 1967, this series covers all facets of the Catholic faith, from its origins to present day. Articles on contemporary Catholics, such as Mother Teresa and Cesar Chavez, are included, as well as articles on the ethical subjects of cloning, abortion, and reproductive technology.

Shaw, Russell, ed. *Our Sunday Visitor's Encyclopedia of Catholic Doctrine.* Huntington, IN: Our Sunday Visitor, 1997. ISBN 0879737468. Catholic doctrine defined and explained in layman's terms, with references and suggested readings for more information.

Thurston, Herbert J. and Donald Atwater. *Butler's Lives of the Saints.* Allen, TX: Christian Classics, 1996. ISBN 0870611372. Available as a multi-volume set or a single paperback, the entries present factual information on the saints as well as detailing their acts of faith and virtue.

Fiction

Most fiction for Catholic teens focuses on teens' interactions with the Catholic school environment. Although there is no comparable Christian fiction genre for Catholic young adults, many titles published by major publishers do include examples of Catholic youth coming to terms with Catholic theology.

Bruchac, Joseph. *The Winter People.* New York, NY: Dial Books, 2002. ISBN 0803726945. Fourteen-year-old Saxso, a member of the Abenaki tribe, maintains both his Catholic faith and belief in Klist, son of the Great Spirit, when he embarks on a dangerous mission to rescue his mother and two younger sisters taken hostage during an attack by the British on their unprotected village.

Cappo, Nan Willard. *Cheating Lessons.* New York, NY: Atheneum, 2002. ISBN 068984378X. Bernadette, a Catholic and a member of an academic quiz team, discovers that her highly respected teacher has cheated, thereby causing her to question adults' perceptions of right and wrong.

Carroll, Jenny. *Shadowland.* New York, NY: Pocket Pulse, 2000. ISBN 0671787918. Susannah, a student at Father Junipero Serra Mission School, is a mediator who helps ghosts find their way to their eternal reward. She and Father Dominic, a fellow mediator, have met their match when Heather, a former student and a ghost bent on revenge, refuses to leave the school. Jenny Carroll is a pseudonym for Meg Cabot.

Connelly, Neil. *St. Michael's Scales.* New York, NY: Arthur A. Levine, 2002. ISBN 0439194458. A Catholic high school student, feeling guilty for the death of his twin brother who died at birth, considers suicide but worries that he won't get into heaven.

Cormier, Robert. *The Chocolate War.* New York, NY: Knopf, 1985. ISBN 0440944597. A high-school boy refuses to be intimidated into selling chocolates at his Catholic prep school, but his defiance causes him to be victimized.

Dana, Barbara. *Young Joan.* New York, NY: HarperTrophy, 1997. ISBN 006440661X. Traces the life of Saint Joan of Arc, from her beginnings as a simple French peasant to the leader of the French army, to her trial and punishment at the stake.

Fiedler, Lisa. *Curtis Piperfield's Biggest Fan.* New York, NY: Clarion Books, 1995. ISBN 0395707331. C.C.'s attempt to survive the ninth grade at St. Bernadette's, a Catholic girls' school, is complicated by her deep crush on Curtis, an eighth grader at the public school.

Lynch, Chris. *Gold Dust.* New York, NY: HarperCollins Juvenile Books, 2000. ISBN 006028174X. In 1975, twelve-year-old Richard befriends Napoleon, a Caribbean newcomer to his Catholic school, hoping Napoleon will learn to love baseball and the Red Sox and will win acceptance in the racially polarized Boston school.

———. *Slot Machine.* New York, NY: HarperTrophy, 1995. ISBN 0064471403. To prepare for high school, overweight fourteen-year-old Elvin attends a Christian Brother summer camp where he tries to find his place among the athletes while his friend tries to fit in with the cool crowd.

Marchetta, Melina. *Looking for Alibrandi.* New York, NY: Orchard Books, 1999. ISBN 0531301427. Josie Alibrandi, an honors student always in trouble at her Catholic school, deals with the reappearance of her absent father, the suicide of a friend, and the temptation of falling in love with the wrong boy.

Murphy, Claire Rudolf. *Free Radical.* New York, NY: Clarion Books, 2002. ISBN 0618111344. Luke's mother makes her peace with God and the Catholic Church and faces up to her past as a protestor during the Vietnam War, when a protest in which she was involved resulted in murder.

Rinaldi, Anne. *The Staircase.* San Diego, CA: Harcourt, 2000. ISBN 0152024301. A young Methodist girl, abandoned by her father at a Catholic convent in Santa Fe, witnesses the miraculous building of a staircase to the choir loft by a wandering carpenter.

For an updated list of Catholic religious fiction, as well as other young adult religious fiction, see the author's Web site at http://www.ancillae. org/library/students/relfic.htm (accessed March 2004).

Nonfiction

Catholic teens are interested in devotional reading that addresses their concerns on a practical level.

Spirituality/Faith Inquiry

Auer, Jim. *10 More Good Reasons to Be a Catholic: A Teenager's Guide.* Ligouri, MO: Liguori Press, 1999. ISBN 0764803220. Auer speaks to teens with questions or doubts about their faith.

———. *Ten Ways to Meet God: Spirituality for Teens.* Ligouri, MO: Liguori Publications, 1989. ISBN 0892432993. Describes how young adults can build a deeper relationship with God.

Bonacci, Mary Beth. *Real Love: Answers to Your Questions on Dating, Marriage and the Real Meaning of Sex.* Ft. Collins, CO: Ignatius Press, 1996. ISBN 0898706130. Discusses the importance of sex within a loving and committed relationship.

———. *We're on a Mission From God: The Generation X Guide to John Paul II, and the Catholic Church, and the Real Meaning of Life.* Ft. Collins, CO: Ignatius Press, 1996. ISBN 0898705673. Reviews the place of the Church in the twenty-first century, and the place of Generation X in the church.

Forliti, John. *Straight Talk for Young Adults: About Faith & Values.* Mystic, CT: Twenty Third Publications, 1997. ISBN 0896227359. Offers guidance and direction to teens on topics such as sex, the Ten Commandments, responsibility and faith.

Gellman, Marc and Thomas Hartman. *How Do You Spell God?* New York, NY: Morrow Junior Books, 1995. ISBN 0688130410. A rabbi and a Catholic priest, known as the "God Squad," host a daily interfaith talk show on cable in New York City explaining the similarities and differences among the world's major religions.

Leach, Michael and Therese Johnson Borchard, eds. *I Like Being Catholic.* New York, NY: Doubleday, 2000. ISBN 0385499515. Celebrities discuss why and how being a Catholic is part of their identity.

McBride, Alfred. *Father McBride's Teen Catechism.* Huntingdon, IN: Our Sunday Visitor Publishing, 1995. ISBN 0879737042. Discusses the teachings of the Catechism, what Catholics believe, and how those beliefs can be incorporated into the everyday life of teenagers.

Pinto, Matthew J. *Did Adam & Eve Have Bellybuttons... and 199 Other Questions from Catholic Teenagers.* West Chester, PA: Ascension Press, 1998. ISBN 0965922804. Easy to understand answers to a variety of questions that young adults have about the Catholic faith.

Devotional

Auer, Jim. *10 Ways to Get into the New Testament: A Teenager's Guide.* Ligouri, MO: Liguori Press, 1991. ISBN 0892433426. Presents various methods of reading the New Testament for young adults.

John Paul II and John Vitek, ed. *My Dear Young Friends: Pope John Paul II Speaks to Teens on Life, Love and Courage.* Winona, MN: St. Mary's Press, 2001. ISBN 0884897249. Fifty-two reflections on Scripture and John Paul's message to youth.

Kielbasa, Marilyn. *Life Can be a Wild Ride: More Prayers by Young Teens.* Winona, MN: St. Mary's Press, 2001. ISBN 0884894843. Prayers for teens by teens.

Saints

Ball, Ann. *Modern Saints: Their Lives and Faces.* Rockford, IL: TAN Books and Publishers, Inc., 1991. ISBN 089555223X. Biographies of well-known saints of the last 200 years. Includes photos for more recent saints.

Lord, Bob and Penny. *Saints and Other Powerful Men of the Church.* Westlake Village, CA: Journeys of Faith, 1990. ISBN 0926143093. Biographies of well-known saints and blesseds in the church.

———. *Saints and Other Powerful Women of the Church.* Westlake Village, CA: Journeys of Faith, 1989. ISBN 0926143085.

History

Dues, Greg. *Catholic Customs and Traditions.* Mystic, CT: Twenty Third Publications, 1993. ISBN 0896225151. Outlines the historical developments of liturgical seasons and devotions.

Fisher, James. T. *Catholics in America.* New York, NY: Oxford University Press, 2000. ISBN 0195111796. Presents an overview of the establishment and growth of the Catholic faith in America, from 1528 to the present day.

Hinds, Kathryn. *The Church.* New York, NY: Benchmark Books, 2001. ISBN 0761410082. Discusses the influence of the Church on European civilization during the Middle Ages.

Johnson, Kevin Orlin. *Why Do Catholics Do That?* New York, NY: Ballantine Books, 1994. ISBN 0345397266. Explains how faith and worship are expressed through customs and culture.

Series

At Issue series. Farmington Hills, MI: Greenhaven Press. Includes primary and secondary sources as well as differing opinions on controversial issues. Also available in paperback. (See also similar titles in the *Current Controversies* series.)
> *The Ethics of Abortion.* 2001. ISBN 0737704691.
> *The Ethics of Genetic Engineering.* 2002. ISBN 0737707992.
> *The Ethics of Human Cloning.* 2002. ISBN 0737704721.
> *Human Embryo Experimentation.* 2002. ISBN 0737712856.
> *Physician Assisted Suicide.* 2002. ISBN 073771056X.
> *Should Abortion Rights Be Restricted?* 2003. ISBN 0737713275.

Opposing Viewpoints series. Farmington Hills, MI: Greenhaven Press. Essays examining the pros and cons of controversial topics. Also available in paperback.
> *Abortion.* 2002. ISBN 0737707771.
> *Biomedical Ethics.* 2003. ISBN 0737712198.
> *The Death Penalty.* 2002. ISBN 0737712244.
> *Euthanasia.* 2002. ISBN 0737701269.
> *Genetic Engineering.* 2001. ISBN 0737705124.
> *Hate Groups.* 2004. ISBN 073772800.
> *Homosexuality.* 1999. ISBN 073770053X.
> *Religion in America.* 2001. ISBN 1565100026.

Turning Points series. San Diego, CA: Greenhaven Press. Essays examining each topic within the historical context.
> Hay, Jeff, ed. *The Early Middle Ages.* 2001. ISBN 0737704810.
> Nardo, Don, ed. *Rise of Christianity.* 1998. ISBN 1565109627.
> Stalcup, Brenda, ed. *The Crusades.* 2000. ISBN 1565109929.
> ———. *The Inquisition.* 2001. ISBN 0737704853.
> Thompson, Stephen P. *The Reformation.* 1999. ISBN 1565109619.
> ———. *The Renaissance.* 2000. ISBN 0737702192.

The Way People Live series. San Diego, CA: Lucent Books. Examines each topic within the context of cultural and political events.
> Netzley, Patricia D. *Life During the Renaissance.* 1998. ISBN 1560063750.
> Rice, Earle. *Life During the* Crusades. 1998. ISBN 1560063793.
> ———. *Life During the Middle* Ages. 1998. ISBN 1560063866.
> Sherrow, Victoria. *Life in a Medieval Monastery.* 2001. ISBN 1560067918.
> Stewart, Gail. *Life During the Spanish Inquisition.* 1998. ISBN 1560063467.

World History series. San Diego, CA: Lucent Books. An overview of each topic, focusing on the establishment and structure of each time period.
> Bachrach, Deborah. *The Inquisition.* 1995. ISBN 1560062479.
> Corrick, James A. *The Early Middle Age*s. 1995. ISBN 1560062460.
> ———. *The Late Middle Ages.* 1995. ISBN 1560062797.
> Dunn, John M. *The Enlightenment.* 1999. ISBN 1560062428.
> Flowers, Sarah. *The Reformation.* 1996. ISBN 1560062436.
> Osman, Karen. *The Italian Renaissance.* 1996. ISBN 1560062371.

Web Sites

The following Web sites provide a general overview of the Catholic faith. Many sites provide teen pages.

American Catholic. Includes seasonal and daily features, minute meditations and online editions of the monthly periodical, *St. Anthony Messenger.* Youth Updates page changes monthly and includes questions and answers. URL: http://www.americancatholic.org/default.asp (accessed March 2004).

Catholic.net. Comprehensive site that includes current events and the latest Catholic news from around the world, as well as information on saints, spiritual living, apologetics, and student life. URL: http://catholic.net (accessed March 2004).

Catholic Goldmine Over 3,000 links, including Youth, History, Documents and Saints. URL: http://www.catholicgoldmine.com/ (accessed March 2004).

Catholic Information Network. Youth page on pull down menu with links to additional youth sites. Large collection of additional pages, including spirituality, prayers, liturgy. URL: http://www.cin.org (accessed March 2004).

Catholic Internet Yellow Pages. Topical subject directory of Internet sites. URL: http://www.monksofadoration.org/directory.html (accessed March 2004).

Catholic Online. The mission of this site is to serve as a center for the exchange of Catholic information. Site is divided into Catholic Traditions, News and Media, Reading and Worship, and Catholic Life. URL: http://www.catholic.org/ (accessed March 2004).

Disciples Now. A partnership with St. Anthony Messenger Press specifically for teens that includes some of the same content as American Catholic, as well as new features such as chat rooms, Catholic topics, and liturgical Scripture readings. URL: http://www.disciplesnow.com (accessed March 2004).

EWTN. Online version of Mother Angelica's Eternal Word Television Network. URL: http://www.ewtn.com/ (accessed March 2004).

Guideposts for Teens. An online Christian magazine offering advice and suggestions for living a Christ-filled life. URL: http://www.gp4teens.com/index.asp (accessed March 2004).

Index of Saints. Brief biographical sketches of saints. URL: http://www.saint-patrickdc.org/ss/ss-index.htm (accessed March 2004).

Life on the Rock. EWTN's (Eternal Word Television Network) show for teens. Site includes the Catholic jukebox, question of the day and religious life. URL: http://www.ewtn.com/rock/ (accessed March 2004).

The Mary Page. Prayers, meditations and Marian research. URL: http://www.udayton.edu/mary/ (accessed March 2004).

New Advent. Includes links to other Catholic sites, as well as resources on documents, councils, and sacraments. Also includes the online version of the fifteen volume 1913 edition of *The New Catholic Encyclopedia.* URL: http://www.newadvent.org (accessed March 2004).

Online Edition of the Catechism of the Catholic Church. Second edition of the English translation of the Latin text, including directions on how to read the online version. URL: http://www.scborromeo.org/ccc.htm (accessed March 2004).

United States Conference of Catholic Bishops. Offers latest news, liturgical resources, daily readings and movie reviews, in addition to information on specific departments and pastoral work promoted by the conference. URL: http://www.nccbuscc.org/ (accessed March 2004).

U.S. Catholic. Online version of monthly periodical. Also includes back issues and additional links. URL: http://www.uscatholic.org/ (accessed March 2004).

The Vatican. The official Vatican web site contains a wealth of information on church documents, Vatican museums, news services, and biographical information on recent popes. The site map is helpful for orientation. URL: http://www.vatican/va/ (accessed March 2004).

The Word Among Us. Online monthly magazine with articles on living your faith. Also includes Saints and Heroes page, which is updated monthly. URL: http://www.wau.org/index.html (accessed March 2004).

You Magazine. Online Catholic Youth magazine focusing on secular and religious issues important to teens. URL: http://www.youmagazine.com (accessed March 2004).

WORKS CONSULTED

Barry, John F. *One Faith, One Lord.* New York, NY: William H. Sadlier, Inc., 1994.

Cahoon, Joanne M. "Catholic Youth Challenge the Church—and Themselves." *The Catholic World* (March/April 1990): 86–89.

Carotta, Michael. *Sometimes We Dance, Sometimes We Wrestle.* Dubuque, IA: Harcourt Religion Publications, 2001.

Carotta, Mike. "Young, Catholic and Capable." *The Catholic World* (Sept./Oct. 1995): 236–239.

Eipers, Carole M. "Adolescent Faith Development: Facing the Tough Questions." *The Catholic World* (Sept./Oct. 1994): 215–218.

Johnson, Kevin Orlin. *Why Do Catholics Do That?* New York, NY: Ballantine Books, 1994.

Kohmescher, Matthew F. *Catholicism Today.* New York, NY: Paulist Press, 1999.

Martos, Joseph. *Doors to the Sacred.* Ligouri, MO: Triumph Books, 1991.

McBrien, Richard P., ed. *Harper Collins Encyclopedia of Catholicism.* New York, NY: HarperSanFrancisco, 1995.

Niebuhr, Gustav. "Hope and Dismay in Catholic Survey." *The New York Times* (August 31, 1996): 10.

Pollard, John E. *Exploring Our Catholic Faith.* Mission Hills, CA: Benziger Publishing Co., 1996.

Savelesky, Michael. *Catholics Believe.* Dubuque, IA: Brown-ROA, 2000.

ACKNOWLEDGMENTS

Catholic section reviewed by Rev. Henry A. Cassel, O.S.A., July 2002.

4

◈ ◈ ◈

THE CHURCH OF JESUS CHRIST OF LATTER-DAY SAINTS

L. Kay Carman

The Church of Jesus Christ of Latter-day Saints— denomination of Christianity

Beginnings:

Organized by Joseph Smith, Jr. (1805–1844) in 1830 in Fayette, New York. He received Book of Mormon from angel Moroni on golden tablets.

Joseph Smith, Jr. was founder, first prophet and president of the Church. Brigham Young (1801–1877), second president, led the Saints to what is now Utah in 1847.

Beliefs and practices:

God the Father and Jesus Christ are two separate beings.

Scriptures used are the Bible (Old and New Testaments), Book of Mormon, Doctrine and Covenants, and Pearl of Great Price. Members regard Book of Mormon as a supplement to the Bible and a second witness of divinity of Jesus Christ.

Latter-day Saints believe marriages performed in LDS temples are for eternity and family life continues after death.

(continued)

> *(continued)*
> ## Demographics:
>
> Current number of members in United States is estimated to be over 5 million.
>
> ## Information point:
>
> The official Web site of the Church, *The Church of Jesus Christ of Latter-day Saints,* URL: http://lds.org (accessed March 2004).

The Church of Jesus Christ of Latter-day Saints is the fifth largest religion in the United States and one of the fastest growing faiths in the world, nearing twelve million adherents in 2003. Founded in western New York in 1830, it has been called America's most successful homegrown faith.

The Church has never been officially called "the Mormon Church," yet its members are often improperly referred to as "Mormons" due to their acceptance of the Book of Mormon as a volume of scripture. Latter-day Saints[1], as they prefer to be known, accept the Bible as scripture but it is the Book of Mormon, and events surrounding its advent, that sets the Church apart from other Christian denominations.

HISTORY

Latter-day Saints believe that during Christ's ministry on earth, he established a church that functioned as the source of authority and doctrine. An essential component was Christ's ordaining of twelve Apostles, men given authority to lead the Church in his absence. After Christ's crucifixion and resurrection, the apostles continued to conduct the affairs of the church; then, one by one, they were martyred, leaving no one with authority to direct the church. By the end of the first century A.D., church members, lacking a prophet, began to change the organization and doctrine established by Christ. The original church and Christ's authority to direct it disappeared from the earth.

The apostles Paul and Peter prophesied of an apostasy from the pure doctrine and authority established by Christ himself. Peter also taught that in the latter days of earth's history there would be a "restitution of all things." (Acts 3:19–21, New Testament of the Bible) Latter-day Saints believe that this restoration began in 1820 through a young man named Joseph Smith, Jr.

The First Vision

A religious fervor gripped the region of western New York around 1820, and clergymen enthusiastically sought new converts. Joseph Smith, Jr. had been taught to pray, to read the Bible, and to have faith in God but, because of the confusion and dissension between denominations, he could not reach a decision regarding which church to join. He wondered if any of the churches were right and, if there was only one true religion, how it could be recognized.

While reading the New Testament he came across the scripture found in James 1:5: "If any of you lack wisdom, let him ask of God, that giveth to all men liberally, and upbraideth not; and it shall be given him." The scripture struck him with great force. He took to heart God's promise that he would freely give, and he determined to ask God for wisdom. He entered the woods near his home, knelt, and prayed to know which church to join. His prayer was answered with a vision of two beings standing in a pillar of light that identified themselves as God the Father and his son, Jesus Christ. Joseph was directed not to align himself with any of the existing churches.

Several days later Joseph mentioned his vision to a local minister and found that his claim made him the object of ridicule and persecution. Years later he reminisced, "It caused me serious reflection then, and often has since, how very strange it was that an obscure boy, of a little over fourteen years of age...should be thought a character of sufficient importance to attract the attention of the great ones of the most popular sects of the day, and in a manner to create in them a spirit of the most bitter persecution and reviling." (*Pearl of Great Price*, Joseph Smith History 1:23)

The Coming Forth of the Book of Mormon

Three years later Joseph received another visitation, this time from a being that identified himself as Moroni, a resurrected prophet from ancient America. Moroni told Joseph that God had a great work for him to do. Joseph was to be the prophet through whom the Church of Jesus Christ would be restored to earth, with the same organization and priesthood authority as the original church. Moroni told Joseph of an ancient record engraved on metal plates and buried in a nearby hill. The record contained abridged histories of former inhabitants of the Americas, and told of their origins in the land of Palestine. Moroni also told Joseph that the "fullness of the everlasting Gospel was contained in it, as delivered by the Savior to the ancient inhabitants." (*Pearl of Great Price*, Joseph Smith

History 1:34) With heavenly help, Joseph translated the plates from their ancient language and published the English translation as the Book of Mormon.

Growth and Persecution

Through the latter part of the 1820s, Joseph continued to receive further visitations and authority (priesthood) from heavenly beings. The Church of Jesus Christ of Latter-day Saints was officially organized on April 6, 1830, the same year as the publication of the Book of Mormon.

The Church attracted a great deal of religious persecution. One reason was its rapid growth and influx of foreign-born converts, primarily from the British Isles. Another was the perceived unorthodoxy of its doctrines, particularly the claim to exclusive Christian authority.

The body of Saints moved first from New York to northeastern Ohio, then to Missouri. In the fall and winter of 1838 and 1839 they were driven *en masse* from the state of Missouri after an official edict from the governor called for their removal or extermination. An estimated 10,000 to 12,000 people moved to western Illinois and built the city of Nauvoo, where they lived in relative peace for a few years and the Church continued to grow.

In 1844, Joseph Smith and his brother, Hyrum, were shot to death in Carthage, Illinois while incarcerated on charges of treason.[2] Church members today honor Joseph Smith, Jr. as a prophet, like those of Biblical times, and as a martyr for the Christian faith. He is not worshiped but simply held in high esteem.

Exodus to the West

Leadership passed to Brigham Young, who inherited a city of 15,000 whose inhabitants were on the verge of expulsion. In the face of continuing regional violence, most began to abandon Nauvoo in February 1846, leaving all behind and beginning a 1,300-mile cross-country trek that would find its terminus in the valley of the Great Salt Lake, then Mexican territory. Between 1847 and 1869, when the Transcontinental Railroad was completed, more than 65,000 people walked or wagoned along the Mormon Trail.

The Church Today

By 2003, the Church had grown to nearly twelve million members worldwide. Its world headquarters are located in Salt Lake City, and due to its historical prominence in the area, it is often thought of as a Utah church. In 1996, however, a milestone was reached when the membership of Latter-day Saints living outside the United States exceeded those within the States, thus establishing the Church as worldwide. The international growth rate has continued to outpace the U.S. growth rate, and today only fifteen percent of all Latter-day Saints live in Utah.

Gordon B. Hinckley, the current president and prophet of the Church, attributes the growth to the Church's strong moral stand, family-centered emphasis, friendliness of members, and practical answers to questions regarding the meaning of life. The Church also has a very proactive missionary program.

CORE BELIEFS AND VALUES

In answer to an inquiry posed to Joseph Smith, Jr. by a journalist, Joseph summarized the teachings and doctrines of the Church in thirteen basic tenets known as the Articles of Faith of The Church of Jesus Christ of Latter-day Saints. They are:

1. We believe in God, the Eternal Father, and in His Son, Jesus Christ, and in the Holy Ghost.
2. We believe that men will be punished for their own sins, and not for Adam's transgression.
3. We believe that through the atonement of Christ, all mankind may be saved, by obedience to the laws and ordinances of the Gospel.
4. We believe that the first principles and ordinances of the Gospel are: first, faith in the Lord Jesus Christ; second, repentance; third, baptism by immersion for the remission of sins; fourth, laying on of hands for the gift of the Holy Ghost.
5. We believe that a man must be called of God, by prophecy, and by the laying on of hands by those who are in authority, to preach the Gospel and administer in the ordinances thereof.
6. We believe in the same organization that existed in the Primitive Church, namely, apostles, prophets, pastors, teachers, evangelists, and so forth.
7. We believe in the gift of tongues, prophecy, revelation, visions, healing, interpretation of tongues, and so forth.
8. We believe the Bible to be the word of God as far as it is translated correctly; we also believe the Book of Mormon to be the word of God.
9. We believe all that God has revealed, all that He does now reveal, and we believe that He will yet reveal many great and important things pertaining to the Kingdom of God.

10. We believe in the literal gathering of Israel and in the restoration of the Ten Tribes; that Zion (the New Jerusalem) will be built upon this the American continent; that Christ will reign personally upon the earth; and, that the earth will be renewed and receive its paradisiacal glory.

11. We claim the privilege of worshiping Almighty God according to the dictates of our own conscience, and allow all men the same privilege; let them worship how, where, or what they may.

12. We believe in being subject to kings, presidents, rulers, and magistrates, in obeying, honoring, and sustaining the law.

13. We believe in being honest, true, chaste, benevolent, virtuous, and in doing good to all men; indeed, we may say that we follow the admonition of Paul: we believe all things, we hope all things, we have endured many things, and hope to be able to endure all things. If there is anything virtuous, lovely, or of good report or praiseworthy, we seek after these things. (*Pearl of Great Price*, "The Articles of Faith")

The Purpose of Life

LDS doctrine teaches that all people are spirit children of God, the Heavenly Father, and that we lived with him as spirits in a pre-mortal existence. Coming to earth was part of a plan that would allow us to progress as eternal beings. When we die, we can potentially return to live with God and our Savior, Jesus Christ.

Scriptures

Church doctrine is based on teachings found in both ancient and modern scriptures. Latter-day Saints believe the Bible to be God's word but not all of his word. They also accept the Doctrine and Covenants (revelations received by Joseph Smith and other latter-day prophets), as well as the ancient scriptures of the Book of Mormon and The Pearl of Great Price (a collection of translations and narrations from Joseph Smith).

The Book of Mormon is revered as "a new and additional [to the Bible] witness that Jesus Christ is the Son of the living God and that all who come unto him and obey the laws and ordinances of the gospel may be saved." (*Book of Mormon*, Introduction) To Latter-day Saints, its writings support, confirm and in some instances clarify the teachings of the Bible.

The Godhead

One significant way in which Latter-day Saints differ from most other Christians is in their belief of the nature of God. Through Joseph Smith's vision of God and Jesus Christ it was revealed that the two are distinct, embodied personages of unlimited power and glory, and that man is created in God's likeness.

Jesus Christ was the firstborn of Heavenly Father's children in a premortal existence. He offered to come to earth and allow himself to be crucified to break the bonds of death through resurrection. He would serve as the Savior for all mankind; that is, atone for the sins of those who would believe in him, repent, and live according to the laws of his gospel.

For Latter-day Saints, the love, sacrifice, and example of Jesus Christ are commemorated weekly through a sacrament service that is the center of the Sunday worship service. The sacrament, a partaking of bread and water in remembrance of Christ's body and blood, is a time of recommitment. Through it, Church members take upon themselves Christ's name, commit to keeping his memory always before them, and request the constant companionship of the Holy Spirit, the third member of the Godhead.

Heaven and Hell

Latter-day Saint doctrine specifies three degrees of post-mortal glory as constituting what most Christians would refer to as heaven. While all are realms of eternal reward, they ascend in their nature and glory. The highest kingdom in Latter-day Saint doctrine is the Celestial kingdom, correlating in significance with the heaven of most Christian theology. In LDS doctrine, marital and kinship relationships established on earth and sealed in one of the Church's temples (128 worldwide as of 2003) can continue in the Celestial kingdom. The concept that "families are forever" is a pinnacle doctrine of Mormonism and the focus of much of church curricula, publication and effort.

Hell is a not a commonly discussed concept in LDS theology; a similar realm is more commonly referred to as "outer darkness," and it is the final abode of the most unashamedly wicked. Most people, all literal children of God who loves and reaches after them, are believed to inherit a kingdom of glory.

Sunday Worship Services

Sunday worship services and social activities are held in buildings called meetinghouses or chapels. Often a meetinghouse will serve as the home for several congregations called wards or branches. The membership of the ward is determined by geographic boundaries, and members are assigned to a ward based upon their address. The primary Sunday worship service held within the meetinghouse is called Sacrament Meeting and includes the singing of hymns, prayers, partaking of the sacrament (communion), and addresses given by lay members. Additional meetings held before or after the Sacrament Meeting are Sunday School, Primary for children aged three through eleven, Young Women for twelve-year-old through seventeen-year-old girls, Relief Society for women, and Priesthood for men and boys twelve and older.

Leadership

Fewer than one hundred men hold full-time positions in the ecclesiastical structure of the Church. They are called General Authorities and receive a living stipend, if needed. Among them are:

The First Presidency. Gordon B. Hinckley, the president of the church in 2003, is sustained and revered by church members as a prophet, seer, and revelator, and the only person on earth to receive revelation from God for the entire church membership. The president is typically assisted by two counselors, and together they constitute the highest governing body of the Church.

The Quorum of the Twelve Apostles. The second highest governing body, the apostles, are called to full-time ministry by the president of the Church. They have the scriptural charge to be special witnesses of Jesus Christ and to ensure the orderly and correct operation of the Church. At the death of the president of the Church, the senior apostle[3] becomes president of the Church.

Quorums of Seventy. Policies of the First Presidency and the Twelve are implemented mainly through senior leaders known as members of the Quorums of Seventy. Many reside in nations around the world, overseeing the Church's growth and development in that region.

Congregations. On a day-to-day basis, the Church's congregations are managed by unsalaried leaders with a significant amount of local autonomy. The primary geographical subdivisions of the Church are wards (local congregations), stakes (comprised of several wards), and areas. At each level of administration, Church officers support and train individuals over whom they preside. Bishops preside over local Church congregations and are the leaders with whom rank-and-file members most frequently interact.

Stakes and wards have no paid ministry. The substantial volume of labor required to run a stake or ward effectively is carried out by the members, who are asked by their leaders to contribute in various administrative, teaching, or service-oriented positions. Ample opportunity is given every willing member of the congregation to have such a "calling," rendering service, sharing talents, and gaining new skills.

The Priesthood

The Church is administered through the priesthood, the authority to act in God's name. Church members believe that the authority that existed at the time of Christ was restored to the earth through the prophet, Joseph Smith. Boys who are deemed worthy, through an interview administered by their bishop, receive the lesser, or preparatory, priesthood beginning at age twelve. Their tasks include collection of freewill offerings and preparing and passing the sacrament. They also begin to serve with an adult male as "home teachers," priesthood representatives who watch over several families in the congregation and visit them monthly.

Church Finances

Members' voluntary offering of a tithe, ten percent of their income, finances the Church's operations. Tithing is not required to be a practicing member of a ward, but it is required to qualify for participation in temple worship. Tithes are used for the construction of meetinghouses and temples, the missionary program, curriculum materials, genealogy libraries, and church education.

FORMATIVE EXPERIENCES

Eighteen-month-old children enter the nursery program and are taught simple songs with messages such as "I am a Child of God." Three-year-olds through eleven-year-olds progress through the Primary program, grouped by age. The curriculum focuses on gospel doctrine, Church history, and the development of personal moral character. They also have regular opportunities to give short, prepared talks.

At age twelve, boys and girls advance from Primary into the Young Men and Young Women (YM/YW) organizations. Girls are divided into three classes by age groups. Boys are divided into the same age groups but meet in Aaronic Priesthood quorums. Each class and quorum has a presidency comprised of a president, two counselors, and a secretary. They are trained by the organization's adult leaders to conduct and preside at meetings, and to extend fellowship to their peers, both in and out of the Church.

Latter-day Saints value education. Members around the world are encouraged to seek the level of secular education that will best serve them, and the Church endeavors to augment secular education with spiritual training. The religious education program offered to high-school-aged students by the Church Education System (CES) is called Seminary. Students in many parts of the United States attend early morning Seminary in a member's home or church meetinghouse classroom before going to school. High schools in some western states offer release-time in which students may take Seminary as a non-credit elective during their regular school schedule.

The Church owns and operates four institutions of higher education: Brigham Young University (BYU) in Provo, Utah; BYU Idaho in Rexburg; BYU Hawaii in Laie; and the LDS Business College in Salt Lake City, Utah. Religious education is part of the curriculum at these schools. It is also available to LDS students who attend public and other private colleges and universities. College students may take Institute classes in scripture study, church history, and topics of spirituality. Social activities are also an important part of the Institute program.

MISCONCEPTIONS AND STEREOTYPES

The most significant stereotype with which LDS youth struggle are the claims by some Christian denominations that Latter-day Saints are not Christian, or that they are a cult. The idea that polygamy is still an integral part of LDS society, and that women and those of African ancestry are considered inferior to white males are also common misconceptions.

Are Latter-day Saints Christians?

In answer to the question "Are you Christians?" Church President, Gordon B. Hinckley, has said, "We are Christians in a very real sense and that is coming to be more widely recognized..."

> We...accept Jesus Christ as our Leader, our King, our Savior. The dominant figure in the history of the world, the only perfect man who ever walked the earth, the living son of the living God. He is our Savior and our Redeemer through whose atoning sacrifice has come the opportunity of eternal life. (http://www.LDS.org, accessed March 2004)

Plural Marriage

For a few decades in the mid-1800s, the practice of plural marriage[4] was a defining characteristic of Mormon orthodoxy and early Utah culture. Although never practiced by a majority of Latter-day Saint men, the principle was viewed as a direct revelation from God to his prophets, and it continued even under harsh public comment and criticism by national media. Its constitutionality was tested in the nation's courts for several years. In 1890, Church prophet Wilford Woodruff announced a revelation ending the practice. The early stereotype remains, however.

In 1998, President Hinckley said of the Church's stand on polygamy: "This Church has nothing whatever to do with those practicing polygamy....If any of our members are found to be practicing plural marriage, they are excommunicated, the most serious penalty the Church can impose. Not only are those so involved in direct violation of the civil law, they are in violation of the law of this Church" (http://www.LDS.org, accessed March 2004).

Blacks and the Priesthood

Another socially unpopular doctrine for more than twelve decades was that men of black African ancestry, although they could join the Church, could not be ordained to the Church's lay priesthood, and thus serve in positions of congregational leadership. Though the doctrinal rationale for this prohibition was discussed frequently in the highest Church circles, no official position was ever declared by the president of the Church.

The twelfth president, Spencer W. Kimball, announced a revelation in June of 1978: "the long-promised day has come when every faithful, worthy man in the Church may receive the holy priesthood, with power to exercise its divine authority, and enjoy with his loved ones every blessing that flows therefrom, including the blessings of the temple. Accordingly, all worthy male members of the Church may be ordained to the priesthood without regard for race or color" (*Doctrine and Covenants*, Official Declaration 2).

Black membership in the Church has grown considerably since the revelation was announced. In his book, *What is Mormonism All About?*, W. F. Walker Johanson states: "the Mormon Church has missionaries—including Black missionaries—throughout Africa...South America...Asia, and is baptizing Blacks, and many other ethnic groups, in large numbers. The Church has bishops and other church leaders who are Black, has a growing population (both in the U.S. and abroad) of Black members, and is energized by this new infusion of strong members ..." (p. 43).

Women and the Priesthood

Within the Church, the priesthood is given only to males; consequently, some have accused Latter-day Saint doctrine of being sexist. Faced with such accusations, Church leaders have attempted to clarify that it is not the Church, nor the men administering it, who make such determinations but God himself. President Gordon B. Hinckley has stated: "The Church...follows the teachings of prophets, ancient and modern. Its doctrine is based on the scriptures and other revelations to those leaders. In the Church today, the First Presidency declares the doctrines, teachings and practices...[They] have been consistent through the ages that ordination to the priesthood has been reserved for men who have been called of God by those who are in authority" (The Church of Jesus Christ of Latter-day Saints, Public Affairs Department archives).

Although contemporary society may see the policy of ordaining only males to the priesthood as a sign that women are considered inferior, both LDS women and men view it as obedience to God's commandments rather than obedience to a policy set by male leaders of the Church.

> ...nearly all female members would indicate that they fully support the Church's position on only males being allowed to hold the priesthood; and, in fact, most women would state that they have significant responsibilities in the Church, and that, in many ways, they are the driving force behind their husbands' priesthood service. Women hold positions at all levels within the Church. They are teachers, administrators, leaders, and companions...in family and Church decisions. (Johanson, p. 110).

The Word of Wisdom

One way in which LDS youth differ from their peers is their choice not to drink caffeinated beverages, both hot drinks and sodas. Faithful Latter-day Saints follow a health code revealed to Joseph Smith in 1833, commonly called "the Word of Wisdom." Adapted through decades of application, the Word of Wisdom encourages a number of things (the eating of healthful foods including grains, fruits, vegetables and, sparingly, meat) and proscribes the use of others (including coffee, alcoholic beverages, tobacco, and illegal drugs).

Missionaries

Single LDS young men aged nineteen to twenty-six are encouraged to suspend all other pursuits and seek temporary appointment as a missionary. Single young women may also seek a "mission call." Young men serve for twenty-four months, young women eighteen. All are self-sustaining, relying on funds procured through saving, the support of parents or other family members or, in cases of need, from the general missionary fund of the Church. More than 60,000 missionaries currently serve in 120 nations and territories. Thousands become fluent in second and third languages and return home as knowledgeable ambassadors for the nations in which they have served.

WHAT ARE LDS TEENS LOOKING FOR AT THE LIBRARY?

It is generally agreed that more girls than boys use the library and that they are in search of a good story, making selections from both the adult and young adult fiction collections. LDS teen girls read LDS fiction because it suits them as religious young women. They know they will find wholesome stories, devoid of profanity, explicit sex, and violence. Choosing LDS fiction is as close as they can come to an assurance that they will not be offended by a book's content.

In 1999, a survey of reading preferences among LDS youth was conducted by Washington County (Oregon) Cooperative Library Services. The results reflected the preferences of over 2,000 high school students who were asked to list favorite authors and specific titles they would borrow from a library. Adult fiction outnumbered young adult (YA) fiction forty-four to thirty-eight percent, with the most popular authors being Dean Hughes, Gerald Lund, and Anita Stansfield. Young adult authors most often mentioned were Cheri Crane, Chris Heimerdinger, and Jack Weyland. Adult nonfiction titles comprised eleven percent of the total. Young adult nonfiction comprised only six percent, with John Byteway's books accounting for all but one title.

An interesting resource for discovering what LDS church members are reading is the Salt Lake County Library System Web site (http://www.slco.lib.ut.us, accessed March 2004). It is updated monthly and lists both fiction and nonfiction. From the Web site home page, select "Book Lovers Area." From the "Sites for Book Lovers" page, select the "Religious Fiction & Non Fiction" link and then the "LDS Fiction and Non Fiction" text link. Links are included for publishers' Web sites.

BUILDING YOUR COLLECTION

Materials published by LDS publishers and written for an LDS audience are seldom reviewed in library journals. Ruby Cheesman, the LDS fiction buyer for the seventeen branches of the Salt Lake County Library System, makes her selections from catalogs and also makes buying trips to the nearest Deseret Book store. She looks for well-established authors and relies on the reputation of the publishers. Also helpful is the fact that a good relationship with the bookstore manager and employees has been established, and they keep her informed of titles they expect to be especially popular. Since most librarians will not be familiar with the names of LDS authors, name recognition will not be a factor in making selections. Relying on the Best Sellers list on the Web site of an LDS publisher or vendor will simplify and expedite selection.

The essential criteria for selecting books for LDS youth is determining that the materials are written by practicing Latter-day Saints and/or published by an LDS publisher. Youth are looking for both fictional and inspirational stories in which they can see a reflection of themselves, and they also look for role models. Materials authored by people not of the religion seldom correctly portray beliefs and life style. All materials authored by disgruntled former Church members have the potential to offend devout LDS teen readers.

TYPES OF MATERIALS AVAILABLE

Materials for LDS teens include the same classifications, formats, and most of the same genres found in any YA collection: fiction (adventure, historical, intrigue, mystery, romance, series), nonfiction (biography, humor, inspirational, instructional), music on cassette and compact disc, video recordings and DVDs.

Fiction

If there is one author whose books could be classified as LDS fiction classics, it would be Jack Weyland. He was among the first authors of LDS fiction and was *the* first to write for young adults. Weyland has authored more than twenty-five young adult titles since the publication of his first novel, *Charly*, in 1980. *Charly* was subsequently made into a full-length motion picture released in 2002.

Along with Weyland, Cheesman's picks for the most notable authors of fiction are Chris Heimerdinger, Cheri Crane, Donald Smurthwaite, Robert Farrell Smith, Clair Poulson, and Susan Evans McCloud.

Jennie Hansen, the author of eleven books, concurs with Cheesman's picks of Crane, Heimerdinger, and Weyland as the most prominent authors of LDS fiction for teens. Reaffirming the case that girls make selections from both the young adult and adult fiction collections, Hansen says that although she writes for an adult audience, about one-third of her fan letters come from teens. Other authors Hansen considers notable are Kerry Blair, Betsy Brannon Greene, Dorothy Keddington, Clair Poulson, and Anita Stansfield. Each of these authors writes primarily for adult audiences, but their books are accessible to teens.

Several historical fiction series, written for adults but popular with teens, offer librarians the chance to make their money go further by appealing to a larger number of readers. *The Work and the Glory* by Gerald Lund is a hugely popular series about early Church history. Lund's series, *The Kingdom and the Crown,* is set in New Testament times and could be enjoyed by Christians of any denomination. Dean Hughes' *Children of the Promise* series is set during World War II.

Inspirational

Several categories of nonfiction materials fall under the heading of inspirational reading. Books written by the current prophet and president of the Church will always be of interest. For example, *Way to Be!* by President Gordon B. Hinckley was a best seller at both Deseret Book and Seagull Book and Tape in early 2003.

A companion book to the "Especially for Youth" (EFY) program, week-long retreats sponsored by the CES, is published each summer and is always in demand. John Bytheway, a popular EFY inspirational speaker, has enjoyed success in both books and talks-on-tape as an outgrowth of his retreat participation. Popularity of young adult titles is short-lived because they are always being replaced by something new, but Bytheway's books have proven to be exceptions.

Books on Preparing for Religious Observances

Ordination of boys to the Aaronic Priesthood at age twelve marks a coming of age within the Church community as they assume responsibility for being of service to the congregation. John Bytheway's book, *Honoring the Priesthood: As a Deacon, a Teacher and a Priest,* listed in the bibliography, offers twelve-year-old through eighteen-year-old boys advice on conducting themselves properly in the offices of the Aaronic priesthood.

When a mission call is received, youth have about three months to physically prepare before they report to a missionary training center. Spiritual and emotional preparation, however, has been in progress since childhood. Three books appear in the bibliography that focus on mission preparedness, Bytheway's *Honoring the Priesthood* and *What I Wish I'd Known Before My Mission* and *Prepare with Honor* by Randy Bott.

Where Do I Go From Here? Finding Your Personal Mission as a Young Adult Woman, by Irene Ericksen and Jan Pinborough, is aimed at girls who have just graduated from high school.

Compact Discs

Among the most popular CDs are movie soundtracks, currently *The R.M.* and *The Best Two Years.*

Popular singing groups are Jericho Road and Providence.

A recording featuring original works composed for the annual EFY program, available through Deseret Book, is released each summer and is always very popular.

Two women recording artists, Cherie Call and Hillary Weeks, record for adult audiences but enjoy a great deal of cross-over popularity with teens.

Videocassettes and DVDs

God's Army, an independent film produced and directed by a Church member, was released in theaters in 1999 and has subsequently been released on videocassette and DVD. The film marked the first time an LDS movie had been produced for general audiences. It was quickly followed by *Brigham City, The Singles Ward, Out of Step, Charly,* and *The R.M.* Movies currently in theaters that will be released on DVD and VHS soon are *The Book of Mormon Movie v. 1: The Journey, The Best Two Years, The Work and the Story, The Day of Defense,* and *Pride and Prejudice: A Latter-day Comedy.* Additionally, *The Other Side of Heaven,* based on the true-life missionary experiences of Church leader John H. Groberg, was released as a motion picture in 2001 by Disney and is available on DVD and VHS.

Librarians would be able to identify new LDS films by checking the Best Sellers list on the Deseret Book Web site, (http://www.deseretbook.com accessed March 2004) or by talking with a contact person at the LDS distributor with whom they have established an account.

PUBLISHERS AND DISTRIBUTORS

Deseret Book, one of two publishing companies owned by the LDS Church,[5] publishes materials under the imprints of Bookcraft, Deseret Book, Eagle Gate, and Shadow Mountain. Headquartered in Salt Lake City, Utah, it is the single most important vendor from which to purchase print and audiovisual materials for LDS patrons. Managers are receptive to setting up credit accounts for libraries, so purchase orders may be used. Bookstores are located in nine western states and in St. Louis, Missouri. A discount of twenty percent is typical. Libraries not near a store may call the customer service department at (800) 453–4532 to establish an account. There is no special set-up required if ordering is done online with a credit card (http://www.deseretbook.com, accessed March 2004). If the "bill to" and "ship to" information indicates that the purchaser is a library, the twenty percent discount will be applied. Indicate in the "message" field that the purchaser is a library and eligible for a discount.

In navigating the Deseret Book Web site the most useful feature to selectors will be the home page feature, "Bestsellers." By selecting this link, selectors then have the option of choosing to view the top ten best sellers of the previous week in the areas of "LDS music" and "LDS youth." Another feature of the Web site is the ability to sort titles by popularity.

Excel Entertainment Group of Salt Lake City specializes in music and film and offers libraries a thirty percent discount. An account may be established by submitting a credit application prior to the first order. Their Web site is located at http://www.excelentertainment.com (accessed March 2004) and their phone number is (801) 355–1776.

Covenant Communications is headquartered in American Fork, Utah. Their Web site home page states that their "mission is to provide the best products possible to the LDS market." Covenant is a publisher, rather than a vendor, and Deseret Book stocks the majority of their products. They recommend that their titles be ordered from a vendor rather than attempting to establish an account with the publisher.

Covenant's sister company, Seagull Book and Tape, operates a chain of eighteen bookstores in Utah, California, and Arizona (http://www.seagullbook.com, accessed March 2004). They carry some of the same products as Deseret Book.

A problem in ordering LDS materials from companies such as Baker & Taylor or Ingram is that large distributors may have only a few copies of a title in their warehouses and an order may not be filled completely. Although an LDS bookstore may offer only half the discount available through a jobber, the difference becomes insignificant if orders are unfilled. The convenience and time saved by shopping at Deseret Book or another LDS distributor makes up for the smaller discount.

LIBRARY SERVICES AND PROGRAMS

The following are suggestions for drawing LDS youth to the library and providing information or services that satisfy specific interests and needs within the Church community.

Information for Prospective Missionaries

Prepare bibliographies of materials to assist missionaries in their preparation to live in a foreign country for two years. *CultureGrams,* a division of Millennial Star Network and Church-owned Brigham Young University, is a good place to start. Add titles of materials in your collection that can give readers insight into the climate, living conditions, food, transportation systems, communications systems, and health care, plus what it is like to live in a particular country. Both juvenile and adult materials would be appropriate for the list as it will also be of interest to the families of the prospective missionary.

Genealogy

Genealogy is a very important topic to LDS Church members because of their belief in the eternal nature of families. Workshops on using print genealogy materials and Web sites offer another opportunity for outreach. If your library has a multi-station computer lab, perhaps it could be reserved for a class offered to youth by a reference librarian or a genealogy specialist from the Church. Although genealogy libraries are located in many LDS meetinghouses, most are small and can seat only a few people. You may be able to provide a learning experience by providing a space for a larger group of youth to explore Web sites and receive instruction on how to navigate sites and research their ancestral lines.

Boy Scouts of America

The activity program for LDS boys living in the United States is the Boy Scouts of America. Let members know if your library owns a set of Merit Badge Handbooks and other scouting resources. If an LDS Scout is interested in the library setting for an Eagle Scout project, you and he can arrive at a mutual agreement for service that will fulfill the Scouting requirement and benefit the library and its patrons.

Book Talks at Relief Society

Once word begins to spread within the Church community that LDS materials are available in the library, staff members may receive requests to give book talks or present classes on selecting good books for children and teens at a Relief Society Enrichment meeting, an evening ward meeting held monthly for women.

Marketing information on library materials to the mothers of teens has proven to be an effective method for disseminating information to youth. To reach the most mothers in your service area, check the telephone directory for The Church of Jesus Christ of Latter-day Saints. Phone numbers for stakes and wards will be listed. Select the stake or ward whose address places it nearest your library. If leaving a message, ask for the name of the Stake or Ward Relief Society Education Counselor. A stake counselor will pass the information on to her ward counterparts; by using her as a contact you can reach the families of six to ten congregations with one phone call. If you provide her with masters of your LDS literature booklist, she can distribute them and duplication will be done within each ward.

Recruiting LDS Youth as Volunteers

Because of the goal-oriented programs of the Young Men's and Young Women's organizations, both boys and girls are anxious to find meaningful service projects. Recruit teen advisory committee members and volunteers by contacting the Young Women's and Young Men's presidents, who are adult leaders, within the local ward or stake boundaries. Ask for contact information for the stake or ward Young Women's president. She will share the information with her counterpart in the Young Men's organization.

Tours

Your library is probably already providing tours for Achievement-age girls and Cub Scouts. Girls in the Achievement Program are eight through eleven years old, corresponding in age to Cub Scouts. Both have program requirements to become familiar with resources within the library. These children will be teens soon, and tours provide an opportune time to mention materials that are specifically of interest to Church members, as well as volunteer opportunities available to teens.

SELECTED TITLES
Fiction

Andersen, C.B. *The Book of Mormon Sleuth*. Salt Lake City, UT: Bookcraft, 2000. ISBN 1573456640. A great aunt gives fourteen-year-old Brandon her rare edition of the Book of Mormon, expecting him to follow its teachings and keep it safe from the menacing thief who is determined to take it from her. Sequel: *The Book of Mormon Sleuth 2: The Lost Tribe*.

Crane, Cheri. *The Girls Next Door*. American Fork, UT: Covenant Communications, 2002. ISBN 1591560721. Four young women rooming together at BYU Idaho discover new friendships and, through their trials, learn to rely on the Lord to watch over them.

———. *Kate's Turn*. American Fork, UT: Covenant Communications, 1994. ISBN 1577346602. Sixteen-year-old Kate, chafing under what she considers to be the old-fashioned restrictions of the Church, travels back in time and learns from an ancestor what it really means to be a Latter-day Saint. Sequels: *Kate's Return; Forever Kate; Following Kate; Sabrina & Kate*.

Hansen, Jennie. *Abandoned*. American Fork, UT: Covenant Communications, 2002. ISBN 1591560705. Just as she settles into a new job and relationship, Tisa's frightening childhood memories and the reality behind them threaten to ruin her life.

———. *Beyond Summer Dreams*. American Fork, UT: Covenant Communications, 2001. ISBN 1577348893. Taylor falls for her grandmother's boarder, a veterinarian with powerful enemies, and they team together to keep their loved ones safe.

Heimerdinger, Chris. *Tennis Shoes Among the Nephites* (*Tennis Shoes Adventures* series, v. 1). American Fork, UT: Covenant Communications, 1999, 1989. ISBN 1577344677. Two unlikely friends working out the mystery of an Indian legend suddenly find themselves transported to the ancient world of Book of Mormon times. Sequels: *Gadiantons and the Silver Sword; The Feathered Serpent, Parts 1 and 2; The Sacred Quest; The Lost Scrolls; The Golden Crown; The Warriors of Cumorah; Tower of Thunder*.

Hughes, Dean. *Rumors of War* (*Children of the Promise* series, v. 1). Salt Lake City, UT: Deseret Book, 1997. ISBN 1573451991. Set at the outbreak of World War II, a missionary in Germany and his family in Utah are both affected by unfolding world events. Sequels: *Since You Went Away; Far From Home; When We Meet Again; As Long as I Have You*.

———. *The Writing on the Wall* (*Hearts of the Children* series, v. 1). Salt Lake City, UT: Bookcraft, 2001. ISBN 1570087253. LDS families face the upheaval of sixties-era politics, threats of nuclear war, and racial injustice. Sequels: *Troubled Waters; How Many Roads?*

Lund, Gerald. *Fishers of Men* (*The Kingdom and the Crown* series, v. 1). Salt Lake City, UT: Shadow Mountain, 2000. ISBN 1573458201. Set in the days of Christ's ministry, leaders in the rebellious Zealot movement are cautious in their examination of Jesus' teachings and his claim to be the Messiah. Sequels: *Come Unto Me; Behold the Man*.

———. *Pillar of Light* (*The Work and the Glory* series, v. 1). Salt Lake City, UT: Bookcraft, 1990. ISBN 088494770X. Benjamin moves his family from Vermont to New York and crosses paths with Joseph Smith, the young prophet who claims to have seen God and Jesus Christ. Sequels: *Like a Fire is Burning; Truth Will Prevail; Thy Gold to Refine; A Season of Joy; Praise to the Man; No Unhallowed Hand; So Great a Cause; All Is Well.*

McCloud, Susan Evans. *Palmyra.* Salt Lake City, UT: Bookcraft, 1999. ISBN 1570087040. Five girls come of age in a town shaped by a new religion and the teachings of the young prophet Joseph Smith. Sequel: *Kirtland.*

Nunes, Rachel. *Ties That Bind.* American Fork, UT: Covenant Communications, 2002. ISBN 1577349393. Rebekka's fiancé develops serious health problems, and she has to decide whether she should marry him and risk losing him to death or free herself to find love and happiness with another.

Poulson, Clair. *I'll Find You.* American Fork, UT: Covenant Communications, 2001. ISBN 157734801X. Working in a prison, Jeri thinks she recognizes one of the inmates as a childhood friend whose kidnapping she witnessed.

———. *Lost and Found.* American Fork, UT: Covenant Communications, 2002. ISBN 1591560926. Amnesiac Coleen is searching for her past and someone is searching for her—a man who would be imprisoned if she remembers him.

Smith, Robert Farrell. *All is Swell: Trust in Thelma's Way (Trust Williams Trilogy, v. 1).* Salt Lake City, UT: Deseret Book, 1999. ISBN 1573454664. Trust Williams envisioned a foreign mission but finds himself in a Tennessee backwater ministering to misfits. Sequels: *Falling for Grace: Trust at the End of the World; Love's Labors Tossed: Trust and the Final Fling.*

———. *Captain Matrimony.* Salt Lake City, UT: Bookcraft, 2001. ISBN 1573459690. Besides teaching math at Mishap High School, Andy is tricked into teaching a course that will require him to unravel the mystery of a local curse.

———. *For Time and All Absurdity.* Salt Lake City, UT: Bookcraft, 2002. ISBN 1570088233. When Ian loses his dream girl and his dad runs into trouble with the law, he thinks things can't get any worse. Then he returns to college where he's saddled with the world's most irritating roommate, and begins a string of dating misadventures.

Smurthwaite, Donald. *The Search for Wallace Whipple.* Salt Lake City, UT: Deseret Book, 1994. ISBN 0875798306. Having been challenged by his bishop to keep a journal, sixteen-year-old Wally records the ups and downs, joys and fears, of his sophomore year. Sequel: *Do You Like Me, Julie Sloan?*

Stansfield, Anita. *Someone to Hold.* American Fork, UT: Covenant Communications, 2002. ISBN 1577349911. Christy finds friendship and love when she helps a stranger stranded on a lonely road during a blizzard.

Weyland, Jack. *Charly.* Salt Lake City, UT: Deseret Book, 1980. ISBN 0877478147. Charly and Sam, two mismatched characters, find romance. Sequel: *Sam.*

———. *Cheyenne in New York.* Salt Lake City, UT: Bookcraft, 2003. ISBN 1570089094. A love story between an LDS girl from Idaho and a New York advertising executive plays out in the aftermath of the September 11, 2001 terrorist attacks.

Nonfiction

Beckham, Janette Hales and others. *Living the Young Women Values.* Salt Lake City, UT: Bookcraft, 1999. ISBN 1570087067. Faith-promoting messages focusing on the values of the Young Women's program.

Bott, Randy. *Prepare with Honor.* Salt Lake City, UT: Deseret Book, 1995. ISBN 087579954X. Provides practical advice for young men and women planning to serve full-time missions for the LDS Church.

Bytheway, John. *A Crash Course in Teenage Survival.* Salt Lake City, UT: Bookcraft, 2001. ISBN 1573459305. Advice for teenagers about topics of self-esteem, prayer, friendship, morality, dealing with tragedy, and learning to love the scriptures.

———. *Honoring the Priesthood: As a Deacon, a Teacher and a Priest.* Salt Lake City, UT: Bookcraft, 2002. ISBN 1570088632. Advice for members of the Aaronic Priesthood on proper conduct.

———. *What I Wish I'd Known Before My Mission.* Salt Lake City, UT: Deseret Book, 1996. ISBN 1573452076. Practical advice on helping elders and sisters get off to a good start on their missions.

———. *You're Gonna Make It.* Salt Lake City, UT: Deseret Book, 1997. ISBN 1573453013. Offers advice and encouragement on facing some of the common difficulties experienced by young people as they move from seventh grade through high school.

Daybell, Chad. *The Youth of Zion: Guidance from Modern Prophets on Dozens of Timely Topics Facing Today's Families.* Springville, UT: CFI Books, 2002. ISBN 1555176313. Advice from modern prophets on what God expects of his people.

Ericksen, Irene. *Where Do I Go From Here? Finding your Personal Mission as a Young Adult Woman.* Salt Lake City, UT: Bookcraft, 2002. ISBN 157008839X. Advice and spiritual insights into making decisions on education, mission, marriage, and career.

Gould, Jeanni. *Perfect Projects for Personal Progress.* American Fork, UT: Covenant Communications, 2002. ISBN 1591560357. Hands-on value experiences and projects with original songs.

Hawkins, Chad. *Youth and the Temple: What You Want to Know and How You Can Prepare.* Salt Lake City, UT: Bookcraft, 2002. ISBN 1570088462. Explores the history and meaning of LDS temples and suggests how to keep the temple of the body worthy of entering the temple building for ordinances and worship.

Hinckley, Gordon B. *Way to Be! 9 Ways to Be Happy and Make Something of Your Life.* Simon & Schuster, 2002. ISBN 0743238303. Provides young adults with a plan for discovering and embracing the things in life that are truly valuable and worthwhile.

Jeffery, R. Dale and V. Ruth Jeffery. *Devotionals for LDS Youth.* Houston, TX: DaVinci Publishing Group, 2001. Ready-to-use spiritual thoughts and devotionals for Seminary and talks.

Sunshine for the Latter-day Saint Teenager's Soul. Salt Lake City, UT: Bookcraft, 1999. ISBN 1570086591. Upbeat stories and poems to motivate, encourage and caution LDS teens.

Tolman, Blair. *The Dance Book: 333 Ways to Ask, Answer and Plan for Dances.* Fruita, CO: Legacy Book Publishing, 1997. ISBN 096558352X. Creative ideas for inviting someone to a dance, responding, dinners, themes, decorations, and music.

———. *Group Dating! 30 Ideas.* Fruita, CO: Legacy Book Publishing, 1999. Ideas for get-togethers with friends, or church activities.

Audiovisual Formats

Cassettes

Bytheway, John. *Bytheway, It's John.* Thousand Oaks, CA: Vision Records, no date available. ISBN 6877471792. Humorous skits, routines, verses, song parodies, impersonations, and one-liners aimed at LDS youth.

————. *Bytheway, It's John: The Second Verse.* Salt Lake City, UT: Deseret Book, 2000. ISBN 1573456483.

Compact Discs

The Best Two Years soundtrack. Orem, UT: Hale Yeah! Records, 2004. ISBN 9692407192.

Bytheway, John. *Are Your Standards Fences or Guardrails?* Salt Lake City, UT: Bookcraft/Deseret Book, 2001. ISBN 1570087415. Uses stories and humor to explain Church standards regarding the media, modesty, and morality.

————. *Five Scriptures that Will Get You Through Almost Anything.* Salt Lake City, UT: Bookcraft, 2002. ISBN 1570087490. Using scriptures and quotations from Church leaders, perspective is offered on surviving personal trials and tragedies.

The Home Teachers soundtrack. Orem, UT: Hale Yeah! Records, 2002. ISBN 9692406912.

Jericho Road. *True North.* Salt Lake City, UT: Shadow Mountain, 2002. ISBN 6877479688.

Not Your Mother's LDS Music. Salt Lake City, UT: Deseret Book, 2003. ISBN 8302761852.

Providence. *Providence.* Salt Lake City, UT: Shadow Mountain, 2004. ISBN 6875791048.

The R.M. soundtrack. Orem, UT: Hale Yeah! Records, 2002. ISBN 9692406912.

The Singles Ward soundtrack. Salt Lake City, UT: Guapo Recording Co., 2002. ISBN 9692406912.

Whatever It Takes: Music to Inspire and Strengthen the Youth. Salt Lake City, UT: Deseret Book, 2002. ISBN 6877479564.

Videorecordings and DVDs

Brigham City. Spartan Home Entertainment, 2002. ISBN 0486870932 (DVD). Sheriff Clayton must serve both justice and mercy to uncover Brigham's deepest secrets, find the serial murderer and keep the small town from ripping itself apart.

God's Army. Zion Films, 2002. ISBN 2590623872 (DVD), ISBN 2590623853 (VHS). Life as a Mormon missionary is not what nineteen-year-old Brandon Allen expected, but by persevering amidst the harsh realities of missionary life in Los Angeles he realizes that his most important convert may be himself.

The Other Side of Heaven. Burbank, CA: Walt Disney Home Entertainment; distributed by Buena Vista Home Entertainment, 2003, 2001. ISBN 0788844393 (DVD), ISBN 0788844377 (VHS). Sent on a three-year mission to Tonga, 19-year-old John Groberg finds himself in the midst of a culture as remote to him as the island is to his Idaho Falls home. Not understanding the language and lonely for his fiancée Jean, John faces suspicion, distrust, typhoons, tidal waves, mosquitoes, and other perils of man and nature as he reaches out to the people of Tonga.

Out of Step. Thomson Productions, 2002. ISBN 0926100463 (DVD), ISBN 0926100453 (VHS). A coming of age story of a Utah girl who goes to New York to become a professional dancer and is challenged in her attempt to secure a scholarship, her values, and her testimony of the gospel.

The R. M. Orem, UT: Halestorm Entertainment; distributed by Halestone Distribution, 2003. ISBN 9692407049 (DVD), ISBN 9692407033 (VHS). A recently returned LDS missionary is anxious to return to his family, girlfriend, and job. Despite his confidence that he will be blessed for his faithful service, he's surprised to find his life turned upside down.

The Singles Ward. Salt Lake City, UT: Halestorm Entertainment, 2002. ISBN 2526110008 (DVD), ISBN 2526110003 (VHS). Recently divorced Jonathan Jordon is thrust back into the dating scene and pressured into joining the local singles ward.

Web Sites

Beliefnet. Features articles on God, faith, prayer, the nature of spirituality, society and ethics. All religions respected. Mormonism is listed as a Christian religion. Includes a bulletin board for Mormon teen chat. URL: http://www.Beliefnet.com (accessed March 2004).

Cheri Crane. Author's Web site. URL: *http://www.chericrane.com* (accessed March 2004).

Chris Heimerdinger. Author's Web site. URL: http://www.cheimerdinger.com (accessed March 2004).

Deseret Book. Web site for the Church-owned publisher. URL: http://deseretbook.com (accessed March 2004).

Jack Weyland. Author's Web site. URL: http://www.jackweyland.com (accessed March 2004).

Jeff Lindsay's Cracked Planet. Articles by BYU graduate and chemical engineer Lindsay examine topics of scientific interest within the context of the gospel, and responds to critics of the church. URL: http://jefflindsay.com (accessed March 2004).

John Bytheway. Web site for popular author and presenter at EFY programs. URL: http://johnbytheway.com (accessed March 2004).

LDS Chat. Chat rooms for teens and young adults. URL: http://www.ldschat.com (accessed March 2004).

LDS Music World. Search by genre, artist or popularity for music by LDS musicians. URL: http://ldsmusicworld.com (accessed March 2004).

LDS Today. News and resources for Church members. Includes links to sites on LDS music, YW/YM program, Seminary, and missions. URL: http://www.ldstoday.com (accessed March 2004).

Meridian Magazine. An online magazine that explores life's challenges through the context of the gospel and clarifies principles "while talking about the cur-

rent, contemporary and immediate." URL: http://www.meridianmagazine.
com (accessed March 2004).

Official Information About the Church of Jesus Christ of Latter-day Saints. A site for
those interested in learning more about the Church. URL: http://mor-
mons.org (accessed March 2004).

Seagull Book and Tape. Web site for the chain of stores that is owned by the same company that owns publisher Covenant Communications. URL: http://www.
seagullbook.com (accessed March 2004).

WORKS CONSULTED

The Book of Mormon, The Doctrine and Covenants, The Pearl of Great Price. Salt Lake
City, UT: The Church of Jesus Christ of Latter-day Saints, 1981.

The Church of Jesus Christ of Latter-day Saints. URL: http://lds.org (accessed March
2004). The official Web site of the Church.

Gold, LauraMaery. *Mormons on the Internet, 2000–2001.* Roseville, CA: Prima Publishing, 1999.

The Holy Bible, King James Version. Salt Lake City, UT: The Church of Jesus Christ of
Latter-day Saints, 1979.

Johanson, W. F. Walker. *What is Mormonism All About?* New York, NY: St. Martin's
Griffin, 2002.

Kidd, Clark L. and Kathryn H. Kidd. *A Convert's Guide to Mormon Life: A Guidebook
for New Members of The Church of Jesus Christ of Latter-day Saints.* Salt Lake
City, UT: Bookcraft, 1998.

Millet, Robert L. *The Mormon Faith: A New Look at Christianity.* Salt Lake City, UT:
Shadow Mountain, 1998.

Newell, Coke. *Latter Days.* New York, NY: St. Martin's Press, 2000.

Official Information About the Church of Jesus Christ of Latter-day Saints. URL:
http://mormons.org (accessed March 2004).

ACKNOWLEDGMENTS

Thank you to Coke Newell, Manager of Domestic Area Relations, The
Church of Jesus Christ of Latter-day Saints, Public Affairs Department, for
invaluable assistance with the following sections: History, Core Beliefs
and Values, Formative Experiences, and Misconceptions and Stereotypes.

NOTES

1. The term "saints" is used as it was in the Bible, denoting simply a baptized
member of Christ's church.

2. Joseph had activated the Nauvoo militia in response to published threats of
violence against the city.

3. The seniority of an apostle is determined by length of service as an apostle,
not by his age.

4. Polygamy, or the practice of having more than one spouse at a time, is the term often used in connection with the practice of plural marriage among early Church members. It was, however, polygyny, the simultaneous marriage of one man to more than one woman, which was the practice.

5. The other publisher is Church Distribution, which prints official publications and curriculum materials.

5

◇ ◇ ◇

ORTHODOX CHRISTIANITY

Presvytera Ruth Uhl and Reverend Luke Uhl

Orthodox Christian Church—considers itself not a denomination but the original Christian Church from which other churches have separated because of doctrinal disagreements

Oldest continuously practiced Christian tradition; has had no changes in dogma since beginnings of Christian Church.

Beginnings:

Origins of Church date from day of Pentecost, A.D. 33, in Jerusalem when Holy Spirit was sent by God to Apostles.
Founder considered to be Jesus Christ, through the Holy Spirit.

Beliefs and practices:

Believes in one God only; has one Trinitarian God: God the Father, God the Son (Jesus Christ), God the Holy Spirit.
Scriptures used are the Holy Bible, (both Testaments); other writings include those of Fathers of the Church, holy people who have commented on Scriptures.
Priests and deacons may be married.

(continued)

(continued)
Demographics:

Current number of members in United States is estimated to be near three million.

Information points:

Antiochian Archdiocese. URL: www.antiochian.org (accessed March 2004).
Greek Orthodox Archdiocese of America. URL: www.goarch.org (accessed March 2004).
Orthodox Church in America. URL: www.oca.org (accessed March 2004).

The Orthodox Church is the gathering of people who worship God in truth according to the oldest of continuously practiced Christian traditions. The term "orthodox" comes from two Greek words: "orthós" meaning "correct" and "dóxa" meaning "belief or glory or implying worship," depending on the context. Thus the Orthodox Church is one that considers itself to have a "true worship of" and "true belief about" God.

Orthodox customs, traditions, and practices are firmly rooted in Holy Scripture, in the living tradition or practices of the Church, and in the decisions of the Ecumenical Councils.

Orthodox Christians usually refer to themselves simply as Orthodox, sometimes adding a reference to the national origin of their ancestors—for example, Greek Orthodox or Russian Orthodox. It is not uncommon, however, for those of other faiths to refer to the "Eastern Orthodox" Church which, while not incorrect, does not fully describe the Church as the worldwide entity it is.

Despite the establishment of a Greek Orthodox Church in St. Augustine, Florida in 1768, and the Russian Orthodox Church mission to Alaska beginning in 1794, the Orthodox Church is not generally well known in America. Immigrants from Greece, Russia, and other countries have generally tended to stay out of the public eye, as a result of living under the persecutions of Christians both under the Ottoman Empire and the Communist yoke. This self-effacement has lead some people who do not know history to conclude either that there is no longer a church that can be called "Orthodox" or that it is an insignificant entity. These conclusions are mistaken. Indeed, there are approximately 300 million Orthodox Christians in the world, second in membership only to the Roman Catholics; and in the United States there are approximately three million Orthodox Christians.

HISTORY

Orthodox Christianity was established in Jerusalem in A.D. 33, at Pentecost, when the Holy Spirit descended upon the Apostles. They then went out into the world, preaching the news of Jesus Christ to the nations. Orthodoxy holds fast to the tenets of the faith laid down by the Apostles and confirmed by the Ecumenical Councils that came after them. While welcoming those who seek the Truth as it has been taught from Apostolic times, Orthodox Christians believe that the best "advertising" is the reflection of how they live their lives.

The Origins of the Orthodox Church

The roots of Orthodox Christianity are in the Old Testament. Orthodox Christians consider themselves to be heirs of the promise of salvation that God made to His chosen people, the children of Israel. Orthodox Christians also believe that they are the New Testament church that is "built on the foundation of the Apostles and prophets, Jesus Christ Himself being the chief Cornerstone" (Ephesians 2:20).

Orthodox Christians consider themselves to be historically consistent with, and a continuation of, the earliest Christian church. However, they also recognize several historical splits, or schisms, within the single Christian church.

The first occurred in the fifth century when a dogmatic disagreement over the nature of Jesus Christ resulted in the separation of the churches in Egypt and Ethiopia from the other churches. The resultant Coptic (Egyptian) and Ethiopian "Oriental Orthodox" churches remain distinct from the "Eastern Orthodox" to this day, although they adhere to the same Apostolic Creed. Many Orthodox Christians today regard the schism as having both theological and political causes, the latter because the peoples in the Middle East and Northeast Africa wanted greater freedom from the Roman Byzantine emperor at Constantinople due to heavy taxation.

A second major schism occurred in the eleventh century, resulting in the fracture between the Orthodox and Roman Catholic churches. Although theological disagreements (principally over the ecclesial jurisdiction of the bishop, or pope, of Rome) existed at the time, most Orthodox Christians today see the split as resulting from cultural, societal, and linguistic distinctions that were dividing the western and eastern segments of the Roman Empire from one another. Orthodox Christians generally maintain that the western Roman Empire politically and ecclesially developed into a more centralized system, in contrast to the more politically pluralistic and ecclesially synodal eastern Roman empire. Theologically, most Orthodox Christians consider that the development of scholastic theology in the West, grounded in Platonic philosophy and expounded by Tertullian, Augustine, and Thomas Aquinas, created a new and distinct western Church.

The formal breakdown in communion between the Eastern Orthodox churches and the western Roman Catholic church is generally acknowledged to date from A.D. 1054, when the bishops of the two senior sees, the Patriarch of Constantinople and the Pope of Rome, mutually excommunicated one another. The ostensible reason given by both sides was that the Eastern Churches did not recognize the Pope of Rome as the highest spiritual authority over all Christians. The Eastern Churches considered this to be a blatant attempt by the Roman Patriarch to claim temporal and spiritual power over the entire church.

Another major source of disagreement at the same time was the addition of the *filoque* ("and the Son") to the Nicene Creed by the Roman church. The addition said that the Holy Spirit descended from both the Father and the Son. In addition to disagreeing with this change of a basic theological belief, all of the other churches said no changes could be made to the Creed or, indeed, any doctrine, without a council of the whole Church. The pope and his supporters said that he could unilaterally make any changes he wished.

It should be noted that in 1967 their successor bishops, Patriarch Athenagoras I and Pope Paul VI, formally rescinded these mutual excommunications, acknowledging that there had been difficulties in understanding between the two sides (partly because of language and administrative differences, partly from personality issues) that eventually led to a total breakdown between the two main parts of Christendom.

Orthodox Christians also consider a third major schism within Christendom to be the breach that occurred at the time of the Protestant Reformation within the western, or Roman Catholic, Church.

Church Organization

While at first glance the hierarchical organization of the Orthodox Church seems to be similar to that of the Roman Catholic Church or the Anglican Church, it actually has a more collegial quality because decisions made are based on a consensus among the bishops. Every hierarch is considered equal to the others, and no one person is thought to have more "power" than another. Each bishop, as a successor to the Apostles, is believed to be responsible for "teaching all that [Christ] has commanded" (see Matthew 28:20), and is therefore the chief spiritual authority within his geographic area, which is called a diocese; he is affectionately referred to as "dèspota," meaning "master" or "sole authority."

Although each bishop is equal to every other in authority and responsibility as an Apostolic successor, some are given administrative responsibilities over a large territory or region that may encompass many dioceses. These have the administrative title of Archbishop, Metropolitan, or Patriarch.

The Orthodox Christian Church is a communion, or fellowship, of sixteen principal, self-governing Churches. Among these sixteen Churches are the four ancient Patriarchates of Constantinople, Alexandria, Antioch, and Jerusalem. Up until the Great Schism in A.D. 1054, Rome was considered the senior in honor. Eventually, because of historical factors including invasions and wars, along with human mistakes and pride, the one Christian Church separated into two distinct sections—the Eastern (Orthodox), and the Western (Catholic). Even so, the Orthodox Church is seen by its followers as complete and undivided and all Patriarchal sees, except for that of Rome, remain in full communion with one another, keeping their ancient beliefs and practicing the same liturgical services and rituals, allowing for local traditions. The Patriarchate of Constantinople is therefore given a primacy of honor within the Orthodox Church, but its senior bishop has no authority comparable to that of the pope. He presides only over his own synod of bishops that govern the Patriarchate.

The unity of the Orthodox Church does not depend on the primacy of a single hierarch or on a centralized administration but in a commonly held faith and practice primarily defined through the seven ecumenical councils.

BELIEFS AND LIFE IN THE CHURCH
The "Laws" of the Church

Orthodox Christians believe that human beings are created in the image of God; humans not only reflect the characteristics of the Maker, but they also are called to develop God-like qualities. The image of God in which humans are formed is considered complete, however, only when it involves male and female.

Orthodox Christians believe that the Church is the Body of Christ and, since Jesus Christ is the Son of God, the laws of the Church are fundamentally God's laws. It is important to remember, though, that Orthodoxy is not so much concerned with law as with life. Orthodoxy takes into account our humanity and works to bring the faithful into communion, or an extremely close relationship, with God.

Orthodox Christians consider the Bible to be the repository of God's revelation and also understand the Bible to be only one part of a Living and Sacred Tradition. God is eternal and changeless, and his Laws are likewise constant. Orthodox Christians thus believe that the Tradition of the Church must be the vehicle for preserving and transmitting God's unchanging truth from generation to generation.

Holy Tradition

A tradition is a belief or custom handed down from our forebears; Christian tradition is the faith and practice delivered to us from the Apostles. Within the Orthodox Church, Holy Tradition is comprised of a number of principal sources, including Holy Scripture, the Seven Ecumenical Councils, the Creed, the Fathers of the Church, the Divine Liturgy, and Icons or Holy Images.

Holy Scripture

The Orthodox Church is preeminently a Scriptural Church—all the services, inspired writings, and administrative rules are filled with direct biblical references and quotations because the Bible constitutes God's principle revelation. The Book of the Gospels is venerated by the faithful during the Liturgy, and, during all types of Orthodox services, if any part of the Gospels are read or sung the congregation stands in respect.

Orthodoxy always understands and interprets Scripture within the context of the Church; indeed the Bible derives its authority from the Church and not the other way around. It was the Church that originally decided which books would form part of the Bible, and the Church alone—as the Body of Christ—interprets Holy Scripture. The books we now consider to comprise Old and New Testaments were formally accepted as truly essential to the Faith in A.D. 364. It is important to remember that the Orthodox Bible uses the Septuagint (Greek) Old Testament, compiled in approximately 200 B.C. to exacting standards. A number of the modern versions of the Scriptures delete passages which one group or another has decided are unimportant. Orthodoxy, as a rule, having once decided that something is true, does not change, so the Church can thus point to a continuously held tradition of common interpretation unchanged over the history of the faith.

Orthodox Christians believe that they are not free to understand or interpret Scripture on their own but need a guide. The Orthodox hold that there is only one Truth when interpreting Scripture—and if everyone in a church is free to believe what they want about a verse in the Bible, and there are differences of opinion, they cannot all have the Truth equally.

The Seven Ecumenical Councils

When disputes have arisen regarding the teachings and administration of the Orthodox Church, the bishops in a region have gathered together to deliberate these matters. Orthodox Christians believe their bishops have always been guided by the Holy Spirit to denounce heresies and proclaim orthodox dogmas (absolute truths). The bishops are charged with teaching authority by virtue of their consecration and Apostolic succession. For example, important decisions were made at the seven Ecumenical Councils, so called because the clergy and the people of all areas of Christianity came together to ask the Holy Spirit for guidance.

In these councils the Scriptures were acknowledged as divinely inspired, and the set of administrative rules called the Canons were put in place. These councils were convened to discuss regulations necessary for governing the Church and dogmatic and doctrinal statements necessary for preserving truth. They worked to condemn certain erroneous beliefs, called heresies, that contradicted the doctrinal truths about God and his plan for our salvation by falsely representing that Christ is either not a true man or a true God.

The Ecumenical Councils firmly asserted that Jesus Christ is both perfect God and perfect man, having two natures, divine and human, which exist unconfused, unchanged, indivisible, and inseparable. Theoretically, even today a council could be called to discuss matters of faith. However, traditionalist Orthodox believe that the Orthodox Church is the *entire* church. Since contemporary Christendom is divided into many groups, each with its own beliefs that differ from the early Church, a common conciliar gathering is impossible.

For further information on these councils, see http://www.goarch.org/en/ourfaith (accessed March 2004).

The Creed

The seven articles of faith proclaimed at the First Ecumenical Council in A.D. 325, together with the five articles proclaimed at the Second Council in A.D. 381, form the Nicene-Constantinopolitan Creed or "Symbol of the Faith." It is effectively a short catechism, or brief summary, of the doctrinal truths about God and his plan for salvation. Orthodox theologians traditionally have been reluctant to state a truth about the nature of God or proclaim a dogma. Since God is unknowable in his essence, mere humans cannot define him. However, when disputes have arisen regarding the true, Apostolic teachings of the Church, all the bishops have gathered at an Ecumenical Council, as described above.

The Orthodox faith is summarized in the Nicene-Constantinopolitan Creed, which was produced at the first two Ecumenical Councils held in Nicaea in A.D. 325 and in Constantinople in A.D. 381. Each Article was considered essential for all Christians to believe. Today, only the Orthodox Church continues to accept the Creed in its entirety as completed at the Councils. The Orthodox position is that no changes can be made unless the whole Church meets and agrees on those changes or deletions. In fact, a major disagreement between the Orthodox and the Roman Catholic Churches is the Catholic addition of the word *"filioque"* to the Creed. For the full text of the Creed, see http://www.antiochian.org/theology (accessed March 2004).

The Fathers of the Church

The Orthodox Church has a special term for those truly devout people who wrote detailed explanations regarding the beliefs and teachings of the Church—Fathers of the Church. Their writings help the faithful to understand the why and wherefore of Orthodox dogma and practice. In order to be considered a Father, one must have written in agreement with all other writings done on a particular subject, in relation to Holy Scripture, which is the preeminent authority, as agreed upon by the Councils, thereby confirming divine inspiration.

The Ecumenical Councils decreed specific guidelines for the general administration of the Church, and they also declared that rulings from various local synods were applicable to the universal Church. Together these rules form the "Canon Law" of the Orthodox Church. Thus the rules or laws of the Church were written between the time of the Apostles and the seventh and final Ecumenical Council at Nicaea in A.D. 787. Administrative regulations in Canon Law are not immutable; they may be changed by a subsequent Council, or the local Church authority may provide a dispensation from them for the spiritual well being of an individual. Bishops and clergy are bound to uphold these sacred canons.

The Divine Liturgy

Just as the construction of an Orthodox house of worship is based on that of the Jewish Temple, Orthodox Christians believe that their daily cycle of services follows the pattern of worship used in the Synagogue and in the daily services at the Temple in Jerusalem: psalms, hymns, prayers, and Scripture readings. This is understandable, since the majority of the first Christians had been raised as Jews.

The word "liturgy," from the Greek word "litourgia," means the "work of the people," specifically the public worship services attended, and participated in, by the faithful. There are several important characteristics of the Liturgy: it is beautiful, it is mystical, it is theological, and it is communal. The Liturgy takes place in the church where it is an experience that involves all of the senses given to us by God—colorful gold-embellished Icons covering the walls and ceiling or dome catch the eye; the voices of the chanter and people chanting the hymns of the Liturgy mirror the singing of the angels at the Throne of the Lord; the fragrance of the incense used to reverence the Icons and the people fills the holy space; and the gifts of bread and wine offered by the priest and the people become the body and blood of the Lord. Orthodox Liturgy is meant to be an "other-worldly" experience. It shows us what we can expect to participate in when we enter eternal life. Divine beauty is emphasized in the Orthodox Liturgy; heaven is wonderful to behold and worship expresses this celestial magnificence. The Liturgy is mystical because it simultaneously embraces heaven and earth. In the Eucharistic celebration the faithful are drawn up into the heavens where they behold and experience God.

The Liturgy is also the living expression of Orthodox faith; this is evident not only in the prayers and hymns but in the very essence of the Eucharist. Christianity is not passive but rather active; the local church is a worshipping community. Worship of the Lord comes first; doctrine and discipline follow. The best way to "know" Orthodoxy, or to "be" Orthodox, is to participate in the life of the worshipping church. Often, those who are interested in joining the Church are advised to attend the various services offered, on a regular basis, even before officially becoming members, so as to get into a rhythm of learning as they worship.

Orthodox worship is not limited to one main Sunday service or ritual; there are a number of sacraments (Mysteries), services, and celebrations that together make up an extensive and complex collection of public worship services. For example, there are services for times of sorrow or great need and a thanksgiving service for special occasions.

Icons or Holy Images

Holy Tradition is expressed in words, such as writings of the Fathers and other holy people, gestures, such as the Sign of the Cross, and Icons, which are holy images. Orthodox Christians consider Icons not as art, nor merely as religious pictures, but rather as a means for God's revelation to mankind. Icons are called "theology in color" since they express dogma in visual form, just as the Bible expresses it in the form of written letters. They are also referred to as "windows to heaven" since God's Word reaches the senses through them and they become vehicles for prayers and communication with God.

The word "Icon" is derived from the Greek word for image, "ikóna." Orthodox Christians do not see Icons as the "graven images" forbidden by the Ten Commandments. Instead, they believe that Icons are critical to understanding Orthodox theology. An Icon of Christ assures us that although Christ is fully God, he nonetheless became fully human, thus assuming in himself the totality of our humanity. The reasoning is that, if Christ was a human with real physical dimensions and was seen by people in his time, he could be portrayed in a painted image. Today this is perhaps more obvious than in the early days of Christianity—if Christ lived today we would have photographs and videotapes.

Orthodox Christians absolutely accept the divine command that God, and God alone, is to be worshipped, not objects or images or persons. Even though God commanded that man should not make and worship "graven images," God also directed that carved and woven images be crafted for use in the sacred services and rituals that were directed toward worshipping him.

Orthodox Christians do not worship Icons; they worship God alone. They do venerate, or show respect to, Icons of Christ, his Mother, and various saints, indicating their regard for them as individuals and for the heroic example they give of steadfast obedience to the will of God. In addition, just as believers ask each other on this earth to pray for them, they also ask those in heaven to pray for them.

Icons are an important part of worship practices for the Orthodox. Visiting an Orthodox Church for the first time can be overwhelming for those who are used to the simplicity of many American churches. An Orthodox church is filled with Icons—on the ceiling, the walls, and around the altar. The highest Icon is that of Jesus Christ, considered the most important of all the Icons in the church. The second largest Icon in a church is that of Mary, the Mother of God, communicating to the Orthodox faithful that the Lord Jesus Christ was truly human, having been born of a woman, and that she extends her loving embrace to those who pray with her, and through her, to her Son.

Orthodox Christianity—The Way

For Orthodox Christians, life in the Orthodox Church consists above all else of being obedient to God's will as expressed in his commandments and laws. Being alive in Christ also means participating in the Mysteries (sacraments) of the Church, the principal ones being Baptism, Chrismation, Repentance, Holy Eucharist, Holy Unction, Holy Orders, and Marriage. These are all public ceremonies, or sacramental services, celebrated in the orthodox house of worship referred to as a church or temple.

A mystery is something not fully understood; in theology, it is a truth incomprehensible to the reason, and knowable only through divine revelation. A sacrament is something sacred or consecrated. These words are used interchangeably, although mystery is the more exact theological term used by the Orthodox Church, for the precise operation of the sacraments/mysteries is unknowable. Orthodox Christians believe that six Mysteries are primarily concerned with forgiveness and remission of sin:

1. Baptism, through which Orthodox Christians believe they are joined to Christ who forgives and remits all sins
2. Chrismation, by which they believe they are sealed with the gifts of the Holy Spirit
3. Repentance, by which they believe they are forgiven by, and reunited to, Christ
4. Holy Unction, in which they are anointed for the healing of body and soul
5. Holy Eucharist, in which the faithful receive Christ's Body and Blood given for the remission of sins and eternal life
6. Holy Orders, by which deacons, priests, and bishops are ordained to celebrate the Mysteries for the forgiveness and remission of sins

There are other Mysteries as well. The Mystery of Marriage is particularly special and important, inasmuch as it is the usual situation in which Orthodox Christians work out their salvation.

To the Orthodox, it is considered truly a mystery that God's grace can be granted to them individually in an inconceivable manner that radically transforms their souls. For instance, at Baptism, Orthodox Christians believe they are "joined" to Christ and participate in his death and resurrection. Saint John Chrysostom wrote about the Eucharist saying: "Not by sight do I judge the things that appear, but by the eyes of the mind" (Homily VII on 1 Corinthians). In other words the consecration of bread and wine into the body and blood of Jesus Christ is a Mystery for Orthodox Christians because what they believe is not what they see; they see one thing and believe it to be something else. Every Mystery of the Orthodox Church combines an outward visible sign with an inward spiritual grace. The Mysteries are therefore at once visible and invisible. In Baptism, for example, there is an outward washing with water and at the same time an inward cleansing of sins.

The Orthodox House of Worship

Orthodox Christians believe that in the Old Testament the Lord gave mankind directions through the Prophet Moses as to how a sacred space should be set aside in this world for worship of the heavenly God. Orthodox Christians understand that earthly worship is only a shadow of the perpetual worship of God in heaven. They therefore believe it is critical for believers to follow the directions of God for earthly worship so that they will know how to worship him forever in the Kingdom of Heaven. Orthodox churches are consequently constructed on the basis of the Old Testament Temple. As directed by God, it had three sections: a Courtyard, a Holy Place, and a Holy of Holies.

Like the Temple in Jerusalem, the New Testament Orthodox church building is also constructed out of solid materials and has the same three sections: the Narthex, or vestibule, corresponding to the Courtyard; the Nave, corresponding to the Holy Place or Sanctuary and usually called such; and the Altar area, corresponding to the Holy of Holies, and often referred to as such.

In the Narthex is usually found a candlestand on which the faithful place lighted candles, reminiscent of the "burnt offering" made to God. For the Orthodox, the candle is a symbol of prayer. It represents the desire of the individual lighting it to stand faithfully in prayer before God. The Nave, or Church Proper, of an Orthodox Church is the area where the faithful assemble for public worship.

In an Orthodox church, the Holy of Holies is separated by an icon-screen (iconostasion), and the entrance is usually closed by a curtain. The Holy of Holies may only be entered by the clergy in the performance of their duties. The Holy of Holies contains an Altar Table that corresponds to the Ark of the Covenant. On the Altar is placed the Book of the Gospels, which Orthodox Christians consider most important, as this book contain the words of Jesus Christ. This corresponds to the Ten Commandments in the Old Testament Ark of the Covenant.

Orthodox churches are built with the Altar at the eastern end, oriented toward the direction from which the light of the morning sun rises. Orthodox Christians usually pray facing east, mindful that they expectantly await the coming of the true Light, the Light of the world, Jesus Christ.

Prayer and Fasting

Orthodox Christians believe in the exhortation of Saint Paul that they must "Pray without ceasing" (1 Thessalonians 5:17). They do so by repeating ceaselessly a brief prayer, commonly referred to as the "Jesus prayer," which may be "Lord, have mercy," or "Lord, Jesus Christ, have mercy on me," or, in its most common form, "Lord, Jesus Christ, Son of God, have mercy on me, a sinner."

For Orthodox Christians, the term "fast" does not mean little or no food; to fast means to modify the amount of food eaten and also to eliminate meat products from the diet, taking into account one's health and circumstances.

Orthodox Christians are asked to fast or abstain from certain foods on about half the days of the year in order to follow the example of Christ as he prayed and fasted. In addition, they fast in order to strengthen the will and to discipline the body—if one cannot do without a certain kind of food for a period of time, how then can one abstain from sin? Orthodox Christians fast on Wednesday to recall the day on which Judas betrayed Jesus and on Friday to commemorate the day on which Jesus died on the Cross and was buried. Other fasts center on religious observances and last fourteen to forty days. On these days Orthodox Christians are expected not to eat animal products, fish, alcoholic beverages, and oils. Fasting is seen as a way of preparing physically and, most importantly, spiritually for the feasts that follow.

Those receiving Holy Communion fast from all food and drink following the evening meal on the day before the Divine Liturgy and do not eat anything until after receiving the body and blood of Christ. When fasting, the faithful are reminded that it is not what goes into their mouths which causes sin but that which comes out. Fasting from food is meant to help believers learn to fast from sin, which is far more difficult. It is important to remember that fasting is not done to gain the respect or envy of others but to be strengthened spiritually. Also, one does not fast from these foods because they are considered evil but rather because the faithful are in training to become stronger in their hearts and minds. Saint Paul makes a number of comparisons to athletes when he writes about the spiritual struggle in the world. Just as athletes follow strict diets in order to be in the best physical condition, so should Christians watch what they eat so that they can learn to watch what they do and say.

Pious Practices

Orthodox Christians have a number of pious traditions and practices that serve to reinforce their faith, such as lighting a candle upon entering a church. An Orthodox then reverences the Icon nearby and makes the Sign of the Cross, then enters into the church. The candle is an offering and a symbol of prayer. The one lighting a candle might wish they could stand faithfully in prayer before God, just as the candle faithfully and patiently burns, but the cares and preoccupations of life often do not allow such attentive prayer. In fact, it is not uncommon to see someone light a candle, kiss the Icon, stand in prayer for a few brief moments, then leave to go on to work or school. Candles or lamps are also used in the Icon corner at home or work.

The newcomer to an Orthodox service will also notice that the worshippers very frequently make the Sign of the Cross. This is a reminder that the thought of God should always be in their minds and hearts, indeed, their whole being. Also, as a rule, Orthodox Christians do not fold their hands in prayer, as many other traditions do. Instead, an Orthodox will bow the head, or make the Sign of the Cross repeatedly, or even make prostrations, bowing all the way to the ground.

Water is an important symbol in the Orthodox Church—Christ is the Living Water, so Christians thirst for him; believers are baptized with water so as to wash away their sins. The priest blesses water on the Feast of the Baptism of Christ, Theophany, and gives it to the faithful to take home. Orthodox Christians use Holy Water to bless their homes, workplaces, automobiles, and so forth. They even drink the Holy Water when ill. In addition, it is very common for a spring to be associated with a place of religious significance, so the water from these springs is also considered blessed and used for spiritual and physical reasons.

Incense is also used in church and at home. The symbolism of burning incense is the hope that God will favorably receive prayers offered up to Him in heaven, just as the believers smell the fragrant smoke that rises heavenward.

Very often someone wishing to have prayers offered for a family member or a special intention will make bread and take it to the priest, who blesses it and distributes it to the whole congregation. This practice is not the same as the Eucharist, of course. It represents God supplying our material needs in this world.

After someone has died, or fallen asleep in the Lord, there are memorial services held at intervals, beginning with the fortieth day after death. A family member, sometimes a friend, will often make (in the Greek tradition) *kolyva*, boiled wheat mixed with spices and dried fruits and nuts. This is to remind those still on earth that Christ said that unless a grain of wheat dies, it will not live again; the one who has died is thus like that wheat, dying and leaving this earthly life and then entering eternal life.

In Conclusion

When reading through this information, it is important to remember that this is by no means all there is to know or learn about the Orthodox Church. After all, this Church and its faith and learning have existed since Apostolic times. In addition, one cannot truly appreciate the ageless and age-old beauty of the Orthodox Church unless and until one participates in even a small way in one of the worship services, for example, by visiting a church.

Within the last twenty years, more and more people have discovered the Orthodox Church as they have searched for a faith that in both beliefs and practice has held constant from Apostolic times. Unlike other churches, the Orthodox Church has preserved its traditions in their entirety throughout its whole history. Today, the Orthodox Churches in the United States and elsewhere are showing steady growth, whether receiving whole congregations who choose to become Orthodox or welcoming individuals seeking the stability of the most ancient, continually practiced Christian tradition.

FORMATIVE EXPERIENCES

Orthodox Christian teens will have received Baptism, Chrismation, and the Eucharist in infancy. According to Father Jerry Markopoulos of Holy Trinity Greek Orthodox Church in Portland, Oregon, teens "also have many opportunities to re-experience their own Baptism and Chrismation as they mature. When I am baptizing an infant...I call all children to come and see what is happening. The faithful are not mere spectators at Baptisms, Weddings, Funerals, etc., but rather participants" (e-mail correspondence, March 2003).

Boys may be altar servers, and many service opportunities are available to both boys and girls. Summer camping programs and vacation church schools provide additional opportunities for youth to grow in their faith.

The most significant formative experiences for Orthodox teens, however, occur as they participate liturgically throughout the year. For example, on Palm Sunday, teens prepare cross-shaped palms for distribution. On the Sunday of Orthodoxy, teens commemorate the restoration of Icons and victory over iconoclasm by carrying Icons around the church's exterior and then back inside. On Holy Friday, teens remove Christ's body from the cross, anoint it, and wrap it in a shroud. They decorate the burial tomb that will be carried in a nighttime procession, followed by an all-night vigil by the tomb.

Father Markopoulos describes teens' formative experiences in these words:

> Orthodox Christianity is about experiencing God through worship, service, fellowship and witness....When it comes to worship, our message is simple yet profound. We say to teens, and all the faithful, "Come, see, partake, receive, participate." Liturgy means "work of the people," clergy and laity working together to make up the worship experience. When they participate in the liturgical life of the church, they have, on a daily basis, many opportunities to experience God personally and profoundly. When we say to one another in the Divine Liturgy that "Christ is in our midst" we mean that He indeed is in our midst. When we say, as each communicant approaches the chalice, that the "servant of God (who is called by name) receives the body and blood of Christ," we mean it. We receive Christ in the Eucharist each time we partake. It doesn't get any more personal or profound than that. (E-mail correspondence, March 2003)

MISCONCEPTIONS AND STEREOTYPES

Orthodox teens most often attend public schools, although many are in private schools or are homeschooled. Their peers sometimes assume they are Jewish because of the term "Orthodox." When they explain that they are Christian, the next assumption is that they are Catholic or just like the Catholics. Since Orthodoxy has been referred to as "a well-kept secret" (Nicozisin), their peers are often totally unfamiliar with their religion. This places youth in the position of explaining and teaching about their faith, and some are more comfortable with that than others.

If they have been identified as Greek Orthodox, young adults are sometimes faced with the misconception that Greek Orthodox Christians worship the gods and goddesses of Greek mythology.

The 2002 film, *My Big Fat Greek Wedding*, provided a first look for many at Greek families and their Orthodox religion. It deals in part with how a family tries to maintain its religious and cultural traditions in mainstream America. Although the film contained some inaccuracies, it did depict the closeness and unity of Greek Orthodox families.

WHAT ARE ORTHODOX TEENS LOOKING FOR AT THE LIBRARY?

High school students who attend Holy Trinity Greek Orthodox Church in Portland, Oregon, were surveyed in February 2003 regarding their use of the local public library. Sixty-seven percent indicated that they were library users. Movies and compact discs, school report materials, books to read for enjoyment, college preparation guides, and books on "things I personally want to learn about" were mentioned as items the young patrons found useful.

When asked what would make the library a more inviting place to them and their friends, they described teen areas where materials were easy to find and where they could talk freely with their friends. They want more movies, better books, and no fines. Two items listed, teen reading programs and access to the library's database of holdings from home via the Internet, are already offered by the Multnomah County (Oregon) Library system, reinforcing the need for librarians everywhere to better promote library programs and services to teens to raise awareness of existing services.

One hundred percent of the teens polled indicated that Orthodox Christian materials in the library's young adult collection would be of interest to them. In larger parishes, youth have the option of accessing materials in their own church library or through the religious education resource department. These materials may not be readily available to them, however, if their parish is not large enough to own such a collection, and then the library would provide a valuable resource to them.

BUILDING YOUR COLLECTION

As with most religions discussed in this book, the best method of assuring that materials purchased will be useful to Orthodox teens is to buy from an Orthodox press that falls under a Patriarchate or purchase items that are sanctioned by a Patriarchal clergy member. Your local Orthodox diocese will be glad to work with you to assist in your selections. Light and Life Publishing Company and the Greek Orthodox Archdiocese, Office of Youth and Young Adult Ministries, are both excellent publishers from which to make selections.

There appear to be no anti-Orthodox materials being published, which removes the risk of ordering items that inaccurately reflect the religion's doctrine.

TYPES OF BOOKS AVAILABLE

Very few Orthodox Christian materials are geared specifically toward teens. Only a few fiction titles are available. Even the nonfiction titles listed in the bibliography are not geared exclusively toward adolescents but are appropriate for the age range. A few video recordings and CD-

ROMs are listed in the bibliography, with video series on the lives of saints being most popular.

Publishers of music are included in the section on publishers. Byzantine chant is popular with some teen groups as they have youth choirs within their diocese that perform chant.

Publishers

Christ the Saviour Brotherhood Publishing and Unexpected Joy Press
14617 West Farm Road 74
Ash Grove, MO 65604
(417) 751–3183

Conciliar Press
P.O. Box 76
Ben Lomond, CA 95005–0076
(800) 967–7377
URL: http://conciliarpress.bizhosting.com (accessed March 2004)

Ecumenical Publications
P.O. Box 717
Westfield, NJ 07091
(908) 232–6118

Greek Orthodox Archdiocese of America, Department of Education
50 Goddard Avenue
Brookline, MA 02445
(800) 566–1088
URL: http://www.religioused.goarch.org (accessed March 2004)

Greek Orthodox Telecommunications (GOTelecom)
Greek Orthodox Archdiocese of America
8 East 79th Street
New York, NY 10021
(800) 888–6835
URL: http://www. gotel.goarch.org (accessed March 2004)
Also distributes video recordings.

Holy Cross Seminary Bookstore
50 Goddard Avenue
Brookline, MA 02445
(617) 731–3500 or (800) 245–0599
URL: http://www.goarch.org/access/hcbks (accessed March 2004)

Light and Life Publishing Company
4818 Park Glen Road
Minneapolis, MN 55416
(952) 925–3888
URL: http://www.light-n-life.com (accessed March 2004)

Orthodox Christian Publications Center
P.O. Box 688
Wayne, NJ 07474–0588
(973) 694–5782

Regina Orthodox Press
P.O. Box 5288
Salisbury, MA 01952
(800) 636–2470
URL: http://www.reginaorthodoxpress.com/index.html (accessed
    March 2004)

Saint Ignatius of Antioch Press
442 Charles Street
Lima, OH 45805–3365
(419) 222–2029
URL: http://home.surge.net/orthodox/stignatius/index.html
    (accessed March 2004)

Saint Innocent/Firebird Videos, Audios, Books
27 Menlo Park Drive
Belleville, MI 48111
(734) 699–0870
URL: http://www.firebirdvideos.com (accessed March 2004)

Saint Isaac of Syria Skete Bookstore
25266 Pilgrims Way
Boscobel, WI 53805
(800) 814–2667
URL: http://www.skete.com (accessed March 2004)

The Saint John of Kronstadt Press
1180 Orthodox Way
Liberty, TN 37095–4366
(615) 536–5239
URL: http://www.kronstadt.org (accessed March 2004)

Saint Nectarios Press
10300 Ashworth Avenue N.

Seattle, WA 98133–9410
(800) 643–4233
URL: http://www.stnectariospress.com (accessed March 2004)

St. Nikodemos the Hagiorite Publication Society
2101 Ritchie Street
Aliquippa, PA 15001–2124
(724) 375–7867

Saint Tikhon's Seminary Bookstore
Saint Tikhon's Road
P.O. Box "B"
South Canaan, PA 18459–0130
(888) 454–6678
URL: http://www.stots.edu/bookstore.htm (accessed March 2004)

Saint Vladimir's Seminary Bookstore
575 Scarsdale Road
Crestwood, NY 10707–1699
(800) 204–2665
URL: http://www.svots.edu/SVS-bookstore (accessed March 2004)

Publishers and Distributors of Orthodox Music

Musical selections (compact discs and cassettes) can also be purchased from the bookstores previously noted.

EIKONA
P.O. Box 4674
Englewood, CO 80155
(303) 221–1355
URL: http://www.eikona.com (accessed March 2004)

National Forum of Greek Orthodox Church Musicians
Ms. Vicki Pappas
1700 North Walnut Street, Apt. 302
Bloomington, IN 47404
(812) 855–8248
Email: pappas@indiana.edu
Hymns of the Orthodox Church Music Education series.

Saint Gregory Palamas Monastery
934 C.R. #2256
Perrysville, OH 44864
(419) 368–5335

URL: http://www.bright.net/~palamas (accessed March 2004)
Lists other Orthodox music sites.

Publishers and Distributors of Videorecordings

Ellinas Multimedia
18 Country Walk Drive
Aliso Viego, CA 92656
(949) 305–2620
URL: http://www.ellinasmultimedia.com (accessed March 2004)

Greek Orthodox Archdiocese, Office of Youth and Young Adult
    Ministries
8 East 79th Street
New York, NY 10021
(212) 570–3561
Orthodox Teen Video series.

Homeschooling Resources

Orthodox Christian Social Studies & History Curriculum, K-8
Drs. David and Mary Ford
P.O. Box 18
South Canaan, PA 18459
(717) 937–4309

Orthodox Christian Schools of Northeast Ohio
755 S. Cleveland Avenue
Mogadore, OH 44260
(330) 929–9126

Saint Isaac of Syria Skete
25266 Pilgrims Way
Boscobel, WI 53805
Attention: Father Simeon
(800) 814–2667
URL: http://www.skete.com (accessed March 2004)

Scouting in the Eastern Orthodox Church

Eastern Orthodox Committee on Scouting
George Boulukos, National Chairman
862 Guy Lombardo Avenue
Freeport, NY 11520
(516) 868–4050
URL: http://www.eocs.org (accessed March 2004)

LIBRARY SERVICES AND PROGRAMS

It may not occur to Orthodox teens and the adults who work with them to contact the library or to explore options for working together; therefore it is the librarian's responsibility to make contact. Locate Orthodox teen groups by searching local churches' Web sites or looking in the yellow pages under Churches—Orthodox. When calling, ask to speak to the parish youth coordinator or parish priest.

Orthodox teen groups are often involved in community service projects that could be adapted to the public library. February is often celebrated by parishes as Youth Month, and youth groups may appreciate suggestions for special projects at that time of the year.

The Orthodox Church in America has a Youth, Young Adult and Campus Ministry Web site at http://yya.oca.org (accessed March 2004) that offers a variety of ideas for community involvement. A little creativity is all that is needed to change these to library-specific projects. For example, in the section titled "20-Something Ideas to Involve Youth in Christ-like Service to Others," (http://yya.oca.org/TheHub/20somethingways/service.htm, accessed March 2004) they suggest choosing an area of town to keep clean for six months. Both the exterior and the interior of the library could benefit from this project, and the youth involved would gain a much deeper understanding of how the library works, how it is organized, and its mission.

The Neighborhood Labor Day project could be adapted into a short-term project at the library, with teens assisting library staff in cleaning the bookshelves and tidying the collections. Groups who were willing to be more formally trained in shelf reading could be of great assistance in a longer-term project, the never-ending job of keeping the library's materials in order on the shelves.

Another service suggestion is to collect recyclables and donate the proceeds to charity. Donations made to the library could be used either to buy materials of interest to teens in general, or materials regarding the Orthodox faith, providing a tie-in between the church's youth group and the greater community at large. Similarly, the "Closet Cleaning" project could be changed to a "Bookcase Cleaning," and the books could be donated to the local library either for addition to the collection or to be offered in the library's fundraising book sales.

The "Buy a Toy" campaign could morph into a "Buy a Book" campaign, with the youth group consulting with their local children's or teen library department to identify social service agencies that would benefit from book donations for their clientele, such as homeless and domestic violence shelters or facilities which house incarcerated youth.

SELECTED TITLES
Basic Reference Materials

These materials may be ordered from any of the publishers listed in the section on publishers.

Harakas, Father Stanley. *The Orthodox Church: 455 Questions and Answers.* Minneapolis, MN: Light and Life Pub. Co., 1988, 1987. ISBN 0937032565 (pbk.). Provides easy-to-understand answers to common questions people have about the dogma, faith practices, and traditions of the Orthodox Church.

Martin, Linette. *Sacred Doorways: A Beginner's Guide to Icons.* Brewster, MA: Paraclete Press, 2002. ISBN 1557253072. Explains the theological significance of Icons, where they came from, how people are represented, and the reasons for the colors, placement of figures, and composition of Icons.

Nasr, Father Constantine. *The Bible in the Liturgy.* Oklahoma City, OK: Theosis Publishing Co., 1988. ISBN 1880321017. Covers how the Old and New Testaments are used in Orthodox liturgical services.

Patrinacos, Nicon D. *A Dictionary of Greek Orthodoxy.* Minneapolis, MN: Light and Life Pub. Co., 2001. ISBN 1880971526.

The Prayer of Jesus: Its Genesis, Development and Practice in the Byzantine-Slavic Religious Tradition. New York, NY: Desclee, 1967. No ISBN available. Written by a Monk of the Eastern Church. Explains the origins of this simple prayer in Apostolic times, and how to use this prayer to approach God.

Snyder, Robert. *Celebration: Feasts and Holy Days.* Yonkers, NY: Orthodox Christian Education Commission, 1995. No ISBN available. A listing and explanation of the special days in the Orthodox Church and why they are celebrated.

Ware, Bishop Kallistos. *The Orthodox Church.* London; New York, NY: Penguin Books, 1993. ISBN 0140146563. Covers the history of the Church from the time of Jesus through Apostolic times, the Seven Councils, the Great Schism, and the effects that the Moslem Conquest and the Bolshevik Revolution have had on the Church.

———. *The Orthodox Way,* 2002 rev. ed. Crestwood, NY: St. Vladimir's Seminary Press, 2002. ISBN 0913836583 (pbk.). Covers all dogma, doctrine, Tradition, and services.

Other Recommended Books

Baggley, John. *Festival Icons for the Christian Year.* Crestwood, NY: St. Valdimir's Seminary Press, 2000. ISBN 0881412015.

Bobosh, Father Theodore. *Am I Saved: Scriptural Thoughts on Salvation.* Minneapolis, MN: Light and Life Pub. Co., 1984. ISBN 0937032387. A title in the *Know Your Faith* series.

Boojamra, John. *Foundations for Orthodox Christian Education.* Crestwood, NY: St. Valdimir's Seminary Press, 1989. ISBN 0881410500.

Carras, Presvytera Roberta. *The People of God: A History of the Orthodox Church.* Toronto: Saint Nektarios Church, 1999. A church history text written for teen use, with review questions at the end of each chapter. Illustrations, maps and diagrams enhance the text.

Chryssavgis, Father Deacon John. *Repentance and Confession in the Orthodox Church.* Brookline, MA: Holy Cross Orthodox Press, 1990. ISBN 0917651561.

Clement, Olivier and Bartholomew, Ecumenical Patriarch of Constantinople. *Conversations with Ecumenical Patriarch Bartholomew I.* Crestwood, NY: St. Vladimir's Seminary Press, 1997. ISBN 0881411787.

Dunaway, Father Marc. *What is the Orthodox Church?: A Brief Overview of Orthodoxy.* Ben Lomond, CA: Conciliar Press, 1995. Twenty-four-page pamphlet. No ISBN available.

Eleftheriou, Basil E. *Encyclopedia of the Major Saints and Fathers of the Orthodox Church.* Minneapolis, MN: Light and Life Pub. Co., 2000. ISBN 1880971518 (v. 1), ISBN 1880971666 (v. 2).

Feofan, Saint Bishop of Tambov and Shatsk. *Raising Them Right: A Saint's Advice on Raising Children.* Mount Hermon, CA: Conciliar Press, 1989. ISBN 0962271306 (pbk.).

Frazier, Father T. L. *Holy Relics: The Scriptural and Historical Basis for the Veneration of Relics of the Saints.* Ben Lomond, CA: Conciliar Press, 1997. ISBN 1888212098 (pbk.).

Gillquist, Peter E., Alan Wallerstedt and Joseph Allen. *The Orthodox Study Bible: New Testament and Psalms, New King James Version.* Nashville, TN: T. Nelson, 1997. ISBN 188821211X. Includes commentaries by the Fathers and other Orthodox writers.

Harakas, Father Stanley. *Contemporary Moral Issues Facing the Orthodox Christian.* Minneapolis, MN: Light and Life Pub. Co., 1982. ISBN 0937032247.

Keller, Aidan. *A Pocket Church History for Orthodox Christians.* Austin, TX: St. Hilarion Press, 1994. ISBN 0923864083.

Mack, Father John. *Preserve Them, O Lord: A Guide for Orthodox Couples in Developing Marital Unity.* Ben Lomond, CA: Conciliar Press, 1996. ISBN 1888212012.

Magdalen, Sister. *Children in the Church Today: An Orthodox Perspective.* Crestwood, NY: St. Vladimir's Seminary Press, 1991. ISBN 0881411043. Discusses aspects of Christian life such as the family, parent and child, education, and social life.

Matusiak, John. *Our Faith: A Popular Presentation of Orthodox Christianity.* Wayne, NJ: New Life Publications, 1986. No ISBN available.

Nicozisin, Father George. *The Orthodox Church, a Well-Kept Secret: A Journey Through Church History.* Minneapolis, MN: Light and Life Pub. Co., 1997. ISBN 188097133X (pbk.).

O'Callaghan, Father Paul. *An Eastern Orthodox Response to Evangelical Claims.* Minneapolis, MN: Light and Life Pub. Co., 1984. ISBN 0937032352 (pbk.).

Orthodox Mysteries: Sacraments and Worship of the Orthodox Church. Translated from the Finnish by Tuija Vänttinen Newton. Oxford: St. Stephens Press, 1998. ISBN 0951903764 (pbk.).

Pulcini, Father Theodore. *Orthodoxy and Catholicism: What are the Differences?* Ben Lomond, CA: Conciliar Press, 1995. No ISBN available. Twenty-four-page booklet.

Rogers, Father Gregory. *Apostolic Succession,* 2nd ed. Ben Lomond, CA: Conciliar Press, 1994. ISBN 0962271373.

Schaeffer, Frank A. *Letters to Father Aristotle: A Journey through Contemporary American Orthodoxy.* Salisbury, MA: Regina Orthodox Press, 1995. ISBN 0964914107.

———. *Portofino*. E. Rutherford, NJ: Berkley Pub. Group, 1999. ISBN 0425166945 (pbk.).

Sisters of the Orthodox Monastery of the Transfiguration. *Bodily Resurrection*. Ben Lomond, CA: Conciliar Press, 1997. No ISBN available. Thirty-two-page booklet.

Stefanatos, Joanne. *Animals and Man: A State of Blessedness*. Minneapolis, MN: Light and Life Pub. Co., 1992. ISBN 0937032905 (pbk.).

Vrame, Anton. *The Educating Icon: Teaching Wisdom and Holiness in the Orthodox Way*. Brookline, MA: Holy Cross Orthodox Press, 1999. ISBN 1885652283.

Ware, Bishop Kallistos. *How Are We Saved? The Understanding of Salvation in the Orthodox Tradition*. Minneapolis, MN: Light and Life Pub. Co., 1996. ISBN 1880971224 (pbk.).

Whiteford, Father John. *Sola Scriptura: An Orthodox Analysis of the Cornerstone of Reformation Theology*. Ben Lomond, CA: Conciliar Press, 1996. No ISBN available. Forty-seven-page booklet.

Interactive Multimedia

From Glory to Glory: Great and Holy Week: Lazarus Saturday to Pascha Sunday. (CD-ROM) [Thessaloniki]: MLS Media. Users select one of the days in holy week, then choose narration, commentary, gospel reading, divine services, or patristic homilies; other options include choice of Greek or English, variations on the selection, and chant in both languages.

Magazines

In Kolya's Classroom
Niki Krause, Editor
Orthodox Christian Schools of Northeast Ohio
755 S. Cleveland Avenue
Mogadore, OH 44260
(330) 929–9126

Little Falcons
P.O. Box 371
Grayslake, IL 60030
(847) 223–4300
Email: littlefalcons@owc.net
Items of interest to all ages, with specific sections for each age group—a family magazine.

Orthodox Family Life
St. Nicholas Church
755 S. Cleveland Avenue
Mogadore, OH 44260
(330) 929–9126

URL: http://theologic.com/oflweb (accessed March 2004)
A family magazine especially helpful for those wanting to teach
   their children at home.

Praxis
Department of Religious Education
50 Goddard Avenue
Brookline, MA 02445–7415
(617) 850–1218 or (800) 566–1088
URL: http://www.religioused.goarch.org (accessed March 2004)
Concise articles of interest to parents, educators, and teens.

Video Recordings

Furris, Nicholas J., Apostolos Fliakos and Yanni Simonides. *History of Orthodox Christianity, Part 1, The Beginnings.* Astoria, NY: GOTelecom, Inc.; Worcester, PA:
   Gateway Films/Vision Video, 1994. First in a series of three programs that
   introduce the history, tenets, and traditions of the Christian Orthodox Church.
   This segment examines the establishment and spread of Christianity up
   through its role in unifying the Byzantine Empire. Illustrated with art works of
   the period. Sequels: *Part Two, Byzantium; Part Three, A Hidden Treasure.*
———, Gary Vikan and Olympia Glaros. *Holy Image, Holy Space: Icons and Frescoes
   from Greece.* Astoria, NY: GOTelecom, 1988.
A Light Still Bright: The Ecumenical Patriarchate of Constantinople. Astoria, NY:
   GOTelecom, 1990.
Praxis Institute. *A Thousand Years are as One Day: Monks from Athos the Holy Moun-
   tain.* Newbury, MA: Praxis Institute Press, 1981. Follows the daily routine
   and religious life of the monks of Simonos Petras monastery on Mount
   Athos.
Stephens, Sue. *Contemplating Icons: An Introduction to Icons and Prayer.* Middle
   Green, Slough: Donnellson, IA: St. Paul Audio Visual Production, UK;
   Heartbeat [distributor], 1989. Prepares the viewers for a spiritual journey
   into the experience of praying with Icons, while the presentation reveals the
   symbolism and theological insights of Icons.

Web Sites

Antiochian Orthodox Archdiocese. URL: http://www.antiochian.org (accessed
   March 2004).
Basics of the Orthodox Church. URL: http://www.goarch.org/en/ourfaith (accessed
   March 2004).
The Cross and the Quill. An online publication written by Orthodox teens. URL:
   http://www.antiochian.org/christianeducation/cq/ (accessed March
   2004).
A Dictionary of Orthodox Terminology. URL: http://www.goarch.org/en/our
   faith/articles/article8049.asp (accessed March 2004).

The Ecumenical Patriarchate of Constantinople. URL: http://www.patriarchate.org
(accessed March 2004).

Lives of the Saints Daily Calendar. URL: http://www.goarch.org/access/calendar
(accessed March 2004).

Monasticism. URL: http://www.goarch.org/en/ourfaith/monasticism (accessed
March 2004).

Orthodox Church in America. URL: http://www.oca.org (accessed March 2004).

Orthodox Ministry ACCESS. URL: http://www.goarch.org/access (accessed
March 2004).

Orthodox Religious Education. URL: http://www.religioused.goarch.org (accessed
March 2004).

Orthodox World Links. URL: http://theologic.com/links (accessed March 2004).

Youth and Young Adult Ministry. URL: http://www.youth.goarch.org (accessed
March 2004).

WORKS CONSULTED

Cavarnos, Constantine. *Guide to Byzantine Iconography, Volume One.* Brookline,
MA: Holy Transfiguration Monastery, 1993.

Coniaris, Anthony (Reverend Father Anthony Coniaris). *Introduction to the Orthodox Church.* Minneapolis, MN: Light and Life Pub. Co., 1997.

Gillet, Lev (Archimandrite Lev), A Monk of the Eastern Church. *The Jesus Prayer.*
Crestwood, NY: Saint Vladimir's Seminary Press, 1987.

Harakas, Stanley (Reverend Father Stanley Harakas). *The Orthodox Church: 455
Questions and Answers.* Minneapolis, MN: Light and Life Pub. Co., 1987.

The Holy Bible, New King James Version. Nashville, TN: Thomas Nelson Publishers,
Inc., 1982.

Kantiotes, Augoustinos (Augoustinos of Florina). *Orthodox House of Worship.*
Translated by Asterios Gerostergios. Belmont, MA: Institute for Byzantine
and Modern Greek Studies, 1994.

Nasr, Constantine (Reverend Father Constantine Nasr). *The Bible in the Liturgy.*
Oklahoma City, OK: Theosis Publishing Co., 1988.

Ware, Timothy (Bishop Kallistos of Diokleia). *The Orthodox Church.* New York,
NY: Penguin Books, 1997.

———. *The Orthodox Way.* New York, NY: Penguin Books, 1993.

ACKNOWLEDGMENTS

We wish to express our gratitude to His Eminence Metropolitan Isaiah
of Denver for his blessing to work on this project.

We also wish to thank the following who assisted us directly or indi-
rectly in our search for the most appropriate resources for this endeavor:
Reverend Dr. Frank Marangos of the Religious Education Department of
the Greek Orthodox Archdiocese of America; Reverend William Christ,
Proistamenos of Holy Trinity Greek Orthodox Church, Tulsa, Oklahoma;
Reverend Mark Leondis, Director of Youth and Young Adult Ministries for

the Greek Orthodox Archdiocese of America; Reverend Deacon Paul Zaharas, Director of Youth and Young Adult Ministries for the Metropolis of Denver; Hieromonk Simeon of Saint Isaac of Syria Skete; Ms. Irene Cassis, Religious Education Coordinator for the Metropolis of Denver; Ms. Kathleen Mehan, Branch Manager, and Ms. Judith Wayne, Reference Librarian, Ridgewood Branch, The Nicholson Memorial Library System, Garland, Texas; Ms. Christina Marneris, Parish Activities Coordinator, and Father Jerry N. Markopoulos, Holy Trinity Greek Orthodox Church, Portland, Oregon; and Mr. Robert Andrew Uhl.

6

◆ ◆ ◆

SEVENTH-DAY ADVENTISTS

Sue Plaisance

Seventh-day Adventists—Christian evangelical movement that developed in the nineteenth century as outgrowth of general advent awakening

Beginnings:

Began in early 1800s when many people in Europe and America became interested in doctrine of Christ's second coming. Formally organized in 1863.

Rooted in the teachings of Baptist minister William Miller, the visions and teachings of SDA founder, Ellen Gould Harmon White (1827–1915), still in use today to apply scriptures to the individual's daily life.

Beliefs and practices:

Christian God is comprised of the Father, Son, and the Holy Ghost.

Central belief of SDA: scriptures found in the Holy Bible, both Old and New Testaments, are without error.

Members believe Christ will return in person at time unknown but close at hand.

(continued)

(continued)
Sabbath observed on Saturday.
Principles of healthy living advocated (vegetarianism, abstention from alcohol, tobacco, drugs).

Demographics:

Nearly one million members in the United States.

Information point:

Official Web site of the Church. URL: http://www.adventist.org/ (accessed March 2004).

Seventh-day Adventists share many characteristics of the evangelical Christian sects, but they do not consider themselves part of any mainstream evangelical or Protestant religion, nor does any group include them. When the founders formally organized in 1863, they adopted a name, Seventh-day Adventists, which reflected the two central tenets of their belief: that the Sabbath is celebrated on the seventh day, Saturday; and that the literal second coming or "advent" of Christ is imminent.

A BRIEF HISTORY

During the 1800s, belief in the second coming or "advent" of Christ experienced a resurgence of attention. William Miller, a farmer and lay preacher in New York, predicted several dates in 1843 and 1844 on which the advent would occur. When it did not, an offshoot of this Millerite movement founded a new order that observed the Sabbath on the seventh day, Saturday. Taking their name from this observance, the Seventh-day Adventists have gone on to become the largest of the Adventist movements, with 10,000,000 to 12,000,000 members in more than 200 countries, including nearly one million residing in the United States.

CORE BELIEFS AND VALUES

Seventh-day Adventists are members of a Christian sect that believe the literal second coming of Christ is imminent. At the time of this cataclysmic event, it is believed the righteous dead will be resurrected and the righteous living will join them to meet God. The wicked will be slain and await final judgment along with Satan and the fallen angels.

The significance of observing the Sabbath on Saturday, the seventh day of the week, is that it was the day God completed creation of the heavens and earth and made the Sabbath, resting and blessing that day.

Central to the religion is the belief that the scriptures found in the Holy Bible are without error.

The writings of Ellen Gould Harmon White play a significant role in the faith of Seventh-day Adventists. Mrs. White, a nineteenth-century visionary and founder, is thought to have had the spiritual gift of prophecy. Her teachings are accepted by Adventists "as directly inspired by God" (*Encyclopedia Americana*, 2002, v. 1, p. 193). Her writings, however, are not considered a substitute for scripture, nor are they placed on the same level, but they are used to apply the scriptures to an individual's daily life.

Guests attending a Seventh-day Adventist church service may participate in any of the service's rituals. Adventists practice "open" communion, which means believers are welcome to participate regardless of their denominational affiliation.

The ritual of foot washing is an important part of the quarterly communion service. It represents "a higher purification—a cleansing of the heart" and demonstrates Christ's dedication to a life of selfless service and the willingness of the individual to serve others in the spirit of Jesus (Cockerham).

A balanced vegetarian diet and healthy lifestyle are emphasized, and consumption of alcohol or narcotics is actively discouraged. Community seminars and support groups are available to provide instruction in nutrition and exercise and avoidance of alcohol, tobacco, and narcotics.

The Church demonstrates a great deal of concern for youth, evident through its extensive education and Youth Ministries programs, and administers a large parochial school system. Each local church's Youth Ministries program sponsors activities such as summer camps, youth rallies, and mission projects where youth share their talents and contribute to their church. The Church's goal "is for the youth to experience the joy of being accepted and intimately involved in the mission of the church" (McFarland, p. 13).

FORMATIVE EXPERIENCES
Missions

Evangelism and proselytizing are important in the faith, and members are encouraged to reach out to others through personal witnessing and extending invitations to worship services and evangelistic seminars.

Much effort is also put into sponsoring missions to almost every nation on earth. Seventh-day Adventists take to heart the admonitions found in the books of Matthew and Revelation in the New Testament of the Holy Bible to preach the gospel, make disciples of all nations, and baptize them. Teens are an integral part of the international mission efforts, participating in both fundraising activities and actual missions.

Baptism

Parents are expected to accept the responsibility for their children's spiritual growth and character development. Teens are not considered members of the Church until they are baptized, which is done by immersion. Individuals are considered ready to be baptized when they are old enough to understand its meaning, have surrendered to Christ and are converted, understand the fundamental principles of Christianity, and comprehend the significance of church membership.

MISCONCEPTIONS AND STEREOTYPES
"It's a Cult"

Some religious groups have labeled the SDA church a cult, but the Church is a fully recognized church in America and a religion practiced throughout the world.

The Branch Davidians

The Branch Davidians began as a sectarian splinter from the SDA church in 1929 after their leader, Victor Houteff, was disfellowshipped because of his deviations from Church teachings. In February 1993, when the Davidian compound near Waco, Texas, was besieged, the SDA church immediately disavowed any affiliation with the Davidians, stating "although the Seventh-day Adventist Church has no affiliation with the Branch Davidians or any other cult, our hearts go out to those who have lost loved ones in the Waco, Texas, tragedy. As compassionate, peace-loving people, our prayers are with these families" (Lawson).

Work Habits

Many SDA members choose not to work on Saturday because it is their day of worship, but SDA employees in crucial fields such as medicine often work Saturdays.

Pacifism, Military Service, and Patriotism

Over the years the Church has softened its original stance from "declining all participation in acts of war and bloodshed" to a position in which noncombatant roles are acceptable to fulfill military duties (Lawson). The Church has determined that the bearing of arms should be a matter of individual conscience. It encourages obedience to civil authorities and offers spiritual support to members in military service.

WHAT ARE SDA TEENS LOOKING FOR AT THE LIBRARY?

Many SDA teens follow the teachings of their Church in regard to healthy living and are vegetarians, so information on physical health and nutrition would be of interest.

SDA teens in Oregon expressed interest in materials published by the Review and Herald Publishing Association, a major publishing house for the SDA Church in the United States, and books written by Ellen Gould Harmon White. Naturally, they want books that present an accurate representation of their faith, rather than presenting it as a cult.

Biographies of people who have survived great hardships through their faith in God are popular with this group, as well as novels that focus on loving families and Christian values.

Many SDA teens attend church-run boarding schools so you may never have a significant population of SDA teens using your library. They tend to stay within their church group for work and recreation, limiting interaction with the general populace.

BUILDING YOUR COLLECTION

Marian McGhee, a book buyer for the Adventist Book Center in Clackamas, Oregon, shared the following criteria used in selecting titles for the young adult section. Look for books that emphasize family values, religious freedom, Christian principles, and high moral standards. She is somewhat careful about selecting books in which characters die because the SDA concept of death is that the individual goes to sleep until the resurrection occurs, which differs from the mainstream Christian concept of death.

McGhee has found that historical fiction is a perennial favorite with teen SDAs, as well as fictionalized biographies. Kay Rizzo, a Seventh-day Adventist, was recommended as a popular Christian author. Rizzo writes the *Serenity Inn* series for teen girls. Jan Karon, author of the *Mitford Years* series, was also recommended as a reliable author of fiction for SDA teens.

TYPES OF BOOKS AVAILABLE

Adventist publishers provide a full line of books and periodicals for children and adults, including many books dealing with biblical and inspirational topics. Books for Christian women are a specialty of some publishers. There are also nondenominational books for adults that are Bible-based and include guides to healthful living principles and more effective Bible study. It appears that much more nonfiction is published than fiction, although the children's book line includes several fiction series.

Publishers

Bethany House Publishers
P.O. Box 6287
Grand Rapids, MI 49516–6287
(800) 877–2665
URL: http://www.bethanyhouse.com (accessed March 2004)

Broadman and Holman Publishers
127 Ninth Avenue North
Nashville, TN 37234
(800) 251–3225
URL: http://www.broadmanholman.com (accessed March 2004)

Family Heritage Books
P.O. Box 232
Wildwood, GA 30757
(800) 777–2848; fax (256) 597–3548
URL: http://www.familyheritagebooks.com (accessed March 2004)

Hartland Publications
P.O. Box 1
Rapidan, VA 22733
(540) 672–3566 or (800) 774–3566; fax (540) 672–3568
E-mail: sales@hartlandpublications.org
URL: http://www.hartlandpublications.com (accessed March 2004)

Harvest House Publishers
990 Owen Loop North
Eugene, OR 97402
(541) 343–0123
URL: http://www.harvesthousepubl.com (accessed March 2004)

Multnomah Publishers
P.O. Box 1720
Sisters, OR 97759
URL: http://www.multnomahbooks.com (accessed March 2004)

Pacific Press
P.O. Box 5353
Nampa, ID 83687–5353
(208) 465–2500; fax (208) 465–2531
E-mail: webmaster@pacificpress.com
URL: http://www.pacificpress.com (accessed March 2004)

Review and Herald Publishing Association
55 W. Oak Dr.
Hagerstown, MD 21740
URL: http://www.rhpa.org (accessed March 2004)
The main SDA publisher in the United States, publications are
    usually distributed through Adventist Book Centers. For a list
    of stores by state, see http://www.adventistbookcenter.com/
    ABC_Locator.tpl/ (accessed March 2004), or phone (800)
    765–6955.

TEACH Services, Inc.
254 Donovan Road
Brushton, NY 12916–3605
(518) 358–3494; fax (518) 367–1844; orders (800) 367–1844
E-mail: info@TEACHServices.com
URL: http://www.tsibooks.com (accessed March 2004)

Thomas Nelson, Inc.
P.O. Box 141000
Nashville, TN 37214
URL: http://www.thomasnelson.com (accessed March 2004)
No phone listed on Web site; they appear to prefer online con-
    tact.

LIBRARY PROGRAMMING IDEAS

Since many SDA high school students attend church-sponsored boarding schools you may not see many students of this age in your library.
However, SDA young adult singles or young married couples may be
interested in attending programs that support their values.

Wellness or Healthful Living Workshops

Programs on vegetarianism, exercise, and healthful living may be of particular interest to these patrons. Contact the nearest SDA Providence hospital for potential speakers on subjects of interest.

Teen Travelogues

Invite teens or young adults who have participated in international missions to make presentations at your library. Teens talking to teens can be an effective way of attracting young people to programs. Set up a presentation graphics program in your meeting room and help the teens load digital photos from their travels into the computer for an informal slide show.

SELECTED TITLES

Jones, Veda Boyd. *The New Citizen.* Uhrichsville, OH: Barbour Publishing, Inc., 1998. ISBN 1577483928. *American Adventure* history series for children and teens, v. 31. Set at the beginning of the twentieth century, Irish immigrant Maureen becomes a citizen and meets President Theodore Roosevelt.

Kirkpatrick, Jane. *A Gathering of Finches.* Sisters, OR: Multnomah, 1997. ISBN 1576730824. Cassie Stearns Simpson crossed the Oregon coastal tidewaters in 1899 to begin her life with prosperous entrepreneur Louis Simpson. He created Shore Acres garden for her, now one of Oregon's loveliest state parks.

Maxwell, C. Mervyn. *Tell It to the World: The Story of Seventh-day Adventists.* ISBN 0816302170. A popular history of the Great Second Advent Movement in North America, it combines stories, historical information, and inspirational passages to illuminate the founders and events that led to development of the modern church.

McFarland, Ken. *Let's Get Acquainted: An Introduction to the Seventh-day Adventist Church.* Nampa, ID: Pacific Press Publishing, 1996. ISBN 0816306915. Written especially for the recent convert, this paperback booklet includes a look at the organization of the church and a brief introduction to the services and literature offered through the church. It is small in size and will require special handling to prevent it from getting lost on the shelves, but it does contain a lot of good information.

Melina, Vesanto, R.D. *Becoming Vegetarian: The Complete Guide to Adopting a Healthy Vegetarian Diet.* Summertown, TN: Book Publishing Co., 1995. ISBN 1570670137. A well-written, well-organized, comprehensive approach to adopting a vegetarian diet. The chapter on vegetarian nutrition for the growing years includes a particularly good section on nutritional needs of adolescents and how to meet those needs. There is even a chapter on vegetarian diplomacy with tips on how to maintain one's vegetarian diet without alienating family and friends.

Ministerial Association, General Conference of Seventh-day Adventists. *Seventh-day Adventists Believe...A Biblical Exposition of 27 Fundamental Doctrines.* Hagerstown, MD: Review and Herald Publishing Association, 1988. ISBN 0828004668. If you have shelf space in your library for only one volume on the Seventh-day Adventist Church, this is the book to buy. Authoritatively prepared by the Ministerial Association of the SDA General Conference, it was rigorously reviewed by leaders from the Church's ten world divisions. It clearly and concisely summarizes the present beliefs of the Church and includes the Biblical passages upon which each is founded.

Rizzo, Kay D. *Lilia's Haven* (*Serenity Inn* series, v. 4). Nashville, TN: Broadman and Holman Publishers, 1999. ISBN 0805416854. In the late 1800s, Lilia defies her parents and elopes with a charming man who she soon learns is a gambler and thief. How she finds the courage to accept the Lord and change the direction of her life makes this book an exciting, romantic adventure, with unseen dangers and unexpected heroes.

White, Ellen G. *Steps to Christ.* Nampa, ID: Pacific Press Publishing, 1908, 1892. ISBN 0816300461. An original founder of the SDA Church and its most prolific writer, White's books are still in use today and play a major role in the education of students of the religion. This particular text includes instruction on becoming a disciple of Christ and moving along the pathway of Christian life.

WEB SITES

Insight Magazine Online. Specifically targeted to SDA teens and young adults, this online magazine offers articles on family relationships, careers, writing, sports, advice to teens, and youth group ideas. URL: http://www.insight magazine.org/ (accessed March 2004).

Seventh-day Adventist Church. This main Web site for the worldwide SDA Church presents information about the church and its members and provides links to related sites. URL: http://www.adventist.org (accessed March 2004).

TagNet. Hosts a large number of Adventist churches' and institutions' Web sites and provides a feature to search these sites. An entire section is devoted to youth and teen groups. URL: http://topics.tagnet.org/youth/teens/ listing1.html (accessed March 2004).

Yahoo Groups. A list for Seventh-day "Adventist youth who want to hang out and talk and meet other" SDA youth. URL: http://groups.yahoo.com/group/ AdventistYouth/ (accessed March 2004).

_____. A list for Seventh-day Adventist youth "passionate about God who enjoy hanging out socially and recreationally." URL: http://groups.yahoo. com/group/bickleyyouth/ (accessed March 2004).

_____. A "group created to bind all SDA" youth members in "service to God" and fellow Christians. URL: http://groups.yahoo.com/group/SDAY_ CLUB/ (accessed March 2004).

_____. SDAYYA is a group for Seventh-day Adventist youth in their late teens and young adults in their early twenties. Includes chats, Bible studies, and book and music recommendations. Also open to non-SDAs who are inter-

ested in learning more about the denomination. URL: http://groups.
yahoo.com/group/SDAYYA/ (accessed March 2004).

Youth Faith—Are You at the Crossroads? This Canadian site for SDA teens includes
links to British Broadcasting Company news articles concerned with religion, the Bible online, frequently asked questions, chat room, book and
movie reviews, and career information. URL: http://www.youthfaith.org/
index.php (accessed March 2004).

Youth Pages—Get Connected. Designed by youth to serve and inspire other youth,
this site connects teens by providing opportunities for ministry and outreach. URL: http://www.youthpages.org/ (accessed March 2004).

WORKS CONSULTED

Chang, Jillyn. High school student. E-mail interview and survey on Seventh-day
Adventist teens, October 2002.

Cockerham, Mark. Pastor, South Park Seventh-day Adventist Church, 22222 S.W.
Grahams Ferry Road, Tualatin, Oregon, (503) 692–2915. E-mail interview,
November 2002.

Encyclopedia Americana, International Edition. Danbury, CT: Grolier Incorporated,
2002.

Lawson, Ronald. "Seventh-day Adventists." Religious Movements Homepage.
URL: http://religiousmovements.lib.virginia.edu (accessed March 2004).

Magida, Arthur J. and Stuart M. Matlins, eds. *How to Be a Perfect Stranger,* v. 1.
Woodstock, VT: Skylight Paths Publishing, 1999.

McFarland, Ken. *Let's Get Acquainted: An Introduction to the Seventh-day Adventist
Church.* Nampa, ID: Pacific Press Publishing, 1996.

McGhee, Marian. Book buyer, ABC Christian Family Book Store, 13455 SE 97th
Ave., Clackamas, OR 97015. Telephone interview, February 2003.

Ministerial Association, General Conference of Seventh-day Adventists. *Seventh-
day Adventists Believe...A Biblical Exposition of 27 Fundamental Doctrines.*
Hagerstown, MD: Review and Herald Publishing Association, 1988.

Toropov, Brandon and Father Luke Buckles. *The Complete Idiot's Guide to the World's
Religions.* New York, NY: Simon & Schuster Macmillan, 1997.

7

JUDAISM

Elaine Daniel and Linda Smith

Judaism—the oldest religion in the Western world, and the first monotheistic religion in the world, based on the belief that God is Creator and Ruler of the universe

Beginnings:

Founded by the patriarch, Abraham, who lived approximately 1300 B.C.E. in Palestine.

Moses received from God first five books of Bible called Pentateuch or Torah, basis of Jewish religion. Judaism founded on teaching and laws of Hebrew Bible (Old Testament) and Talmud, book of law.

Beliefs and practices:

"Torah" means instruction or guidance.

Christianity and Islam both derive from Judaism although they differ in beliefs and practices.

Demographics:

About 5,700,000 members in the United States.

(continued)

(continued)

Information points:

Union for Reform Judaism. URL: http://www.uahc.org/ (accessed March 2004).

Maven. URL: http://www.maven.co.il/ (accessed April 2004). Web directory with over 7,000 Jewish and Israel links.

The Jewish religion originated over 4,000 years ago in the desert of Canaan, now Palestine and Israel. The patriarch of a nomadic family, Abraham, began to worship one God, and the long, complex history of Judaism began. Judaism was the first monotheistic religion and is one of the oldest religions still in practice today. Many Jewish festivals and religious doctrines are based in their extensive history, and therefore the section on festivals will also provide basic historical background.

HISTORY AND DOCTRINE

Judaism is a complex religion with a multiplicity of viewpoints. The main point of agreement between all Jews, however, is the importance of the Jewish Bible. The Bible, known to Christians as the Old Testament, contains the original collection of laws, religious beliefs, ethics, histories, codes of conduct, and social and moral values that are still in use today.

The Bible is divided into three main sections: the Torah (also called the Pentateuch or the Five Books of Moses), the Prophets, and the Writings. During weekly synagogue services, consecutive portions of the Torah are read aloud. This is considered a great honor for both the reader and those who recite the blessings before and after the reading.

All Jews worship one God and read the same Bible, but they are a widely diverse group. There is no central authority deciding on religious or social practices, nor is there any universally accepted interpretation of the sacred writings. Over the course of 4,000 years, three main groups of Jews have developed, and practices vary from group to group. The main divisions are Orthodox, Conservative, and Reform.

The Orthodox observe the laws in the Bible the most faithfully. Since the Orthodox Jews believe that the Bible was written by God and given to Moses on Mount Sinai, they believe that God's law is immutable. They follow strict religious practices, social mores, and dietary laws (referred to as *kashrut*, or keeping kosher). Men wear *kippot* (skull caps) at all times, and sometimes *tallit katan* (prayer shawls worn under clothing) to show their devotion and piety in the presence of God. Women practice modest dress and cover their hair, sometimes with wigs or scarves. Orthodox synagogues practice gender separation with women and men sitting in different areas and synagogue services are in Hebrew. The Sabbath (sundown Friday to sundown Saturday) is a day of rest; Orthodox households do not use lights, cars, or any other electrical or mechanical equipment during the Sabbath.

The various groups of Hassidic Jews are part of the Orthodox sect and are sometimes called the ultra-Orthodox. They follow the Biblical laws (as interpreted by Hassidic rabbis) very strictly.

The Conservative movement began in the United States in the late nineteenth century as a response to the call for Judaism to adapt to the modern world. Conservative Jews have modified religious observances and social customs. For example, services are held both in English (or the vernacular of the region) and Hebrew, and the women and men may sit together. Both women and men may wear the kippot and the tallit.

Women take part in all aspects of Conservative Judaism, including being rabbis (teachers) and cantors (leaders of the services). There is emphasis placed on the religious education of children as well as increasing interest in adult Jewish education.

The most liberal of the three major groups, Reform Judaism, began in Germany in the late nineteenth century and maintains that Jewish thought and practices need to be frequently updated and modified. Services are held mostly in English and may include instrumental accompaniment. Friday night services are emphasized more than in the other groups. Again, men and women may sit together, and either can wear the kippot and prayer shawls.

Recently, a modern radical movement has arisen called Jewish Renewal. A world-wide, trans-denominational movement, Jewish Renewal was founded by Rabbi Zalman Schacter-Shalomi and is grounded in Judaism's prophetic and mystical traditions, including the Kabbalah and other classic Jewish sources. The focus is on making Jewish spirituality more accessible in an egalitarian and participatory environment. Jewish Renewal promotes justice, freedom, responsibility, and caring for the earth. The movement acts to fully include people who have not always felt welcomed by more traditional congregations, including sexual minorities, singles, and women.

Historically, there are two Jewish groups based on geography and culture. The Sephardic Jews lived for centuries in Spain. After being expelled in 1492, they settled in Northern Africa, Italy, Egypt, Palestine, Syria, the Balkans, and the Ottoman Empire. In 1497 the Sephardic Jews who had taken refuge in Portugal were expelled as well. They settled in Western Europe, the West Indies, and in North America.

Ashkenazi Jews lived in modern Germany and Poland and, after the Crusades and the resultant hate crimes against them, they began to migrate throughout Europe and eventually to North America.

These two groups are distinguished by different histories, different pronunciation of Hebrew, different religious practices, and differences in their social habits, literature, and clothing. When the modern State of Israel was formed in 1948, Hebrew was declared the official language. Sephardic Hebrew was chosen as the preferred pronunciation, and today most synagogues in the United States have adopted the Sephardic pronunciation.

FESTIVALS

The festival and holiday cycle begins every year with Rosh Hashanah, the Jewish new year, which falls in autumn, usually in September or October. The following ten days are a time for contemplation leading up to the most solemn holy day, Yom Kippur—the Day of Atonement. Together the days are called the "Days of Awe." Yom Kippur is observed for one day, and adults abstain from eating, bathing, and all other regular occupations of daily life. This is considered a time for repentance and for considering one's relationships in the world and with God. These days are solemn and serious but also have elements of joy and sweetness, as repentance can create forgiveness and reconciliation.

The festival of Sukkot is celebrated four days after Yom Kippur. For seven days, Jewish families eat and sometimes sleep in a *Sukkah* (hut or booth), which is built outdoors and decorated with fruit and vegetables. Sukkot is a thanksgiving and harvest festival and is one of the oldest Jewish holidays.

Immediately following Sukkot are the holy days of Shemini Atzert and Simhat Torah, or Rejoicing in the Law, which celebrate the significance of the Torah. In the synagogue, the last verses of the Torah are read and then the first verses of Genesis, the beginning of the Torah, are read to begin the cycle once more. During the service, the Torah scrolls are removed from the Ark (a container or cabinet for the scrolls), and congregation members dance and sing as the Torah is carried around the building.

Hanukkah is probably the festival most familiar to Christians because it coincides with the timing of the Christmas holidays. In Jewish homes, candles are lit for eight nights to commemorate the victory of a revolt against the dominant Syrians in 165 B.C.E. Songs, games (especially involving the dreidel, a four-sided top), gifts, and potato latkes or pancakes make this minor holiday a happy and popular celebration. (It is not necessary for libraries to make Hanukkah a sort of "substitute Christmas" in December. If your library wants to have holiday displays for different religions,

Passover or Yom Kippur would be more appropriate choices since they are major Jewish holy days.)

In late winter or early spring, Purim celebrates Esther's clever rescue of the Jews from the Persian vizier, Haman. This is a celebration that emphasizes fun, food, and sometimes masquerades.

Later in the spring, Passover is celebrated for eight days. Passover commemorates the events in the book of Exodus and deliverance of the Jews from Egyptian oppression. On the first two nights the main service of the holiday, the Seder, is observed in the home. The story of the flight from Egypt is read aloud from a Haggadah, the book of the Passover service. Passover requires special dietary restrictions, including eating only unleavened bread and using special dishes and utensils.

Yom Ha'atamaut—Israel Independence Day—is celebrated in the late spring. This is a secular celebration and not a holy day; many synagogues, however, hold services and traditional Israeli foods are eaten at home.

Shavuot is observed in late May or early June and celebrates God giving the Torah to Moses.

The most important holiday, though, is the Shabbat or Sabbath. It is celebrated each week, beginning on Friday evening at sundown, and it lasts until nightfall on Saturday. In the home, blessings are said over candles, wine, and braided bread called Challah. On Friday night in the synagogue, prayers and songs welcome the day of rest. On Saturday, the Torah is removed from the Ark and read aloud to the congregation. Orthodox Jews refrain from any kind of work, including using any kind of mechanical or electrical device. The concept of a period of rest each week is counted as one of Judaism's greatest gifts to the rest of the world. Herman Wouk, in his book, *This is My God,* wrote a beautiful passage on the Sabbath. An excerpt reads, "this day is the fulcrum of a practicing Jew's existence and generally a source of strength, refreshment and cheer.... Our Sabbath opens with blessings over light and wine.... Our observance has its solemnities, but the main effect is release, peace, gaiety, and lifted spirits" (Wouk, pp. 58–59).

FORMATIVE EXPERIENCES

The first life event of a Jewish person is his naming. If the child is male, he is given his Jewish name and the *brit milah* (circumcision) is performed eight days after his birth. A *mohel* (professional circumciser) performs the circumcision to mark the covenant of God with the child. A baby girl can receive her Hebrew name at any time in a ceremony often performed at home.

At the age of thirteen, a Jewish male child is received by the congregation as a *bar mitzvah* (son of the commandments). Girls are traditionally received at age twelve as a *bat mitzvah*. The child prepares by learning Hebrew, the melodies and chants used when reading the Bible, and the responsibilities of a Jewish person. On the Sabbath of the mitzvah, the child leads some portion of the service and is called to read from the Torah scroll for the first time. The child is then considered an adult with the privileges and obligations to observe Jewish law and follow the *mitzvoth* (commandments or laws).

The next life event is marriage. Usually held in a synagogue or garden, the ceremony begins with the parents of both the bride and groom walking their child to the *chuppah* (wedding canopy), which represents the tents of the nomadic life of the early Jewish people.

The final event for all is death. Judaism forbids embalming, so burial occurs as soon as possible after death, usually within two days. Rituals for mourning are designed to help the mourners with their grief. During the first week after the burial (*shiva*), the family and close friends of the deceased recite the *Kaddish* (a memorial prayer) once a day with a *minyan* (a group of at least ten men for the Orthodox or ten adults for other branches). They remain quietly at home during this week and receive visitors. This is called "sitting shiva." For the year following the death, close family members recite the Kaddish at least once a week with a minyan. Usually the mourners attend services at the synagogue to do this. One year after the death and burial, the family returns to the grave to place a memorial stone or special marker. Thereafter the family members recite the Kaddish on the anniversary of the death and during the memorial services on Yom Kippur, as well as the last day of Sukkot, the last day of Passover, and the second day of Shavuot (holidays during the Jewish year).

MISCONCEPTIONS AND STEREOTYPES

Jews have been one of the most viciously discriminated against minorities in the history of the world. Everything from the small cruelties of the stereotyped statements, "Jews are cheapskates" or "all Jews are upper class or rich," to blatant attempts at complete eradication pervade Western culture. Whether selecting materials that serve a mainly Jewish community or a mixed community, a librarian needs to determine whether the author looks at these issues intelligently.

The Anti Defamation League (http://www.adl.org, accessed February 2003) offers help for dealing with bigotry, as well as suggestions for educational programs and advocacy. Their sections on dealing with hate online, discussing hate in the home and in schools, and anti-bias training are invaluable.

WHAT ARE JEWISH TEENS LOOKING FOR AT THE LIBRARY?

Jewish teenagers are looking for a place that is accepting of them as minorities in Western culture, has resources that are useful to them in work and in play, and is populated by caring professionals who attempt to include them in the library's activities.

A small but helpful tip: teenagers are already self-conscious and frequently feel like outsiders. Respect their privacy to read. Making comments about their material choices, even at the checkout desk, might alienate patrons.

Education is a major focus in the Jewish community, so library programs supporting the educational process would appeal to Jewish youth and their families. Programs exploring Jewish living would also be of interest. Topics could include holiday information (with the focus going beyond Hanukkah, which is actually a rather minor holiday), stress reduction for students, the Kaballah, or teen issues, such as dating, from a Jewish perspective. A teen book discussion group that reads and discusses books with Jewish main characters is another option. Booklists of library materials on such topics are highly recommended.

Public libraries should be particularly careful about having displays for holidays of the dominant religion, Christianity. For example, a nativity display in December will send a negative message to Jews, as well as other non-Christians.

BUILDING YOUR COLLECTION

Every recommended resource mentioned in the bibliography of this chapter would be acceptable to Conservative Jews, Reform Jews, and associated affiliations. However, Orthodox Jews, and especially the ultra-Orthodox, would find much of this material objectionable. Usually young ultra-Orthodox Jews will be educated entirely within Jewish schools. Therefore, a public library in the United States will have the most problem finding materials that will help Orthodox Jews or those who have maintained strong cultural ties with another country.

It would be difficult, if not impossible, to describe criteria that would suit all factions of Judaism. One group would find great offense in an item where another would find the divine. If your library has the potential of serving Jewish congregations, or teen groups who would use the library resources, approach the governing body of the synagogue or the teen group for guidance in choosing materials.

There is one area where all Jews will agree: Christian materials presented as Jewish materials are offensive. Groups such as "Jews for Jesus" offend even secular or cultural Jews with no affiliation to any Jewish group. Also, Christian publishing houses do not publish true Jewish books. They may produce items that are useful in an interfaith discussion, but these should not be used as a main source of information on Judaism.

Non-Jews do create materials that would be a welcome part of a Jewish collection. However, either a Jewish press or a medium to large secular publishing company would publish these materials.

Finally, materials on the "Holocaust Hoax" theories need to be represented in the library's collection since informative materials for young adults should be made available for research papers on these topics.

Publishers and Distributors

Jewish Lights Publishing
P.O. Box 237
Sunset Farm Offices, Rt. 4
Woodstock, VT 05091
(802) 457–4000; fax (802) 457–4004
URL: http://www.jewishlights.com/ (accessed March 2004)
Publishes books that reflect the Jewish wisdom tradition for people of all faiths and all backgrounds.

KTAV Publishing House, Inc.
930 Newark Avenue, 4th floor
Jersey City, NJ 07306
(201) 963–9524; fax (201) 963–0102
URL: http://www.ktav.com (accessed March 2004)
Publishes Jewish books for children and young adults, including prayer books, games, school supplies, and textbooks. KTAV also produces scholarly books on a range of topics including biblical study and contemporary issues.

Jason Aronson
230 Livingston St.
Northvale, NJ 07647
(800) 782–0015; fax (201) 767–1576
URL: http://www.aronson.com/shop/catalog/default.php (accessed March 2004)
Spans the entire spectrum of approaches to Jewish tradition: Orthodox, Hasidic, Reconstructionalist, Reform, Conservative,

Renewal, unaffiliated, and secular. Topics include Anti-Semitism, Classics in Translation, Family, Folklore and Storytelling, Hasidism, History, Holidays, Holocaust, Israel, Jewish Law, Kabbalah, Marriage, Meditation, Prayer, Talmud, Theology, Torah, Travel, Women's Studies, and more.

Jewish Publication Society
2100 Arch St., 2nd Floor
Philadelphia, PA 19103
(215) 832–0608 or (800) 234–3151; fax (215) 568–2017
URL: http://www.jewishpub.org/index.htm (accessed March 2004)
The oldest publisher of Jewish literature published in the English language. Since 1888, JPS has been providing titles that further Jewish culture and education.

Powell's Books
1005 W. Burnside
Portland, OR 97209
(866) 201–7601
URL: http://www.powells.com/psection/Judaica.html (accessed March 2004)
Powell's is a respected bookseller with a well-chosen selection of resources on Judaism.

LIBRARY SERVICES FOR JEWISH YOUTH

Observant Jews follow dietary laws known as *kashrut* or kosher. The dietary observances can be complicated, and various groups follow kashrut to varying degrees. The basic rules are no pork products, no shellfish (or any seafood that lacks both fins and scales), and no mixing of meat and dairy products. Permitted foods include fruits, vegetables, domesticated animals, and fowl. The Kosher symbol is a discreet "K" or "U" on the label and simplifies purchasing refreshments.

If you serve refreshments at library gatherings, a basic understanding of these restrictions will help you be more inclusive. For example, marshmallows are not kosher, and many kinds of hot dogs contain both meat and dairy products.

People keep kosher to different levels; some Jews do not follow the restrictions at all while some will have different kitchenwares so the meat and dairy foods are kept separate. If you serve an Orthodox or ultra-Orthodox population, the local synagogue should be willing to help you find ways to be as inclusive as possible.

Since Muslims also follow dietary restrictions (*halal*) that are somewhat similar to kashrut, being careful with food choices will serve two populations at once. A vegetarian offering is often the simplest way to include any who follow dietary restrictions.

Volunteer community service projects are very important in Jewish life, especially projects with a focus on social justice or social action. Most Jewish community centers have volunteer programs for youth and adults, and the B'nai B'rith Youth organization has a teen initiative with social justice as a focus of community partnerships. Libraries looking for socially conscious partners would do well to contact local Jewish community groups or organizations when exploring potential projects. Teens working on volunteer projects for honors credit would also be another resource available to library staff.

SELECTED TITLES
Professional Reference

Hart, Merrily F. *Creating a Collection: A Resource Booklist for a Beginning Judaic Library.* New York, NY: Association of Jewish Libraries, 2000. ISBN 0929262549. A guide to developing a core collection for a beginning synagogue, school, or community center library.

Silver, Linda. *Developing a Judaic Children's Collection: Recommended Books and Videos.* New York, NY: Association of Jewish Libraries, 2001. ISBN 0929262565. Contains suggestions of books and videos for preschool, elementary and middle schools, organized by subject bibliographies. Indexed by author/illustrator and title.

Fiction

Baer, Edith. *Walk the Dark Streets: A Novel.* New York, NY: Farrar, Straus and Giroux, 1998. ISBN 0374382298. Eva, a young Jewish girl living in Nazi Germany, experiences increasing tensions in daily life while planning to escape.

Banks, Lynne Reid. *Broken Bridge.* New York, NY: Avon Flare Publishers, 1996. ISBN 0380723840. Nili, Lesley's daughter, witnesses an attack that leaves her Canadian cousin murdered in the streets of Jerusalem. She is torn between her loyalty to a Jewish Israeli and her desire to protect the identity of the Palestinian suspect who was instrumental in saving her life. Sequel to *One More River.*

———. *One More River.* New York, NY: Avon, 1993. ISBN 0785706267. Set in 1967, *One More River* is the story of Lesley, a Canadian Jewish girl, whose family decides to leave their secure life and move to a kibbutz in Israel.

Bennet, Cherie and Jeff Gottesfeld. *Anne Frank and Me.* New York, NY: G.P. Putnam's Sons, 2001. ISBN 0698119738. After suffering a concussion while on a class trip to a Holocaust exhibit, Nicole finds herself living the life of a Jewish teenager in Paris during the Nazi occupation. Adapted from the play of the same title.

Carmi, Daniella. *Samir and Yonatan*. New York, NY: Arthur A. Levine Books, 2000. ISBN 0439135230. Samir, a Palestinian boy, is sent to an Israeli hospital where he makes friends with an Israeli boy, Yonatan. Together, they have otherworldly experiences, and Samir finds peace about his brother's death in the war.

Feder, Harriet K. *The Mystery of the Kaifeng Scroll: A Vivi Hartman Adventure*. Minneapolis, MN: Lerner Publications Co., 1995. ISBN 0822507390. When Vivi Hartman's mother suddenly disappears while they are in Istanbul, Turkey, the fifteen-year-old befriends an Arab girl and sets out to find her mother, encountering a mystery involving an ancient Torah scroll along the way.

Laird, Christina. *But Can the Phoenix Sing?* New York, NY: Greenwillow Books, 1995. ISBN 0688136125. Seventeen-year-old Richard discovers the details of the hidden past of his stern and remote stepfather when he reads a manuscript about the Jewish resistance in Poland.

Levitin, Sonia. *The Cure*. San Diego, CA: Harcourt Brace, 1999. ISBN 038073298X. A sixteen-year-old boy living in 2407 collides with the past when he finds himself in Strasbourg in 1348 confronting the anti-Semitism that swept through Europe during the Black Plague.

———. *The Singing Mountain*. New York, NY: Simon and Schuster Books for Young Readers, 1998. ISBN 068983523X. After spending a summer in Israel, Mitch decides to stay and pursue a life of Jewish Orthodoxy.

Matas, Carol. *The Garden*. New York, NY: Simon and Schuster Books for Young Readers, 1997. ISBN 0689807236. After leading a group of Jewish refugees to Israel after World War II, sixteen-year-old Ruth joins the Haganah, the Jewish Army, and fights to keep the land granted to the Jewish people by the United Nations.

Meyer, Carolyn. *Drummers of Jericho*. New York, NY: Harcourt Children's Books, 1995. ISBN 0152004416. Moving story of a fourteen-year-old Jewish girl whose family relocates to a small Southern town and who experiences subtle and even blatant hatred from her high school peers.

Michener, James. *The Source*. New York, NY: Random House, 2002, 1965. ISBN 0375760385. An archeological site offers the story of the Jewish people from the beginnings of the Jewish faith and through thousands of years of history.

Miklowitz, Gloria. *Masada: The Last Fortress*. Grand Rapids, MI: Eerdmans Books for Young Readers, 1998. ISBN 0802851681. As the Roman army marches across the Judean desert towards Masada, Simon and his family prepare to fight and never surrender.

Potok, Chaim. *The Chosen*. New York, NY: Simon and Schuster, 1967. ISBN 0449213447. The classic story of two boys, one an Orthodox Jew and the other the son of a Hassidic rabbi, in Brooklyn, New York in the 1940s. A warm tale of religious faith, families, and friendship.

Pullman, Philip. *The Tiger in the Well*. New York, NY: Knopf, 1990. ISBN 0679826718. In 1881 London, Sally finds her young daughter and her possessions assailed by an unknown enemy, while a shadowy figure known as the Tzaddik involves her in his plot to exploit the Jewish immigrants pouring into the country.

Ragen, Naomi. *Jephte's Daughter*. New York, NY: Warner Books, 1989. ISBN 1902881508. The story of a modern-day arranged marriage between an eighteen-year-old American girl and a devout Torah scholar who lives in Jerusalem. Adult themes. Naomi Ragen writes many adult books with Jewish women as their main characters.

Rosenberg, Liz. *Heart and Soul.* New York, NY: Harcourt, 1996. ISBN 0613022750. Willie Steinberg is a promising seventeen-year-old cellist and composer who leaves her private school in Philadelphia for a long summer in Virginia with her hapless mother.

Schur, Maxine. *Sacred Shadows.* New York, NY: Dial Books, 1997. ISBN 0803722958. When her German hometown becomes part of Poland after World War I, Lena, a young German Jew, suffers from the anti-Semitism growing around her.

Uris, Leon. *Exodus.* Garden City, NY: Doubleday, 1958. ISBN 0517207982. The birth of the state of Israel is told through the story of an American nurse and an Israeli freedom fighter.

Voigt, Cynthia. *David and Jonathan.* New York, NY: Scholastic, 1992. ISBN 0590451650 (hardcover); ISBN 0590451669 (pbk.). The relationship between two close friends, Henry and Jonathan, changes when Jonathan's cousin David, a victim of the Holocaust, comes to live with the family. Appropriate for older teens.

Nonfiction

Anti-Semitism

Chaikin, Mariam. *A Nightmare in History: The Holocaust, 1933–1945.* New York, NY: Clarion Books, 1987. ISBN 0395615801. Traces the history of anti-Semitism from biblical times through the twelve years of the Nazi era, and describes Hitler's plans to annihilate European Jews.

Cohn-Serbok, Dan. *The Crucified Jew: Twenty Centuries of Christian Anti-Semitism.* Grand Rapids, MI: W.B. Eerdmans, 1997. ISBN 0802843115. Surveys the persecution of Jews from ancient times to the present, focusing on how the seeds of anti-Semitism were sown in Christian sources and nurtured throughout the history of the Church.

Crossan, John Dominic. *Who Killed Jesus: Exposing the Roots of Anti-Semitism in the Gospel Story of the Death of Jesus.* San Francisco, CA: Harper, 1995. ISBN 0060614803.

Reeve, Simon. *One Day in September: The Full Story of the 1972 Munich Olympics Massacre and the Israeli Revenge Operation "Wrath of God."* New York, NY: Arcade, 2000. ISBN 1559705477.

Zakim, Leonard P. *Confronting Anti-Semitism: A Practical Guide.* Hoboken, NJ: KTAV, 2000. ISBN 0881256293.

Devotionals

Tanakh: A New Translation of the Holy Scriptures According to the Traditional Hebrew Text. Philadelphia, PA: The Jewish Publication Society, 1985. ISBN 0827603665. A translation of the Holy Scriptures based on the traditional Hebrew text, this is a work by rabbis representing the three largest branches of Judaism in North America.

History

Dimont, Max I. *Jews, God, and History*. New York, NY: Mentor Books, 1994. ISBN 0451628667. A secular history of the Jewish people; revised and updated edition.

Eban, Abba. *Heritage: Civilization and the Jews*. New York, NY: Summit Books, 1984. ISBN 067162881X. The companion to the award-winning television series of the same name, this is a colorful and easy-to-read book with illustrations and photographs of art, historical sites, cultural items, and Jews of the last 5,000 years.

Howe, Irving. *World of Our Fathers: The Journey of the East European Jews to America and the Life they Found and Made*. New York, NY: Galahad Books, 2001. ISBN 0883658828.

Holocaust

Aharoni, Zvi. *Operation Eichmann: The Truth about the Pursuit, Capture and Trial*. New York, NY: J. Wiley, 1997. ISBN 0471193771.

Baumel, Judith Taylor. *Kibbutz Buchenwald: Survivors and Pioneers*. New Brunswick, NJ: Rutgers University Press, 1997. ISBN 0813523370.

Brecher, Elinor J. *Schindler's Legacy: True Stories of the List Survivors*. New York, NY: Dutton, 1994. ISBN 0452273536.

Frank, Anne. *Diary of a Young Girl: The Definitive Edition*. New York, NY: Doubleday, 1995. ISBN 0385473788.

Goldhagen, Daniel Jonah. *Hitler's Willing Executioners: Ordinary Germans and the Holocaust*. New York, NY: Alfred A. Knopf, 1996. ISBN 0679446958.

Keneally, Thomas. *Schindler's List*. New York, NY: Simon and Schuster, 1982. ISBN 0671516884.

Rosengarten, Israel J. *Survival: The Story of a Sixteen-year-old Jewish Boy*. Syracuse, NY: Syracuse University Press, 1999. ISBN 0815605803.

Spiegelman, Art. *Maus: A Survivor's Tale: My Father Bleeds History*. New York, NY: Pantheon Books, 1986.

———. *Maus II: A Survivor's Tale: And Here My Troubles Began*. New York, NY: Pantheon Books, 1991. ISBN 0394556530 (hardcover); ISBN 0679729771 (pbk.).

Israel

Ackerman, Susan. *Warrior, Dancer, Seductress, Queen: Women in Judges and Biblical Israel*. New York, NY: Doubleday, 1998. ISBN 0385484240.

Bar-Am, Micha. *Israel, a Photobiography: The First Fifty Years*. New York, NY: Simon & Schuster, 1999. ISBN 068484513X.

Bard, Mitchell Geoffrey. *The Complete Idiot's Guide to the Middle East Conflict*. New York, NY: Alpha Books, 1999. ISBN 0585278784.

Fleisher, Robert Jay. *Twenty Israeli Composers: Voices of a Culture*. Detroit, MI: Wayne State University Press, 1997. ISBN 081432648X.

Gold, Stephanie. *Israel Guide: Your Passport to Great Travel!* New York, NY: Open Road, 1996. ISBN 1883323754.

Holliday, Laurel, ed. *Children of Israel, Children of Palestine: Our Own True Stories*. New York, NY: Pocket Books, 1998. ISBN 0613177754.

Horovitz, David, ed. *Shalom, Friend: The Life and Legacy of Yitzhak Rabin.* New York, NY: New Market Press, 1996. ISBN 0788158651.

Horovitz, David P. *A Little Too Close to God: The Thrills and Panic of a Life in Israel.* New York, NY: Knopf, 2000. ISBN 0375403817. An emigrant reflects on his decision to live in Israel, discussing the country's response to Yitzhak Rabin's assassination, the role of ultra-Orthodox Jews, and his fears as his children prepare for military service.

Humphrey, Andrew. *Israel and the Palestinian Territories: A Lonely Planet Travel Survival Kit.* Oakland, CA: Lonely Planet Publications, 1996. ISBN 0864426917.

Kaiser, Walter C. *A History of Israel: From the Bronze Age through the Jewish Wars.* Nashville, TN: Broadman & Holman, 1998. ISBN 0805462848.

Lukacs, Yehuda. *Israel, Jordan, and the Peace Process.* Syracuse, NY: Syracuse University Press, 1997. ISBN 0815628552.

Ofrat, Gideon. *One Hundred Years of Art in Israel.* Boulder, CO: Westview Press, 1998. ISBN 0813333776.

Perdue, Leo G. et al. *Families in Ancient Israel.* Louisville, KY: Westminster John Know Press, 1997. ISBN 0664255671.

Rabinovich, Itmar. *Waging Peace: Israel and the Arabs at the End of the Century.* New York, NY: Fararr, Straus, and Giroux, 1999. ISBN 0374105766.

Thomas, Gordon. *Gideon's Spies: The Secret History of the Mossad.* New York, NY: St. Martin's Press, 1999. ISBN 0312252846. Since its formation in 1951, the intelligence-gathering agency of Israel has been a vital part of the country's survival. This exposé offers anecdotes, blunders, and rumors from throughout Mossad's history.

Winter, Dave. *Israel Handbook: With the Palestinian Authority Areas.* Lincolnwood, IL: Footprint Handbooks; Passport Books, 1998. ISBN 1900949482.

Preparing for Religious Ceremonies (Observances)

Burghardt, Linda. *Jewish Holiday Traditions: Joyful Celebrations from Rosh Hashanah to Shavout.* New York, NY: Citadel Press, 2001. ISBN 0806522062.

Cardin, Nina Beth. *The Tapestry of Jewish Time: A Spiritual Guide to Holidays and Life-cycle Events.* Springfield, NJ: Behrman House, 2000. ISBN 0874416450.

Feinstein, Edward. *Tough Questions Jews Ask: A Young Adult's Guide to Building a Jewish Life.* Woodstock, VT: Jewish Lights, 2003. ISBN 158023139X.

Gilman, Neil. *The Way into Encountering God in Judaism.* Woodstock, VT: Jewish Lights, 2000. ISBN 1580230253.

Isaacs, Ronald H. *Every Person's Guide to Purim.* Northvale, NJ: J. Aronson, 2000. ISBN 0765760460.

Kimmelman, Leslie. *Dance, Sing, Remember: A Celebration of Jewish Holidays.* New York, NY: Harper Collins, 2000. ISBN 0060277254. Explains eleven major Jewish holidays and how they are celebrated.

Klagsbrun, Francine. *Jewish Days: A Book of Jewish Life and Culture around the Year.* New York, NY: Farrar, Straus, and Giroux, 1996. ISBN 0374525668. Comprehensive book of Jewish holy days and festivals.

Leneman, Cantor Helen, ed. *Bar/Bat Mitzvah Basics: A Practical Family Guide to Coming of Age Together.* Woodstock, VT: Jewish Lights, 1996. ISBN 1580231519. A practical guide with how-to information about the bar/bat mitzvah process and how to connect and grow as a family through the experience.

Lew, Alan. *One God Clapping: The Spiritual Path of a Zen Rabbi.* New York, NY: Kodansha International, 1999. ISBN 1580231152. By the man known as the "Zen Rabbi," this is the story of a spiritual odyssey that culminated with the formation of the Jewish meditation movement.

Martins, Stuart M. *The Jewish Lights Spirituality Handbook: A Guide to Understanding, Exploring, and Living a Spiritual Life.* Woodstock, VT: Jewish Lights, 2001. ISBN 1580230938. A collection covering many aspects of today's Jewish spirituality including prayer, meditation, Jewish traditions, rituals, and holy days.

Salkin, Jeffrey K. *For Kids—Putting God on Your Guest List: How to Claim the Spiritual Meaning of Your Bar or Bat Mitzvah.* Woodstock, VT: Jewish Lights Publishing, 1998. ISBN 1580230156. A guide for preparing for the bar or bat mitzvah. Discusses the history and significance of this rite of passage and connects it with the core spiritual values of Judaism.

Shendelman, Sara. *Traditions: The Complete Book of Prayers, Rituals, and Blessings for Every Jewish Home.* New York, NY: Hyperion, 1998. ISBN 0786863811. Prayers and traditional services and rituals for Jewish holidays that are celebrated primarily in the home.

Solomon, Lewis D. *The Jewish Book of Living and Dying.* Northvale, NJ: Jason Aronson, 1999. ISBN 0765761017. Jewish mourning customs and spiritual guide.

Weber, Vicki L., ed. *The Rhythm of Jewish Time: An Introduction to Holidays and Lifecycle Events.* West Orange, NJ: Behrman House, 1999. ISBN 0874416736.

Wolf, Laibl. *Practical Kabbala: A Guide to Jewish Wisdom for Everyday Life.* Westminster, MD: Random House, 1996. ISBN 0609803786. This introductory guide to the Kabbala's teachings focuses on achieving an emotionally balanced and nourishing life. The Kabbala, mystical teachings concerning God and the universe considered to provide the means to reach fulfillment, is currently getting a great deal of press.

Audiovisual and Interactive Multimedia Formats

CD-ROMs

Anne Frank House: A House with a Story. Summit, NJ: Cinegram Media, Inc., 2000. ASIN B000053F9D. The story of Anne Frank and her companions as they hid from the Nazis. Uses historical photographs, excerpts from films, Frank family photographs, voice narration, and music. One computer disc and a user guide.

Dead Sea Scrolls Revealed. MPC/MAC, Windows 3.1, Macintosh version. Oak Harbor, WA: Pixel Multimedia LTD, 1994. ISBN 1577991621. Includes color images of the Dead Sea Scrolls, color photos of artifacts, people, and historical sites. Video clips include interviews with leading scholars discussing areas of controversy and parallel English translations of selected manuscripts.

Compact Discs

Tizmoret ha-filharmoit ha-Yisre'elit. *The Israel Philharmonic Orchestra 60th Anniversary Gala.* New York, NY: RCA Victor Red Deal, 1997. ISBN 6304403674.

Video Recordings

Avalon. Burbank, CA: REC/Columbia Pictures Home Video, 1991. ISBN 080010546X. Immigrant Sam Krichinsky and his extended family are followed over several decades, from their first poverty-stricken days in America to increasing prosperity.

Europa Europa. New York, NY: Orion Home Video, 1992. ISBN 1562551051. Based on the true story of Solomon Perel, a German Jew who survived World War II by living seven years as a Nazi.

Great Figures of the Bible series. New York, NY: Yale Roe Films, 1990–1994. V. 1, *The Story of Temptation: Adam and Eve,* ISBN 1560861460; v. 2, *The First Murder: Cain and Abel,* ISBN 1560861479; v. 3, *About Fathers and Sons: Abraham and the Binding of Isaac,* ISBN 1560861487; v. 4, *Suffering and Sacrifice: The Story of Job,* ISBN 1560861495; v. 5, *The Agony of Power: The Story of Moses,* ISBN 1560861509; v. 6, *Greatness and Passion: The Story of David,* ISBN 1560861517. Based in part on Elie Wiesel's *Messengers of God,* biblical portraits and legends. Describes biblical characters in context of their time.

Life Is Beautiful. Burbank, CA: Miramax Home Entertainment, 1999. ISBN 0788814087. The story of a Jewish waiter, his wife, and their son begins as a romantic comedy and ends in a German concentration camp. Walking a fine line between humor and profound sadness, this film affirms the power of life, love, and laughter in the midst of the Holocaust.

Master Race. Burlington, VT; Alexandria, VA: WGBH Educational Foundation (PBS Boston Video, distributor), 1998. ISBN 6305245649. Germans talk candidly about the initial allure of Nazism, and German Jews recall their persecution and internment in concentration camps as Hitler's master race pursued its destiny.

Schindler's List. Universal City, CA: MCA Universal Home Video, 2004, 1994. ISBN 6308308552 (DVD); ISBN 0783211856 (VHS). A truly remarkable experience, this film tells the story of Oskar Schindler, a German businessman who saved more than 1,000 Jews from the Nazi concentration camps. The scenes in the ghettos and camps are frighteningly realistic.

Web Sites

Here are some further resources to explore for offering library services to Jewish youth. If you prepare a bibliography of your Judaica collection, these Web sites will be welcome additions:

Association of Jewish Libraries. Dedicated to supporting Judiaca resources throughout the United States and Canada. URL: http://www.jewishlibraries.org/ (accessed March 2004).

B'nai B'rith Youth Organization. B'nai B'rith Youth Organization is the largest, most widely known and respected youth organization for Jewish teens. URL: http://www.bbyo.org (accessed March 2004).

Jewish National and University Library. The Jewish National and University Library serves a threefold purpose: it is the National Library of the State of Israel, the National Library of the Jewish People, and the Central Library of the Hebrew University. URL: http://jnul.huji.ac.il (accessed March 2004).

Jewish Public Library, Montreal, Quebec, Canada. The collection includes magazines, rare books, archives, pre-World War resources, and the Irving Layton collection. URL: http://www.jewishpubliclibrary.org (accessed March 2004).

Jewish Teen Central. A place for Jewish teens from around the world to hang out and be themselves. URL: http://www.angelfire.com/ny/jewishtgirlcentral/ (accessed March 2004).

Jewish Teens: A Place for Jewish Teens to Talk About Anything. Requires a Yahoo! Account. URL: http://clubs.yahoo.com/clubs/jewishteens (accessed March 2004).

MALMAD – Israeli Center for Digital Information Services. The Israel Center for Digital Information Services acts as a joint framework or consortium for the acquisition, licensing and operation of information services to all the Israeli universities. URL: http://libnet1.ac.il/~libnet/malmad-israelnet.htm (accessed March 2004).

WORKS CONSULTED

Anklewicz, Larry. *Guide to Jewish Films on Video.* Hoboken, NJ: KTAV Publishing House, Inc., 2000.

Jewish Virtual Library (formerly the *Jewish Student Online Research Center*). URL: http://www.us-israel.org/jsource (accessed March 2004).

Kushner, Harold S. *To Life! A Celebration of Jewish Being and Thinking.* Boston, MA: Little, Brown, 1993.

———. *When Bad Things Happen to Good People.* New York, NY: Schoken Books, 1989.

Magida, Arthur J. and Stuart M. Matlins, eds. *How To Be a Perfect Stranger: A Guide to Etiquette in Other People's Religious Ceremonies.* Woodstock, VT: Skylight Paths Publishing, 1999.

Slater, Robert. *Great Jews in Sports.* Middle Village, NY: J. David Publishers, 2000.

Syme, Rabbi Daniel B. and Cindy Frenkle Kanter. *100 Essential Books for Jewish Readers.* Secaucus, NJ: Citadel Press Book, Carol Publishing Groups, 1998.

Wouk, Herman. *This Is My God: The Jewish Way of Life.* Boston, MA: Little, Brown, and Co., 1988.

Readers, Reviewers, and Interviewees

Bell, Charles T., MS, MS/LIS, Champaign, Illinois.

Diamond, Marvin, Librarian, Congregation Beth Israel, Portland, Oregon.

Marks, Dr. Michael, Associate Professor, Willamette University, Salem, Oregon.

Rose, Jackie, MLS, Youth Division Manager, Lake Oswego Public Library, Lake Oswego, Oregon.

8

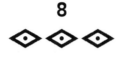

ISLAM

Linda Smith

Islam—Strictly monotheistic religion, whose adherents believe that Allah (God) is Creator of the universe and all humans are equal before Allah

Root word "slm" in Arabic means "to be in peace" or "to be an integral whole." From this root comes "islam," meaning "to surrender to God's law and thus to be an integral whole," submitting to the one God, Allah.

Beginnings:

Originated about 622 C.E. in Mecca on Arabian Peninsula (now Saudi Arabia).

Founded by Muhammad the Prophet (c. 570–632 C.E.). Muslims follow his teachings but do not worship him.

At the time that the Christian West was in its Dark Ages, Islamic countries were renowned for their traditions in art, science and philosophy.

Beliefs and practices:

The Qur'an is the sacred book of the Muslims, revealed to Muhammad by the Angel Gabriel to guide humanity.

(continued)

(continued)
Demographics:

Current number of members in the United States is estimated at six million.

Reported by many reputable organizations to be fastest-growing religion on earth.

Second largest religion in world after Christianity.

Information point:

Islamic City in CyberSpace. URL: http://www.islamicity.com/ (accessed March 2004). "Gateway to Islamic religion and culture."

Islam translates literally into "submission or surrender to the will of God" (*Allah* in Arabic), and a Muslim is one who surrenders to Allah's will. Sometimes non-Muslims think that Muslims worship a different God than Christians or Jews, but all of these religions worship the same Supreme Being.

Islam is a large, diverse faith but there is one underlying belief for all Muslims: that there is a single, all-knowing, omnipotent Being who created the universe. All Muslims are equal before Allah and share in a community based on the ideal of equality, regardless of nationality, race, or any other differences. However, Muslims and non-Muslims have a long history of misunderstanding and lack of communication between communities, worsened by recent terrorist attacks and war in the Middle East.

Muslims worldwide were appalled and repulsed by the actions of those who attacked the World Trade Center towers in New York and the Pentagon in Washington, D.C. in 2001. Nadia Sheikh, a high school junior in Lake Oswego, Oregon, described the way in which her world changed on 9/11, the resulting scrutiny her family endured as Muslims in the United States, and the subsequent loss of part of her identity. She states, "I am suffering for the horrendous acts of a few terrorists representing a minority of Muslims." Conversely, she has also seen the negative turned to positive by accepting neighbors and friends who rallied around her family, and is able to conclude, "As Americans, we need each other. Race and religion are not barriers but bridges."

The editor of this book told me of this project on September 11, 2001. In the months that I've been working on it, I find myself holding the hope that this chapter will, in some small way, lead to greater understanding and a more meaningful dialogue between people. I also hope that it will provide ideas to library selectors on ways to deepen their collections and to allow their patrons to discover the beauty and diversity of Islam.

There is no way to tell what the long-term consequences of the tragedy and the subsequent war will be. If what I have written seems dated or is missing something you find necessary, please contact me, the editor, or the publisher, and write it in the margins of your book for your fellow librarians or students to use.

A BRIEF HISTORY OF ISLAM

Around 600 C.E.,[1] the Western world was split between two super powers: the Byzantine Empire[2] and the Sasanian Empire.[3] Between these two giants lay the sparsely populated Arabian Peninsula. The majority of the Byzantine Empire was Christian and the Sasanians were mostly Zoroastrians,[4] with minority populations of Christians, Buddhists, Manichaeists,[5] and Jews. The Arabs were generally polytheists, loosely organized along tribal lines.

Between the years of 540–629 C.E., the Byzantine Empire and the Sasanians were frequently at war as they vied for control of the Near East. As a result of the spreading Byzantine influence, Christianity was the fastest growing religion of the time.

Less than two hundred years later, the Middle East was transformed beyond imagination by the influence of the prophet Muhammad.

The Change Agent

Around 570 C.E., Muhammad was born in the trading city of Mecca.[6] As a young man, he was very pious, and when he was grown he frequently retreated to a cave on Mount Hira to pray. In 610 C.E., Muhammad experienced a vision of the Angel Gabriel, who gave him a message from God. He began to share the message with his wife, extended family, friends, and eventually the citizens of Mecca. As Muhammad's message of radical monotheism began to take root, it also completely antagonized other pagan, polytheistic citizens of Mecca. In order to avoid death threats, in 622 C.E. Muhammad and his followers fled to Medina,[7] about 200 miles to the north of Mecca. The citizens of Medina had invited Muhammad and his followers to come and try to restore order to their town filled with tribal feuding. In Medina, the followers of Muhammad, or Muslims, were able to create an entirely new community for themselves with rules for both worship and protection based on the revelations given to Muhammad.

These revelations given to Muhammad were collected into the Qur'an. The messages reveal life's meaning and, as such, the Qur'an is the center of Muslim life. The reverence Muslims hold for the Qur'an shows in the care taken in the handling of the text, the effort that many take to memorize the entire Qur'an, and the beauty of the calligraphy in hand-copied versions. It is also considered to be magnificent literature.

Early Islamic History

After the *hijira* (flight from danger) to Medina, conflicts arose between members of the new community. First, the people who followed Muhammad to Medina argued with the people who lived there. Then they both fought with the tribe that controlled Mecca, until Muhammad took over that city. Muhammad was able to control these conflicts with both his secular authority as a community leader and arbiter of disputes and his religious authority based on his credentials as Prophet.

Muhammad established no priesthood or organization for the church. He made no provisions for the succession of leadership, and when he died in 632 C.E., there was considerable confusion in the community. Later that year, Abu Bakr,[8] an early follower of Muhammad's teachings, and also his father-in-law, was chosen as the successor to Muhammad.

Abu Bakr was faced with handling the community's turmoil after Muhammad's death, as well as the broader message Muhammad had begun to preach. At the end of his life, Muhammad had begun to proclaim the world-wide beauty of his message from Allah.

Early success in the spread of Islam also sowed seeds of fragmentation. Friction from the spoils of war and the tension between early converts and later converts started splintering the community shortly after Abu Bakr's death in 634 C.E. The second caliph, 'Umar, was elected in 634 C.E. and assassinated ten years later. The third caliph, 'Uthman, (caliph 644–656 C.E.) seemed at first to offer the ability to reconcile the factions since he was both an early convert and a member of the politically powerful tribe to which Muhammad originally belonged. Unfortunately, his policy of nepotism[9] led to intense opposition, and he was murdered in 656 C.E. The controversy over succession led to civil war in 661 C.E., the result of which was that Mu'awiya, a close relative of 'Uthman and leader of the Umayyad clan, claimed the caliphate.

The Fruits of War

In the early days of Islam, the followers and companions of Muhammad had elected the caliphs. With Mu'awiya's ascent to the caliphate, the nature of power in the Muslim community completely changed. First, he created a hereditary caliphate. Second, he moved the center of power away from the Arabian Peninsula to Damascus in Syria. Third, he changed the nature of government to follow centralized Byzantine or Persian models, as opposed to the tribal, consensus-based models of government previously used.

The split between the Sunni and Shi'i Muslims began with this civil war and Mu'awiya's reign. The Shi'i Muslims believed that 'Ali, caliph 656–661 C.E., was wrongfully murdered and was the rightful claimant to the caliphate. The Sunni Muslims believed that Mu'awiya was the rightful successor. As time passed, the Shi'ites fervently clung to their beliefs, claiming the descendents of 'Ali as the rightful heads of the community. This led to the suppression of the Shi'i since they did not recognize the legitimacy of the authority of the Sunni governments over them.

Long Term Consequences/Golden Age of Islam

After the end of the Umaiyad[10] dynasty founded by Mu'awiya in 750 C.E., the rapid geographic expansion that had marked the first 120 years of Islam came to an end. Instead, art, jurisprudence, literature, mathematics, medicine, science and trade flourished as Muslims focused on internal affairs. This time also saw a decline of political power, and the power of the caliphate itself declined.

Invasions

In the late 900s, the rich, cosmopolitan areas of Iran, Iraq, and the Arabian Peninsula tempted raiding nomads from Central Asia. Just as they had invaded the failing Western Roman Empire in the 600s, these Asiatic nomads now invaded Islamic lands. The invaders were Muslim Turks who fought with great vigor. The Turks, who called themselves the Seljuk,[11] conquered Asia Minor, which previously had resisted all Arab attempts. By 1100 C.E., the Seljuk controlled the caliphate and were one of the major powers in the Islamic world.

The seeds for the Crusades were planted when the Seljuk won a major victory over the Byzantines in 1071 C.E. The Byzantines appealed to the nations of Western Europe for help in their campaign, and in 1095 C.E. Pope Urban II translated a simple call for military help into a Crusade to "free" Jerusalem from Muslim control. What followed was 200 years of military struggle with eight separate invasions by European nations, ending with the Holy Land still under Muslim control.

The next great invasion began in 1220. The Mongols, under the command of Genghis Khan, started in the east and swept west in several brutal waves. By 1260, only Egypt, Arabia, and Northern Africa had escaped the Mongolian conquest. The Mongol invasion was devastating to the local cultures and economies but also energizing in the long run as "the Mongol Khans…patronized Islamic learning, the arts and sciences, as they had never been patronized before" (Robinson, p. 26).

More Peaceful Growth

As opposed to the dramatic, military spread of Islam in the central Islamic lands, Islam in the far east mostly seeped in by more peaceful means. Traders brought Islam to Indonesia from India and Arabia in the eighth century c.e. Islam reached the rest of Southeast Asia by the thirteenth century via trade routes. Sufism, Islamic mysticism,[12] helped Islam blend gradually with the already present Hindu and Buddhist populations. Java and the Philippines were converted in the fifteenth century, and Islam spread into the rest of the archipelago.

Imperialism

By the seventeenth century, Muslim power had begun to wane. At that time, the three major Muslim powers were the Shi'ite Safavid Empire in Persia, the Sunni Ottoman Empire in Asia Minor, and the Mughal[13] Empire in India. These empires declined at different rates and in different ways, but the results of the declines were the same. European and Russian armies were able to wrest territory and trading privileges from Muslims.

In the eighteenth century there was a backlash against European intrusiveness, and a reform movement swept the Muslim world. As the temporal power of the princes waned, the religious scholars (the *ulama*) and the mystics strove to improve their crumbling worlds by advocating an uncontaminated vision of Islam. In order to create this uncontaminated vision, they often encouraged a military backlash against the European presence. The Western view of Muslim *jihads*,[14] or religious crusades, comes from this period.

The Modern Age

The legacies of Western imperialism and the two World Wars, as well as the ubiquity of Western culture, are the keys to understanding the current state of Muslim/non-Muslim relations. The creation of Israel after World War II and the intrusiveness of Western culture into the Middle East and other areas of the world have helped to lay the foundation for current world events, especially those dealing with Muslims from the Central Islamic lands.

The Muslim World Today

Islam is a global religion with the majority of Muslims living in Asia. A full thirty percent live in the Indian subcontinent. The rest of the world's Muslim population is just as diverse: twenty percent in Sub-Saharan Africa, eighteen percent in the Middle East (northern Africa and southwest Asia to the Arabian Sea), seventeen percent in Southeast Asia, and ten percent in countries of the former Soviet Union and China. The remaining five percent live in Europe, North and Latin America, and Australia.

Islam is one of the fastest growing religions in the United States today, with an estimated 6,000,000 to 7,000,000 Muslims currently in the country. This fast growth is due to current immigration patterns as well as conversions. Most U.S. mosques are ethnically very diverse.

CORE BELIEFS AND VALUES

At the very heart of a Muslim is a love of Allah and the belief that God is just, merciful, beautiful, and the Creator of the universe.

In addition to love of Allah, all Muslims believe that Muhammad is the last of the prophets sent by God to help people create a just society on earth and reveal Allah's will in the Qur'an. All who revere Allah are part of this community, regardless of their ethnic origin, country of origin, or language. In the Qur'an, Allah revealed that there will be a Day of Reckoning. A human's struggle to live a moral life will be judged by God at the end of time, and he will determine rewards and punishments. This moral life includes a deep awareness of the suffering of others, caring for those weaker or less fortunate than oneself, and a passion for equality.

In order to assist the community in their quest for surrender to a moral life that embodies surrender to the will of Allah, Muhammad revealed basic principles called the Five Pillars of Islam. These principles were solidified during the life of Muhammad as the way a Muslim could live a righteous life.

Statement of Faith (Shahada)

The statement of faith is a simple, profound, and powerful message: "There is no God but God, and Muhammad is his messenger." The Shahada proclaims the message of radical monotheism, and it proclaims the personal nature of a Muslim's relationship with God, for no other being or person can mediate between God and man.

Prayer *(Salat)* Five Times a Day

Praying five times a day leads a person to discover the role of God in one's everyday life. One is supposed to pray at dawn, at midday, in the afternoon, just after sunset, and in the evening. Prayer can be done anywhere that is quiet and clean, but most people prefer to pray in a mosque (also called a *masjid*) or at home where necessary supplies, such as water for ablution, are available. Men tend to pray in a mosque when possible; otherwise they may pray wherever they are as long as it is in a clean setting. Women also pray at a mosque, or in their home or work place.

At its most basic, a mosque is a "wall so orientated that a line drawn directly from Mecca would strike it at right angles. This ensures that a Muslim knows which way he should face to pray" (Robinson, p. 184). The other essential for a mosque is a fountain or shower for washing.

Several rituals allow people to set aside their daily concerns and pray with the greatest sincerity. When a Muslim prepares to pray, she or he symbolically removes the day's concerns by removing her or his shoes. Then one should wash the face, hands and feet with water (termed "ablution"), or dust if no water is available, to express the desire for purity. The ablution is not just about physical cleanliness—it is a time to remove worldly concerns and serves as a time of transition from the inner to outer world. If water is in short supply, dust can be used for the brief ablution to indicate the transition since this bathing is both a symbolic and literal expression of purity. After cleansing, Muslims face Mecca and perform the cycle of prayers, called a *rakat*, which includes body movements and postures as well as words.

Since Islam is a religion that encourages a personal relationship with God, a priest does not lead prayers, but instead they are led by a *muezzin*, a person learned in the Qur'an. The call to prayer is always in Arabic: "God is most great" is repeated four times; "I bear witness that there is no God but God" is repeated twice; "I bear witness that Muhammad is God's messenger" is repeated twice; "Come to prayer" is repeated twice; "Come to success" is repeated twice; "God is most great" is repeated twice; and finally, "There is no god but God!" (Robinson, p. 182).

The Friday midday prayer is obligatory, and at that time there is also a sermon by a leading Muslim of the area.

Alms *(Zakah)*

It is a Muslim's responsibility to care for those who are in need. Since all things belong to God, the giving of alms reminds people that they are the custodians of God's bounty. Each Muslim determines the level of his or her giving individually, but many people hold to the custom of two and a half percent of one's capital over one's basic needs. Giving should be done privately and not ostentatiously.

Fasting *(Siyam)*

Ramadan is the ninth month of the year in the Muslim calendar and also refers to a fast, held from sunrise to sunset, carried out during this period. The fast includes refraining from eating, drinking, sex, and smoking during the daylight hours of the month. All Muslims who have reached puberty are required to observe this religious obligation. Since the Islamic calendar is lunar, the month can fall during different parts of the year. The purpose of this fast is to create compassion for those who hunger, thirst, and suffer. Good deeds and works of charity are encouraged during Ramadan.

Pilgrimage *(Hajj)*

Hajj is an obligation for those who are physically and financially able to journey to Mecca in Saudi Arabia during the twelfth month of the Islamic year. Hajj celebrates actions in the lives of Abraham, Hagar (his wife), and Ishmael (his son). During hajj, a pilgrim wears a plain garment called the *ihram.* It is made of two white sheets and represents the pilgrim's renunciation of secular life and the equality of mankind.

Hajj begins with the pilgrim walking seven times around the Kaaba.[15] He or she then runs between Mecca and Marwa seven times in remembrance of Hagar's desperate search for water for Ishmael. The pilgrim drinks from the Zamzam well where Hagar found an outflow of water at Ishmael's feet. At sunrise the following day, the pilgrim journeys toward the plain of Arafat to stand before God and worship him. He or she moves on to Mina on the next day, and symbolically throws stones at three pillars in memory of Satan's tempting of Abraham, Hagar, and Ishmael to disobey God. The pilgrim sacrifices an animal[16] to commemorate the willingness of Abraham to submit to God's will. He then shaves his head and removes the ihram. Seven more circuits of the Kaaba are completed and the pilgrim then returns to normal life.

Women as well as men go on hajj. They do not need to wear the ihram, and they do not need to wear a veil, even if they normally do so. Instead of shaving their heads, women generally cut at least a bit from their hair to show humility.

The most famous hajj in Western history is the pilgrimage of Malcolm X. Discouraged and angry from his break with the Nation of Islam (a black separatist religious movement that adopted some of the principles of Islam), he proclaimed his belief in the principles of Islam, and sought to fulfill his religious duty of the hajj to take time away from the United States. During his hajj, he experienced the unity, brotherhood, and lack of racism that Islam at its best can provide. This is one of the purposes of the hajj—it creates a chance for people to meet one another in a holy place where violence is forbidden and all distinctions of class, race, and culture are removed.

The Western media focuses on the central Islamic lands and, in their need to transmit information quickly, often fail to give a deeper understanding of the amazing diversity of the Islamic world.

There are many divisions in Islam, just as there are in Christianity or Judaism. The majority of Muslims are Sunni, with the largest minority population being Shi'ite. Smaller but influential sects include the Sufis (Islamic mysticism) and the Wahhabis (who believe that all ideas added after the third century of Islam are untrue and should be abolished). Islam is a world-wide religion, and regional differences have an impact on how Islam is practiced in different parts of the world. For example, not all Muslim women wear veils or face coverings as is commonly thought in the West. Also, some sects prohibit dancing and music, some encourage them.

For more information on the various Islamic sects and offshoots, see http://www.rickross.com/reference/islamic/islamic27.html   (accessed August 2003).

Dietary Restrictions

Muslims follow dietary restrictions, such as avoiding pork or pork products and eating only *halal* meat—meat that comes from animals that have been ritually slaughtered according to Islamic Law. Muslims do not consume alcohol and only eat fish that have scales or fins, thus avoiding shellfish.[17]

The following products are definitely halal: milk (from cows, sheep, camels, and goats), honey, fish, plants that are not intoxicants, fresh or naturally frozen vegetables, fresh or dried fruit, legumes and nuts (peanuts, cashews, hazelnuts, walnuts, etc.), grains (wheat, rice, rye, barley, and oats), and meat from cows, sheep, goats, deer, moose, ducks, game birds, etc. that are slaughtered according to Islamic rites.[18]

WHAT ARE MUSLIM TEENS LOOKING FOR AT THE LIBRARY?

The revelations in the Qur'an are at the heart of Muslim identity, and Quranic study is a basis for daily conduct. To serve the needs of young Muslim patrons, librarians need to understand and respect this.

The Qur'an is written in Arabic. For a translation to be considered a proper Qur'an, the verse should have the original Arabic on one side and the translation next to it or facing it. There are several excellent translations available both in print and on CD-ROM (see bibliography). In addition to the Qur'an, a library would do well to have a collection of the sayings and teachings of the Prophet Muhammad (the Hadith).[19] There is a variety of materials available on the Hadith in all price ranges.

Muslims from all over the world discuss religious life in Arabic. Depending on your patron base, try to find materials for learning to read and speak Arabic. You may also need materials in Farsi, Turkish, Malaysian, and the languages of Indonesia.

A young person's information needs are based on many things, not only his or her religious affiliation. In order to fulfill a library's goal of inclusiveness, here are some other considerations for collection goals.

Young people need help with their schoolwork. School and public libraries fill this need for other students and are already sensitive to the information needs of a diverse population. The suggestions in the collection development section of this chapter would be a good place to start. If there is an Islamic school in the area (check yellow pages for "Mosques" or "Schools—Religious Education"), you may have already seen the kinds of projects that teachers assign to their students. A library should have a healthy representation of the arts and sciences from the Islamic world. Biographies of Muslim artists, scientists, general art surveys, and the history of science are helpful for Muslims to learn about their past, and these also create resources and information for the non-Muslim portions of the library's patron base.

Teens need information as well as reading for pleasure. Music, fiction, and art help young people make sense of their lives and fuel creative fires. Dive into the literature of the many parts of the world from which Muslims come. These materials validate different experiences and allow youth to explore the world.

Young people need a safe place to do their work and socialize. If a young person wears traditional clothing or is interested in many different topics, then she or he needs a librarian who is accepting of these differences. Like any other minority, young Muslims may be harassed due to their appearance and clothing; inappropriate or malicious behavior should never be tolerated in the public library.

FORMATIVE EXPERIENCES

By the time a Muslim is a young adult, he or she has gone through a number of formative experiences.

There are two major ceremonies in childhood. Around the age of four, both boys and girls are taught the first revelation from the Qur'an (*Sura* 96:1–5) and the *basmala* ("In the name of God most merciful, most beneficent").

"The second ceremony is circumcision, which is generally performed on boys between seven and twelve, although it is permitted to circumcise a child seven days after birth" (Robinson, p. 188). Female circumcision, although practiced by some Muslims, is a highly controversial subject and is not supported by the majority of Muslims.

"[P]ractices such as clitoridectomy and/or removal of the labia…are a grave violence against the person and are strictly forbidden in Islam. Such practices…have absolutely no religious basis, and like all mutilations, are not sanctioned by Islamic law and are legally prohibited in the United States" (Glasse, p. 103).

Two other formative experiences happen during puberty. First, both genders have to decide on their views on modest dress. Men are not supposed to wear silk or gold jewelry. Women's modest dress is observed in a variety of fashions ranging from less revealing Western styles to the enveloping *burka*. Also during puberty, young Muslims begin observing Ramadan.

Finally, by the time they are teens, Muslims will probably have experienced the enormously formative experience of discrimination.

STEREOTYPES AND MISCONCEPTIONS

Sometimes people will call Islam Mohammadism and Muslims Mohammadians. This is a common fallacy that compares Muhammad to Christ. According to Christian thought, Christ was God made flesh. Muhammad was and always has been considered human and fallible. Calling Islam Mohammadism is erroneous and can be considered quite insulting.

Another commonly held belief about Muslims is that they wish to take over the world by military force or terrorist activities. This false belief was heightened after the 9/11 attacks when many Americans assumed that the terrorists were acting on behalf of Islam. This reflects a common fallacy about Islam that Muslims think it is acceptable to kill in the name of God. This kind of belief is denounced by all leading Islamic religious thinkers and is abhorrent to Muslims. The origins of this fallacy are beyond the scope of this chapter, so we merely state that anyone who would commit such an act should not be considered a Muslim.

Some Americans confuse the Black Muslim movement with Islam. In fact, the Nation of Islam was a black separatist religious movement that adopted some of the principles and practices of Islam but had no formal affiliation with the rest of the Muslim community.

One of the dangers of collection development for Muslim youth involves biases in the available resources. The image of Islam as a religion locked in rigid orthodoxy remains alive to this day. The "us against them" attitude can creep into materials written by both Muslims and non-Muslims.

BUILDING YOUR COLLECTION

The first line of defense against further misinformation is a sense of self-awareness. What kinds of authors do you prefer? What formats of materials? Next, consider the knowledge of your patron base and your collection. Do you have mostly non-Muslims who need factual information about Islam, the central Islamic lands, or the Far East? Do you serve a mostly Muslim population or perhaps a minority of Muslims who need special resources?

In evaluating and selecting materials, consider these points:

- Does the author or the reviewer have a pro or anti-Islam agenda? Are they being honest about their biases? What are the credentials of the author or reviewer? Who is the intended audience?

- When was the work created? Do current events play a major part in the review's tone? After the events of September 11, 2001, many books about the Taliban, Osama bin Laden, and terrorism were published. Some were excellent and some were blatantly racist. Will this source be dated in less than a year or two? Was it created as propaganda?

- Where in the world does the author live? Regional differences may account for discrepancies between two items on the same subject. For example, European history commonly considers the Battle of Tours and Poitiers in 732 a major turning point in Western history. The Franks, under the command of Charles Martel, defeated an Islamic army that had been unstoppable in their spread across North Africa, Spain, and Asia Minor. Arab historians looked at the battle very differently. "The Arab historians of the Middle Ages mentioned neither the names of Tours or Poitiers, and know nothing of Charles Martel. The battle is mentioned under the name of Balat al-Shuhada, the Highway of Martyrs, and is presented as a comparatively minor engagement" (Lewis, p. 19). The Arabs knew that France was the limit of their expansion, and the troops that Martel encountered were merely a band of raiders, operating beyond the very edges of the frontiers. Different regions, therefore different priorities and viewpoints. The Arab historians spent their considerable intellectual energy considering the concurrent battles for Constantinople, which were far more influential on the course of Western history than most Western history books analyze.

- How was information for the book collected? Did the author interview eyewitnesses? Do their accounts contain unsubstantiated information or rumor?[20] If the book contains sensationalistic stories and no documentation for them, it might be best to pass.

LIBRARY SERVICES

Programming for Muslim youth can add a layer of complexity to your current programs. If you are already attempting to find inclusive activities that young people will enjoy, however, chances are your programs will also appeal to a Muslim audience.

Try to allow for separate gender spaces. This might mean separating the chairs in a room into two sides so that men and women may sit separately if they wish. If you are serving a religiously mixed community, be sure to ask your local mosque how they prefer to socialize in these situations.

Male library staff should be aware that some Muslim women will not shake hands with men who are not related to them. Wait for the woman to extend her hand before extending your own. Likewise, some Muslim men will not shake hands with unrelated women.

When refreshments are served at an event, avoid serving items containing pork products (marshmallows included) or shellfish, and check that there is no alcohol in any of the foods.

Book groups, poetry groups, reading programs, and storytelling are very popular activities among many Muslims and can be enriching to the rest of the library users since Islamic literature is very beautiful. Consider advertising your reading program at your local mosque if you are not currently reaching young Muslims.

Muslim youth are expected to be respectful and modest and to adhere to the principles and practices of their religion. As the library's relationship with the local Muslim community grows, you will be able to gauge what the standards are for your area and how the library can be welcoming to Muslims. For example, in serving a more conservative population, consider screening library displays for overly immodest images or messages, as well as being alert to the previously mentioned dietary restrictions. The best way to find out what is acceptable is to ask when in doubt.

Displays of the Islamic arts and sciences from around the world including rugs, architecture, calligraphy, painting, medicine, astronomy, and literature are interesting, educational, and enlightening. Such displays are especially nice during Ramadan, the month of fasting. Again, since the Muslim calendar is lunar, you will need to check the dates. Books and CD-ROMs of Islamic clip art are very useful during this time. Resources on learning Islamic calligraphy also encourage cultural sharing.

A bibliography of materials your library owns on Islam is an enormously useful tool to facilitate library service for all patrons. This can be placed in a binder or reproduced as a handout for patrons.

If your library offers musical programming as part of its entertainment schedule, consider including world music and dance, which have become popular and more accessible. Ethnic groceries and restaurants, as well as the area mosque, may provide help in locating performers.

Henna is a plant-based dye used around the world to create beautiful body art. It is often associated with weddings and other festive occasions. A henna party pack can be purchased for library programs, and you may allow the youth to try it independently or hire an experienced artist.

Greeting cards that depict various images of Islamic art and architecture are available from Astrolabe. They can be used for displays or for a program on world art.

Publishers and Distributors

Amana Publications
10710 Tucker Street
Beltsville, MD 20705–2223
(301) 595–5777; orders only (800) 660–1777; fax (301) 595–5888
URL: http://www.amana-publications.com/ (accessed March 2004)
E-mail: amana@igprinting.com

Astrolabe Pictures, Inc.
201 Davis Dr., Suite I
Sterling, VA 20164
(703) 404–6800; orders (800) 392–7876; fax (703) 404–6801
URL: http:// www.astrolabepictures.com; or http://www.islam icmedia.com (accessed March 2004)
E-mail: info@astrolabepictures.com
Books, gifts, software, toys, videos. Has a young adult/teen section.

The Council on Islamic Education
P.O. Box 20186

Fountain Valley, CA 92728
URL: http://www.cie.org (accessed March 2004)
Curriculum guides and teachers' notes.

The Institute of Islamic Information and Education
P.O. Box 41129
Chicago IL 60614–0129
(773) 777–7443; fax (773) 777–7199
Tri-folds and other useful brief handouts.

Islamic Circle of North America
166–26 89th Avenue
Jamaica, NY 11432
(718) 658–1199; fax (718) 658–1255
Educational tri-folds on different subjects.

Islamic Society of North America
P.O. Box 38
Plainfield, IN 46168
(317) 839–8157; fax (317) 839–1840
URL for young adult materials: http://www.isna.com/books-
  teen-and-young-adult.html (accessed March 2004)

Sound Vision
1327 W. Washington Blvd., Suite 105
Chicago, IL 60607
URL: http://www.soundvision.com (accessed March 2004)
Audio, books, gifts, software, syllabi, and videos.

The University of Texas' Center for Middle Eastern Studies
URL: http://menic.utexas.edu/menic/k.html (accessed January
  2003)
Has a useful section with lists of resources for grades K-12.

SELECTED TITLES

A list of suggested resources follows. All can be found at Astrolabe,
  Baker & Taylor, or Sound Vision.

Video Resources, Core Collection

Building Bridges video pack. TV Islam Production, 2002. Sound Vision, SKU 110–306.
  Discussion on how Muslims can bridge the gap with other communities.

The Crusades by Terry Jones and the History Channel. A&E Entertainment, 1995. ASIN 6303454550. Excellent four-part documentary on the causes and events of the Crusades.

The Hajj by ABC Nightline, 1997. ISBN 1562789996. Muslim Michael Wolfe documents his second Hajj trip and explains the origins and meanings of the various rituals.

The Hajj: CNN. Sound Vision, 1998. SKU 147–012. Coverage and practical guides.

Hakeem Olajuwon. Sound Vision, 1999. ISBN 6305338043. Biography of the famous Muslim basketball player.

Hijab: An Act of Faith. Sound Vision, 1998. SKU 110–123. Documentary about the injunction to dress modestly.

Islam: A Closer Look. Tapeworm Video, 1998. ISBN 6304872941. A short documentary on common misperceptions of Islam.

The Message: The Story of Islam. Directed by Moustapha Akkad, 1976. ISBN 0764002929. Available through Astrolabe. Action epic starring Anthony Quinn. One of the few films about Islam and Muhammad from an Islamic viewpoint.

Wonders of Islamic Science. Sound Vision, 1989. SKU 110–066. Highlights the achievements of Muslims in the fields of astronomy, botany, geography, mathematics, medicine, and zoology.

Video Resources, Deeper Collection

Adam's World. Islamic Circle of North America. A multi-volume series produced between 1990 and 2000. Often called the Muslim "Sesame Street." Ages two through thirteen.

Deeper Roots: Muslims in America Before Columbus. Islamic Sound and Vision, 1999. SKU 110–151. Video and book combination.

Islam: Empire of Faith. PBS, 2001. ISBN 0780635353. PBS documentary.

Lion of the Desert. Directed by Moustapha Akkad, 1980. ISBN 6305020078. Story of Libyan Omar Al Mukhtar, who fought the Italian occupation of Libya early in the twentieth century. One of the few films about the resistance to colonialism.

Sources of Music for Entertainment

Amazon.com at http://www.amazon.com (accessed March 2004) has a world music section that includes reviews. Music of the Far East, India, Indonesia, and the Middle East is available.

Araby Music at http://www.arabymusic.com (accessed March 2004) has traditional Arabic, Egyptian and Lebanese music, as well as Arabic pop, Rai (a style of Algerian music), belly dance, Gulf States music, and religious music.

Aramusic at http://www.aramusic.com (accessed March 2004) specializes in pop music.

eWorld Records at http://www.store.yahoo.com/eworldrecords/index.html (accessed March 2004) has Arabic, Armenian, Greek, and Persian music.

Music for Learning and Inspiration

Ali, Dawud Wharnsby. *The Colors of Islam.* Sound Vision, 2000. SKU 710–003. Wharnsby Ali is a Canadian Muslim artist and educator.

———. *Sunshine, Dust, and the Messenger.* Sound Vision, 2000. SKU 213–007.

———. *A Whisper of Peace.* Sound Vision, 1999. SKU 213–300.

Islam, Yusuf (formerly Cat Stevens). *A Is for Allah* (and other titles). Resurgence, 2000. ISBN 6305969825. A collection of songs that reflect the basics of Islam.

Young Adult Novels

Banks, Lynne Reid. *Broken Bridge.* Flare Publishers, 1996. ISBN 0380723840. Nili, Lesley's daughter, witnesses an attack that leaves her Canadian cousin murdered in the streets of Jerusalem. She is torn between her loyalty to a Jewish Israeli and her desire to protect the identity of the Palestinian suspect who was instrumental in saving her life. Sequel to *One More River.* These two books by Banks have Jewish main characters but are included because they deal with Muslim/Jewish, Arab/Israeli interfaith relations.

———. *One More River.* Avon, 1993. ISBN 0785706267. Set in 1967, the story of Lesley, a Canadian Jewish girl, whose family decides to leave their secure life and move to a kibbutz in Israel.

Ellis, Karen. *The Breadwinner.* Groundwood Books, 2001. ISBN 0888994168. Because the Taliban rulers of Kabul, Afghanistan, impose strict limitations on women's freedom and behavior, eleven-year-old Parvana must disguise herself as a boy so her family can survive after her father's arrest.

Emerick, Yahiya J. *Ahmad Deen and the Jinn at Shaolin.* Ahmira Publishing, 1998. ISBN 188972002X. One title in a series of action novels aimed at Muslim youth.

———. *Isabella: A Girl of Muslim Spain.* Ahmira Publishing, 1998. ISBN 1889720070. A retelling of the classic tale of a young girl who finds Islam amidst the religious conflicts of medieval Muslim Spain.

Fletcher, Susan. *Shadow Spinner.* Alladin Library, 1999. ISBN 0689830513. The story of a young girl sent by Scherazade to seek out stories.

Hicyilmaz, Gaye. *Against the Storm.* Yearling, 1993. ISBN 044040892X. The story of twelve-year-old Mehmet whose family moves to Ankara, Turkey, where the pressures of urban poverty and life in a shantytown take their toll.

———. *The Frozen Waterfall.* Farrar Straus & Giroux, 1994. ISBN 0374324824. Twelve-year-old Selda moves from Turkey to Switzerland where she must cope with a new language and culture.

Hutchinson, Haji Uthman. *Invincible Abdullah.* American Trust Publications, 1992. ISBN 0892591218. A series of travel and adventure novels aimed at young Muslims. Four titles include *The Deadly Mountain Revenge, The Car Theft Kidnapping, The Mystery of the Missing Pearls,* and *The Wilderness Survival.*

Laird, Elizabeth. *Kiss the Dust.* Puffin, 1994. ISBN 0140368558. Tara is a Kurd, and when it becomes apparent that her father supports the Kurdish guerillas, the family must flee from Iraq to the United Kingdom.

Napoli, Donna Jo. *Beast*. Atheneum, 2000. ISBN 0689835892. Orasmyn, a Persian prince, makes a terrible mistake that sets free an old curse and causes him to be turned into a lion. He must leave his kingdom before his transformation is discovered and seek redemption in the outside world. A powerful retelling of "Beauty and the Beast" from the Beast's point of view.

Nye, Naomi Shihab. *Habibi*. Pocket Books, 1999. ISBN 0689801491. Liyana, a fourteen-year-old Arab-American girl living in St. Louis, is distressed when her father decides to uproot his American family and return to his home in Jerusalem. All other titles by Nye are also highly recommended, including her poetry.

Temple, Frances. *Beduins' Gazelle*. Orchard Book, 1996. ISBN 0064406695. In 1302, two cousins of the nomadic Beni Khalid tribe who are betrothed become separated by political intrigue between warring tribes.

Nonfiction, Core Collection

Al-Qardawi, Yusuf. *The Lawful and the Prohibited in Islam*. Islamic Book Service, 1999. ISBN 0892590165. Religious life and practices in Islam.

Anway, Carol L. *Daughters of Another Path*. Yawna, 1995. ISBN 0964716909. Written by a non-Muslim mother whose daughter accepted Islam, this book shatters stereotypes and shares testimonials from several American Muslim women.

Austin, Allan D. *African Muslims in Antebellum America*. Routledge, 1997. ISBN 0415912709. Biographies of Muslim slaves.

Badawi, Jamal. *Gender Equity in Islam*. Islamic Book Service, 1995. ISBN 0892591595. Presents an effective overview of the status and rights of Muslim women as defined by the Qur'an and *Sunna*.

Brend, Barbara. *Islamic Art*. Harvard University Press, 1992. ISBN 067446866X. Traces the development of classic Islamic art.

Emerick, Yahiya. *Holy Koran for School Children*. IBTS, 1998. ISBN 1889720224. Recommended for grades five through ten.

Esposito, John. *The Islamic Threat: Myth or Reality*. Oxford University Press, 1999. ISBN 0195130766. Looks at conflict and terrorism in the Islamic nations and analyzes the impact on relations with the West.

———. *Oxford History of Islam*. Oxford University Press, 2000. ISBN 0195107993. Discusses the origins, historical development, and culture of Islam.

Faruqi, Isma'il and Lois Lamya al Faruqi. *Cultural Atlas of Islam*. Prentice Hall, 1986. ISBN 0029101905. This book provides a beautiful and picturesque overview of Islam, covering beliefs and traditions. Older title with useful background information.

Haddad, Yvonne and John Esposito. *Muslims on the Americanization Path?* Oxford University Press, 2000. ISBN 0195135261. Cultural influences on Muslims in the United States.

Hajjaj, Abd-Allah. *The Isra and Mi Raj: The Prophet's Night-journey and Ascent into Heaven*. Dar Al-Taqwa, 1989. ISBN 1870582063. Summarizes the miraculous journey of Muhammad from Mecca to Jerusalem to the heavens.

Kahf, Mohja. *Western Representations of the Muslim Woman: From Termagant to Odalisque*. University of Texas, 1999. ISBN 0292799640.

Maalouf, Amin. *Crusades through Arab Eyes.* Schocken, 1989. ISBN 0805208984. Valuable viewpoint for a diverse collection despite the date of publication.

MacDonald, Fiona. *A 16th Century Mosque.* Peter Bedrick Books, 1994. ISBN 087226310X. Introduces the Islamic faith, explains why and how mosques were constructed, and looks at the people who worked and worshiped at the mosque.

Maqsood, Ruqaiyyah Waris. *After Death, Life!: Thoughts to Alleviate the Grief of All Muslims Facing Death and Bereavement.* Goodword Books, 1998. ISBN 8185063346. This book offers practical advice on Islamic attitudes toward death and the correct procedures of burial.

Maqsood, Ruqaiyyah Waris. *Muslim Marriage Guide.* Amana, 2000. ISBN 091595799X.

Mernissi, Fatima. *Women and Islam.* Cambridge University Press, 1991. ISBN 0631169040. All titles by Mernissi are highly recommended for a core collection. Additional titles are mentioned in the "Works Consulted" section.

Nasr, Seyyed H. *Young Muslims Guide to the Modern World.* Library of Islam, Ltd., 1994. ISBN 1567444768. For Muslims growing up in the West, this book offers pertinent, succinct information that is required to be able to discuss issues on an intellectual level. Slightly dated but still appropriate.

Numanchi, Ali K. and Seyyed H. Nasr. *Mecca the Blessed, Medina the Radiant.* Aperture, 1997. ISBN 089381752X. Photographs show the cities of Mecca and Medina during the holy month of Ramadan.

Nyang, Sulayman S. *Islam in the USA.* ABC International Group, Inc., 1999. ISBN 1871031699.

Wadud, Amina. Oxford University Press, 1999. *Qur'an and Woman: Rereading the Sacred Texts from a Woman's Perspective.* Oxford University Press, 1999. ISBN 0195128362.

Yeomans, Richard. *Story of Islamic Architecture.* New York University Press, 2000. ISBN 081479694X.

Nonfiction, Deeper Collection

Ajram, K. *Miracle of Islamic Science.* Dimensions, 1993. ISBN 0911119434. Recommended for grades six through twelve.

Badri, Malik. *Contemplation: An Islamic Psychospiritual Study.* International Institute of Islamic Thought, 2000. ISBN 1585642678. Describes and compares Islamic contemplation to other meditations.

Diouf, Sylviane A. *Servants of Allah: African Muslims Enslaved in the Americas.* New York University Press, 1998. ISBN 0814719058.

Emerick, Yahya. *What Islam is All About.* International Books & Tapes Supply, 1997. ISBN 1889720143. Recommended for grade seven through adult. Designed to meet the major needs of a basic Islamic education. Prolific author.

Hamid, Abdul Wahid. *Companions of the Prophet.* Mels, 1998. ISBN 0948196130 (v. 1, pbk.); ISBN 0948196122 (v. 2, pbk.). The lives of sixty companions of the Prophet.

Hamid, Azieza. *Fatima, Daughter of Mohammad.* Mels, 1997. ISBN 0948196084.

Hussaini, M. M. *Elementary Book of Halal and Haram.* Iqra' International Educational Foundation, 1997. ISBN 0911119124. Juvenile title about dietary restrictions.

Khalid, Khalid Muhammad. *Men Around the Messenger.* Al Manara, date unavailable. No ISBN available. Obtain through Astrolabe.

Maqsood, Ruqaiyyah. *What Every Christian Should Know about Islam.* Islamic Foundation, 2000. ISBN 0860373754. Discusses political, religious, and social issues using a question and answer format.

Nicolle, David. *Men at Arms* series, especially *Armies of Islam, 7–11th Centuries,* ISBN 0850454484; *The Mamluks, 1250–1715,* ISBN 1855323141; and *Armies of Muslim Conquest,* ISBN 185532279X. Osprey Books, various dates.

Outb, Sayyid. *Islam and Universal Peace.* American Trust Publications, 1993. ISBN 0892591366. Explains the Islamic concept of peace within oneself, at home, and in the universe, and presents Islam's prescription for attaining it.

Rahman, H. U. *The Chronology of Islamic History.* Mansell Publishers, 1988. ISBN 0720119820. Good basic chronology.

Rahman, Syed Azizur. *The Story of Islamic Spain.* Goodword Books, 2001. ISBN 8187570571.

Razwy, Sayed A. A. (translated by Yasien Muhammad.) *Salman El-Farsi = Salman the Persian: A Short Story of His Life.* Tahrike Tarsile Qur'an, 1988. ISBN 0940368838. Life of one of the companions of Muhammad.

Siddiqui, M. Ahmadullah. *Islam, Muslims, & Media: Myths and Reality.* NAAMPS Publications, 1997. ISBN 0964162415.

Thompson, Ahmed. *Asma Bint Abi Bakr.* Ta-Ha Publishers, no date available. ISBN 189794005X. Life of the daughter of Abu Bakr.

Software

Hadith CD ROM Al Bayan. HARF Information Technology, 2000. A Hadith program available in multiple languages.

Islamica Clipart 1. Sound Vision, no date available. SKU 312-075. Over 150 Islamic clipart images, including Arabic letters and numbers.

Islamica Photo CD-ROM. Sound Vision, no date available. ISBN 1590111001. Beautiful, professional photographs from around the world.

Hajj and Umra. Sound Vision, no date available. SKU 376–007. Software to explain the Hajj.

The Qur'an is available on CD-ROM through Astrolabe and Sound Vision in a range of prices.

Adult Titles for Teens and Parents, Core Collection

al Ghazzali, Mohammad. *Thematic Commentary on the Koran.* International Institute of Islamic Thought, 2000. ISBN 1565642600. Interpretation and commentary on each *sura* (chapter).

Armstrong, Karen. *Islam: A Short History.* Modern Library, 2002. ISBN 081296618X. A well-written overview of the religion, including its attitude toward politics.

Beshir, Ekram, M.D., and Mohamed Red Beshir. *Parenting in the West: An Islamic Perspective.* Amana, 1999. ISBN 0915957876. Raising Muslim children in the United States and Europe.

Council for Islamic Education. *Teaching about Islam and Muslims in the Public School Classroom.* Council on Islamic Education, 1995. ISBN 1930109008. Recommended for grades kindergarten through twelve.

Ingram, Brian and Virginia Morris. *Guide to Understanding Islamic Investing.* Lightbulb Press, 2001. ISBN 0965093212. This guide examines which investments are permitted or are forbidden. Adult title useful for teens as well.

Khaldun, Ibn. *Muqaddimah.* Kazi, 1996. ISBN 061421162X. Ibn Khaldun's *Introduction to History* includes his theories on history, sociology, and political science. A classic in the field.

Maqsood, Ruqaiyyah. *Living with Teenagers: A Guide for Muslim Parents.* Ta-Ha Publishers, 1995. ISBN 1897940289. Addresses the issues faced by Muslim families in the West, including depression, drugs, friends, modesty, and more. By the author of *The Muslim Marriage Guide.*

Thousand and One Nights. Viking Press, 1995. ISBN 0140442898. Classic literature.

Von Denfer, Ahmed. *Ulum al-Koran: An Introduction to the Sciences of the Koran.* Kazi, 1998. ISBN 0860372480. The Ulum al Quran are the disciplines of knowledge needed to understand the Qur'an.

Adult Titles for Teens and Parents, Deeper Collection

Al 'Ati, Hammudah 'Abd. *Islam in Focus.* Amana, 1997. ISBN 0915957744. Teaches the belief or act of worship from an explanation of the articles of faith to a detailed guide through prayer and the other pillars of Islam. Also includes "Distortions about Islam."

Al-Kaysi, Marwan Ibrahim. *Morals and Manners in Islam.* Islamic Foundation, 1986. ISBN 0860371689. Lists the various rules for proper Islamic conduct. Still in use despite its publication date.

Al Qaradawi, Yusuf. *Fiqh az-Zakat: A Comparative Study.* International Institute on Islamic Thought, 1999. ISBN 1565642716. Book on the *Zakat* (almsgiving).

Dirks, Jerald F. *Cross and the Crescent.* Amana, 2001. ISBN 1590080025. Written by a former ordained minister, this book reaches out for interfaith dialogues between Islam and Christianity.

Eaton, Charles Le Gai. *Islam and the Destiny of Man.* State University of New York, 1995. ISBN 088706163X. Explores what it means to be Muslim today.

Findley, Paul. *Silent No More: Confronting America's False Images of Islam.* Amana, 2001. ISBN 1590080017. A former congressman discusses the false stereotypes of Islam that linger among non-Muslims.

Gibb, A. R. *Travels of Ibn Battuta.* South Asia Books, 1993. ISBN 8173043728.

Hofmann, Dr. Murad. *Islam the Alternative.* Amana, 2000. ISBN 091595771X. Introduces Islam for "westerners who seek to understand Islam on a personal level."

———. *Religion on the Rise: Islam in the Third Millennium.* Amana, 2001. ISBN 1590080033. Topics discussed include Jesus in the modern world, democracy versus *shura*, and the rights of women.

Islam, Yusuf (formerly known as Cat Stevens). *Life of the Last Prophet.* Mountain of Light, 1996. ISBN 1900675005. Book and compact disc.

Khan, Muhammad Muhsin. *Sahih al-Bukari*. Kazi, 1993. ISBN 1567444962. The complete Hadith.

Maqsood, Ruqaiyyah Waris. *A Muslim Study of the Origins and Doctrines of the Christian Church*. Oxford University Press, 2002. ISBN 0195797175.

Said, Edward W. *Covering Islam: How the Media and the Experts Determine How We See the Rest of the World*. Vintage Books, 1999. ISBN 0679758909.

Zahra, Muhammad. *The Four Imams: Their Lives, Works and Schools of Thought*. Dar Al-Taqwa, 2001. ISBN 1870582411.

WORKS CONSULTED

Abushakrah, Jan. *Islam in the United States*. Portland, OR: Muslim Educational Trust, 2001.

Anway, Carol L. *Daughters of Another Path: Experiences of American Women Choosing Islam*. Lee's Summit, MO: Yawna Publications, 1995.

Armstrong, Karen. *Islam: A Short History*. New York, NY: Modern Library, 2002.

Eggenberger, David. *An Encyclopedia of Battles: Accounts of Over 1,560 Battles from 1479 BC to the Present*. New York, NY: Dover Publications, Inc., 1985.

Esposito, John L. *Islam: The Straight Path*. New York, NY: Oxford University Press, 1998.

Glasse, Cyril. *The New Encyclopedia of Islam*. Walnut Creek, CA: AltaMira Press, 2001.

Hodgson, Marshall G.S., ed. *The Venture of Islam: Conscience and History in a World Civilization. Vol. I, The Classical Age of Islam*. Chicago, IL: The University of Chicago Press, 1974.

Hourani, Albert. *The History of the Arab Peoples*. Cambridge, MA: Belknap Press of Harvard University Press, 1991.

Lewis, Bernard. *Islam in History: Ideas, People, and Events in the Middle East*. Chicago and LaSalle, IL: Open Court Press, 1993.

———. *The Muslim Discovery of Europe*. New York, NY: W.W. Norton & Company, 1982.

Lewis, Bernard. *The Political Language of Islam*. Chicago, IL: The University of Chicago, 1988.

Melville, Charles, ed. *Safavid Persia: The History and Politics of an Islamic Society*. London: I.B. Tauris & Co., Ltd., 1996.

Mernissi, Fatima. *The Forgotten Queens of Islam*. Translated by Mary Jo Lakeland. Minneapolis, MN: University of Minnesota Press, 1993.

———. *Scheherazade Goes West: Different Cultures, Different Harems*. New York, NY: Washington Square Press, 2001.

———. *The Veil and the Male Elite: A Feminist Interpretation of Women's Rights in Islam*. Cambridge, MA: Perseus Books, 1991.

Mirpuri, Gouri and Robert Looper. *Indonesia* (*Cultures of the World* series). New York, NY: Benchmark Books, 2002.

Olesky, Walter. *The Philippines* (*Enchantment of the World* series). New York, NY: Children's Press, 2000.

Robinson, Frances. *Atlas of the Islamic World since 1500*. New York, NY: Facts on File, 1982.

Rodinson, Maxime. *Europe and the Mystique of Islam.* Seattle, WA: University of Washington Press, 1987.

Sheikh, Nadia. "Commentary: In My Opinion: 'Suffering for the horrendous acts of a few.'" *The Oregonian* (August 8, 2003), sec. E, pg. 7.

Skube, Michael. "Either You are a Believer or an Infidel." *The Washington Post* (October 24, 2001).

Smart, Ninian. *The World's Religions,* 2nd ed. London: Cambridge University Press, 1998.

Smith, Huston. *The Illustrated World's Religions: A Guide to Our Wisdom Traditions.* San Francisco, CA: Harper, 1994.

Wormser, Richard. *American Islam: Growing Up Muslim in America.* New York, NY: Walker & Co., 1994.

Interviews

MacDonald, Dr. David. Illinois State University. E-mail correspondence, 2001.

Said, Wajdi. Director, Muslim Educational Trust. Portland, Oregon. December 2001.

Tavakoli, Dr. Mohammad. Illinois State University. E-mail correspondence, 2001–2002.

Chapter reviewed by Dr. Mohammad Tavakoli.

NOTES

1. Common Era (C.E.) and Before Common Era (B.C.E.) are a more inclusive way of denoting date than A.D. and B.C. The dates remain the same but the notation is preferred in the study of non-Christian subjects.

2. The Byzantines controlled modern Turkey, Greece, Israel, Egypt, southern Italy, the North African coast, and Syria.

3. The Sassanid dynasty ruled Persia from C.E. 224–651. The dynasty superseded the Parthian Empire and challenged Roman power in the East. This was the last line of Persian kings before the Arab conquests. The Sasanians covered modern Iran, Iraq, and some of central Asia.

4. Zoroastrianism is the religious system founded in Persia by Zoroaster, teaching a universal struggle between the forces of light and of darkness.

5. Manichaeism was an ancient dualist belief system that originated in third-century Persia—a religious doctrine based on the separation of matter and spirit, of good and evil.

6. Mecca is located on the western edge of the Arabian Peninsula.

7. Then called Yathrib; the old section of an Arab city in North Africa.

8. As the first caliph of Islam, Abu Bakr united Arabia and spread Islam.

9. 'Uthman appointed members of his tribe to important governorships.

10. The Umaiyad family dominated Mecca and later established a dynasty as rulers (caliphs) of Islam.

11. The Seljuk were a Turkish dynasty ruling in central and western Asia from the eleventh to the thirteenth centuries.

12. Sufism is Islamic mysticism. Mystics believe communion with the Divine Presence occurs through intuition or ecstasy rather than rational thought.

13. Mughal, also Mogul or Moghul, was a member of the Muslim dynasty of Mongol origin that ruled large parts of India from 1526 to 1857.

14. The word *jihad* connotes an individual's striving for spiritual self-perfection; also, a struggle.

15. The Kaaba is a cube-shaped structure that is the central holy site of Islam.

16. The animal sacrificed is usually a goat, sheep, camel, or cow and is usually provided onsite and professionally prepared rather than sacrificed by the individual. The meat is distributed to the poor and hungry.

17. URL: http://www.apha.org/ppp/red/indialanguage.htm (accessed February 2003). This page is a service of the American Public Health Association to assist health care providers.

18. URL: http://www.eat-halal.com (accessed February 2003). Answers the question, "What is halal?"

19. The Hadith is a record of the traditions or sayings of the Prophet Muhammad and serves as a major source of religious law and moral guidance, second only to the authority of the Qur'an.

20. Portions of this section have appeared in a different form on the author's Web site, *A Basic Help for Middle Eastern History,* URL: http://www.dragstroke.org/smili/history.html (accessed March 2003), © Linda Smith.

9

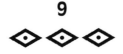

BUDDHISM

Sue Plaisance

Buddhism—Religion considered by its adherents to be a teaching, a combination of paths leading to spiritual discovery and self-awakening

One of the major religions of the world; only major religion that has never been used as rationale to wage war or support a warrior class.

Beginnings:

Founded about 525 B.C.E near Benares, India, when Siddharta Gautama, or Buddha, attained enlightenment.

Beliefs and practices:

Buddhists have faith in the Buddha but do not revere him as a god. Buddhism is nontheistic.

"Buddha" means "the enlightened one."

Tripitaka is scripture that collects the Buddha's teachings, rules of monastic life, and philosophical commentaries on the teachings. Also vast body of Buddhist teachings and commentaries called *sutras*.

(continued)

(continued)

Basic institution of Buddhism is the *sangha,* or monastic order, through which traditions are passed from generation to generation.

Demographics:

Estimates of current number of members in the United States range from 750,000 to 5 million.

Information point:

Buddhist Information Network. URL: http://www.buddhanet.net/ (accessed March 2004).

Buddhism is not considered a religion by its adherents because they do not worship a universal creator as most religions do. Buddhism is a teaching, a combination of paths to spiritual discovery and self-awakening. Buddhism has no Supreme Being, no single creed that must be followed, no ceremonies or rites that must be adhered to, nor does it expect exclusive allegiance from its followers. Buddhism teaches a highly ethical code as the path to individual enlightenment. It asks its followers to abstain from taking life of any kind, and not to lie, cheat, or steal. Buddhism instructs its followers to treat all others with kindness. Buddhism is an ever-changing combination of ways to live a thoughtful life.

BRIEF HISTORY

The Buddhist philosophy and religion was founded in about the sixth century B.C.E. in India by Siddharta Gautama, who became known as the Buddha.

Siddharta was the son of a powerful ruler of a small kingdom in what is now southern Nepal. At his birth, a sage predicted that the prince would become an ascetic or universal monarch. To protect his son from fulfilling the prophecy of becoming an ascetic, the king raised him isolated from the realities of life. The prince lived in luxury confined to his father's palace, and in his early twenties married and fathered a son.

At about age twenty-nine he left his father's palace and ventured into the nearby city. Having been sheltered his entire life, he was shocked when confronted by the realities of old age, illness, and death. After considering what he had seen, he again ventured into the city and encountered a wandering holy man, an ascetic, who owned nothing and desired to own nothing. This experience changed the course of Siddharta's life, and he decided to become an ascetic, leaving his family and his father's palace behind.

After several years of studying with holy men, Siddharta became interested in the Hindu concepts of *samsara* and *moksha,* the cycle of birth, rebirth, and eventual release through unification with the Supreme Being.

He spent several more years meditating and practicing a life of extreme denial, eventually realizing that a middle path between luxury and denial was the most effective way to live. After a lengthy period of deep meditation he achieved enlightenment or "awakening." The Buddha, as Siddharta came to be known, began to teach others how to "awaken" to the essential truth of the impermanent and interdependent nature of all life. His analysis of suffering came to be known as the Four Noble Truths and his solution to suffering, the Eightfold Path. These two basic teachings became known as the "Dharma" or doctrine of Buddhism.

The three major traditions of Buddhism are Theravada, Mahayana, and Vajrayana (Tibetan). The ideal of early Buddhism was the perfected saint who was purified of all desires. The School of Theravada, or doctrine of the elders, is considered representative of the early Buddhist teachings.

Mahayana Buddhism, or the Great Vehicle, is more common today. Its central precept is the potential for enlightenment found within all individuals. Its model is the perfected person who delays entry into nirvana, or total transcendence above desire, until all others are similarly enlightened. The Mahayana tradition embraces several schools of thought, including Zen Buddhism, which emphasizes the practice of meditation to achieve enlightenment.

Zen Buddhism developed as one of the meditation schools of Mahayana Buddhism and became especially popular in Japan. Zen Buddhism emphasizes an intuitive approach to enlightenment. Zen became the religion of the samurai (or warrior class) in Japan because it was simple and emphasized discipline.

Two schools of Zen Buddhism developed in Japan—Rinzai and Soto.

Rinzai was established by Japanese monk Eisai. Rinsai uses *koans,* or paradoxical statements, as an aid to cleanse the mind through meditation. Eisai said about his doctrine in his chief work, *Kozen gokokuron,* "Outwardly it favors discipline over doctrine, inwardly it brings the Highest Inner Wisdom."

The Soto school of Zen Buddhism was founded by Dogen, who used *zazen* meditation as the way to reach enlightenment. (Zazen is essentially sitting meditation.)

Vajrayana Buddhism is an offshoot of Mahayana Buddhism that began during the fifth century B.C.E. in India as an entirely new branch of Buddhism. Vajrayana Buddhism spread from India to Nepal, China, and Japan, and became most widespread in Tibet. Belief in reincarnation is a major distinction between the Vajrayana Buddhist tradition and the Theravada and Mahayana traditions.

CORE BELIEFS
AND VALUES

Buddhism is a way of life, a way of learning about one's place in the universe. For all Buddhists, the essential truth is the impermanent and interdependent nature of all life. When a person awakens to this truth, he or she can be transformed by it.

Some Buddhists have said that Nirvana cannot be described in words. The closest we can come using our Western sensibilities is to say that Nirvana is the extinction of both craving and the ego, or separate self. It is a state of peace and serenity.

All Buddhists seek the same goal—to become an awakened human being, a Buddha, but all Buddhists do not believe the same things. Each Buddhist tradition has its own path for attaining that goal.

Buddhists believe in many god-like beings, all subject to the law of Dharma, which is not a god but Truth or Reality—the way things really are. They strive to awaken to the Dharma, compassion, and selflessness. The central theme of Buddhism is becoming a true student, always searching for the truth, questioning and examining oneself.

The Buddhist concept of life after death is that the existence of an independent soul or ego is an illusion; therefore, there is nothing in humans that survives death. The Buddha taught that all living things must perish. The most fundamental point the Buddha taught is that the real cause of suffering is not impermanence itself but our human tendency to go against impermanence by trying to stay young, by thinking we have some sort of permanent ego-identity, and by becoming attached to possessions or to loved ones. This is why meditation, or self-examination, is the central practice of Buddhists.

The sacred literature of Buddhism has never been restricted to a single book accepted by all Buddhists. The sermons and discourses of the Buddha and his disciples have been studied individually by schools of Buddhist thought. The Buddhist literature best known in the west is the Tripitaka or Three Baskets.

The Four Noble Truths

The Four Noble Truths, or analysis of suffering, form the basis of all Buddhist teaching. This set of basic beliefs has never been used as the rationalization for a war, military crusade, or any other military action against non-believers. This is extremely rare in the history of world religions. The Four Noble Truths are:

1. Truth of suffering—all existence is suffering and cannot satisfy as it is not permanent.
2. Truth of the origin of suffering—the cause of suffering is desire and craving for permanence and sensual pleasure.
3. Truth that suffering can be overcome by ceasing to desire—known as Nirvana, or total transcendence.
4. Truth of the Eightfold path—the way to end desire is to follow the Eightfold path that will lead to the cessation of suffering, craving, and attachment.

The Eightfold Path

1. Right View—a view based on understanding the four Noble Truths.
2. Right Resolve—right intentions, good will, non-harming of creatures.
3. Right Speech—no lying, gossip or slander.
4. Right Conduct—no action conflicting with moral discipline.
5. Right Livelihood—no professions harmful to other creatures.
6. Right Effort—maintaining a wholesome mind.
7. Right Mindfulness—awareness of body, thought, and feelings.
8. Right Concentration—concentration of the mind to be able to achieve full awareness.

FORMATIVE EXPERIENCES

Buddhism does not have any formal rites of passage or coming-of-age ceremonies, but a few schools of Buddhist thought have developed some rites of passage. Initiation and wedding ceremonies are sometimes used in the Theravada tradition of Buddhist thought.

The initiation ceremony is also a name-giving ceremony. It is known as *Jukai* and is practiced by certain Japanese Buddhist sects. This ceremony is the same for males and females and can take place at any age.

There is no standard marriage ceremony in the United States and Canada. The bride and groom design their own ceremony with the overall purpose of reminding guests of "the essential Buddhist principle of non-harmfulness to all sentient beings" (Magida, p. 64). In some Theravada marriage ceremonies, the wedding party goes to the local temple and a long cotton thread is wound first around the image of the Buddha and then around the members of the wedding party, symbolically uniting all into one community.

MISCONCEPTIONS AND STEREOTYPES

"All Buddhists Believe in Reincarnation"

> Tibetan Buddhists teach reincarnation, but most of the other major Buddhist philosophies ignore it.

"Buddhists Welcome Suffering"

> Buddhists try to look upon suffering as an opportunity to learn and grow, as something potentially positive, as a kind of teacher.

"All Buddhists Wear Robes"

> While some Buddhist ministers do wear official robes during worship services, members of most Buddhist sects wear casual clothes.

"Buddhists Must Endure Lengthy Meditations"

> Some Buddhists sects, such as Zen, do emphasize meditation, but many others use a minor form of chanting instead.

"Buddhists *Gassho* to Pray for Good Fortune"

> The act of *gassho* (to put your hands together and bow your head) is not a prayer at all, nor is it a supplication for anything for oneself. It is an expression of humility, of realizing how much one has to be thankful for.

WHAT ARE BUDDHIST TEENS LOOKING FOR AT THE LIBRARY?

Buddhist teens want what most teens want—to be a valued, accepted part of their community and to find their place in the world. They examine their parents' and communities' values, and then determine which are most important to them individually. They seek to assert their individuality while maintaining their place in their extended family. They hope to be hip and religious at the same time, part of the popular teen culture but true to their beliefs and heritage.

Being Buddhist in a predominantly Christian society can create an identity issue with which some teens struggle. Establishing an identity separate from their parents but belonging to a minority group can make the search for personal identity more difficult or intense. Information that introduces Buddhist teachings in clear, simple language (using a non-scholarly approach) and information that compares Buddhist and Christian beliefs can be helpful in a Buddhist teen's search for identity in Western culture. Contacting Buddhist priests and ministers in your community is a good way of determining what information may be of interest to the Buddhist teens who visit your library.

BUILDING YOUR COLLECTION

Books that help with one's search for identity or with general themes of world peace or inner spiritual peace can be of particular interest to Buddhist teens as they reinforce the message of the Buddha. *Living Buddha, Living Christ* by Thich Nhat Hanh addresses the issue of identity and emphasizes the universal teachings of both Buddhism and Christianity.

Older teens are immersed in the dynamic and challenging social climate of senior high school. *What Would Buddha Do? Answers to Life's Daily Dilemmas* by Metcalf and Riegert is a practical, easy-to-read book that addresses actions in specific situations.

Tricycle Magazine and *Shambala Sun Magazine* are up-to-date resources that present Buddhist views on current events. Other recommended Buddhist magazines are *Mandala, Dharmalife,* and *Bodhi.* "These magazines often provide an alternative viewpoint to those in the TV media, especially in these volatile times." (Hata, 2003)

TYPES OF BOOKS AVAILABLE

There are a large number of nonfiction titles available, many written especially for the Western reader who needs very basic information about the tenets of Buddhism. Books on the major types of Buddhist thought are readily available, with Vajrayana (Tibetan) Buddhism currently appearing to be most popular in the mass media. Books by the Dalai Lama, Chogyam Trungpa, D.T. Suzuki, and other well-known Buddhists are popular and can easily be found in most full-service bookstores, through major book jobbers, or on the Internet. Fiction with Buddhist settings or philosophy, especially for teens, is difficult to find in the United States.

Publishers

Chagdud Gonpa Foundation
P.O. Box 279
Junction City, CA 96048–0279
(530) 623–2721; (877) 479–6129; fax (530) 623–6709
E-mail: sales@tibetantreasures.com
URL: http://www.tibetantreasures.com (accessed March 2004)

Dharma Publishing
2910 San Pablo Avenue
Berkeley, CA 94702
(510) 548–5407; (800) 873–4276; fax (510) 548–2230
E-mail: info@dharmapublishing.com
URL: http://www.dharmapublishing.com (accessed March 2004)

Hinduism Online at the Himalayan Academy
Himalayan Academy, Kauai's Hindu Monastery
107 Kaholalele Road
Kapaa, HI 96746–9304
Fax (808) 822–4351
E-mail: contact@hindu.org
URL: http://www.himalayanacademy.com/books/online_books.
   html (accessed March 2004)

Snow Lion Publications
P.O. Box 6483
Ithaca, NY 14851–6483
(607) 273–8519; (800) 950–0313; fax (607) 273–8508
E-mail: info@snowlionpub.com
URL: http://www.snowlionpub.com (accessed March 2004)

LIBRARY SERVICES AND PROGRAMS
"Help the Earth"

Environmental education programs on recycling and conserving
Earth's natural resources and beauty are a natural fit for Buddhists.
Speakers could address recycling, responsible use of natural resources,
and ways to conserve resources in everyday life. Celebrate National
Wildlife Week and Earth Day each April with book displays and book-
lists.

Annotated Bibliographies

Create bibliographies of books suitable for teens on the environment, recycling, wildlife, pet care, and conservation of natural resources.

Pet Care and Wildlife Conservation Programs

The Golden Chain of Buddhism says, "I will be kind and gentle to every living thing, and protect all who are weaker than myself." Since the goal is to live harmoniously with all, offer programs on responsible pet care and local wildlife conservation areas and refuges.

Attracting Birds and Butterflies to Your Backyard

Offer a gardening program on designing gardens that provide food and shelter for native birds and butterflies.

Buddha Goes to the Movies

During the last twenty years, Buddhist philosophies have frequently emerged in popular American movies. The *Star Wars* movies, *The Lion King, Little Buddha, Pocahontas, Seven Years in Tibet, Kundun, The Karate Kid* and sequels, and even the *Teenage Mutant Ninja Turtles* movies contain scenes that speak directly to Buddhist beliefs. Write a do-it-yourself quiz that challenges teens to match the movie with the Buddhist belief. Put together an annotated booklist that features recent popular movies that incorporate the ideals of Buddhist thought. Plan a teen program that focuses on movies and major religious beliefs. (From *The Living Dharma* Web site, URL: http://www.livingdharma.org, accessed March 2004)

SELECTED TITLES

Batchelor, Stephen. *Buddhism Without Beliefs: A Contemporary Guide to Awakening.* New York, NY: Berkeley Publishing Group, 1997. ISBN 1573220582. This book is for the person who is willing to try the exercises included to explore the principles of Buddhism. Clear language and the avoidance of foreign terms and jargon place this text well within the grasp of Western teens and young adults.

Chen, Da. *Wandering Warrior.* New York, NY: Delacorte Books, Random House, Inc., 2003. ISBN 0385900899. For lovers of kung fu action movies, *Wandering*

Warrior offers the same non-stop action in book form. Eleven-year-old Luka carries the birthmarks of the future emperor of China. But with no family left to protect him, Luka needs help. Enter the Buddhist monk Atami who takes Luka under his wing and begins training him as a kung fu warrior. Atami is captured by the enemy, and Luka must make his way alone to meet his destiny. A kung fu coming-of-age novel for aspiring young martial artists.

Conover, Sarah. *Kindness: A Treasury of Buddhist Wisdom for Children and Parents.* Spokane, WA: Eastern Washington University Press, 2001. ISBN 091005567X. This collection of traditional Buddhist tales retold for a Western audience includes thirty-two stories of elephants, mice, monkeys, rabbits, tigers, monks, and men, all striving to live a good life and achieve enlightenment. The author has included a section of sources for the stories, quotations, and sayings presented in the book, as well as further sources on Buddhism for children and teens.

Dalkey, Kara. *The Heavenward Path.* New York, NY: Harcourt Brace & Co., 1998. ISBN 015201652X. This exciting sequel to *Little Sister* sees Mitsuko leaving her refuge in the Buddhist temple to travel through twelfth century Japan, confronting ghosts and dragons with a little help from her supernatural sidekick, the shape-shifter Goranu. Author Dalkey crafts an engaging historical adventure fantasy based on Animist, Shinto, and Buddhist beliefs, which also involves a romance between a mortal and an immortal.

———. *Little Sister.* New York, NY: Penguin Putnam Inc., 1996. ISBN 015201392X (hardcover), ISBN 0140386319 (pbk.). Weaving a unique tale of Animism, Shintoism, and Buddhism, the author tells of an aristocratic young girl, Mitsuko, in twelfth century Japan who must find a way to protect her older sister from supernatural dangers as well as very real warlords. She receives unexpected assistance from a supernatural being, Goranu, who is a shape-shifting demon.

Hanh, Thich Nhat. *Living Buddha, Living Christ.* New York, NY: Riverhead Books, 1995. ISBN 1573220183. Hanh draws parallels between these two venerable religious traditions and explores the intersection of compassion and holiness at which the two meet, enhancing our understanding of both.

———. *Peace Is Every Step: The Path of Mindfulness in Everyday Life.* New York, NY: Bantam Books, 1991. ISBN 0553351397. Hanh, a world leader in Buddhism, promotes a movement that combines traditional meditative practices with active nonviolent civil disobedience known as "engaged Buddhism."

Koja, Kathe. *Buddha Boy.* New York, NY: Farrar Straus Giroux, 2003. ISBN 0374309981. Justin just wants to stay under the radar and out of trouble in high school, but when he reluctantly befriends another student who is a self-styled Buddhist monk, he finds he cannot avoid the school bullies. "Buddha Boy" Jinsen enables Justin to define what is important and unimportant in high school, in life, and in relationships.

Metcalf, Franz. *Buddha in Your Backpack: Everyday Buddhism for Teens.* Berkeley, CA: Seastone, imprint of Ulysses Press, 2003. ISBN 1569753210 (pbk.). A practical guide for teens that covers who Buddha was, what Buddhism is and isn't, and how Buddhism relates to everyday Western life, especially for teens. The author is an enthusiastic Buddhist but makes it clear that incorporating Buddhist principles into one's life need not mean a conversion to Buddhism or renunciation of other religious affiliations. All of the relevant teen angst issues such as dating, school, stress, cliques, family expectations, and peer pressure are covered. A fascinating guide for teens and adults who are curious about Buddhism.

——— and Ray Riegert. *What Would Buddha Do: Answers to Life's Daily Dilemmas.* New York, NY: Gramercy Random House, 2002. ISBN 0517220075. An entertaining and perceptive approach to applying 2,500 years of Buddhist teachings to everyday life. Concerns about personal identity, relationships, materialism, stress, love, and values are handled in a straightforward manner, showing how Buddhist teachings can guide in handling the trials of contemporary life.

Piburn, Sidney, ed. *The Dalai Lama, A Policy of Kindness: An Anthology of Writings by and About the Dalai Lama,* second ed. Ithaca, NY: Snow Lion Publications, 1993. ISBN 1559390220. Includes the Nobel Peace Prize Lecture; an interview about his life; essays on cooperation among world religions, human rights and universal responsibilities; and ethical approaches to environmental protection.

Scheck, Frank Rainer and Manfred Görgens. *Buddhism: An Illustrated Historical Overview.* Hauppage, NY: Barron's Educational Series, 1999. ISBN 0764109103. A basic guide to the subject of Buddhism designed for the student seeking information for a research report.

Whitesel, Cheryl A. *Rebel: A Tibetan Odyssey.* Scranton, PA: HarperCollins, 2000. ISBN 0688167357. Although he rebels against life in the Tibetan Buddhist monastery where he had been sent, fourteen-year-old Thunder comes to some amazing realizations about himself.

WEB SITES

BAUS Youth Group. Buddhist Association of the United States is a group affiliated with a Buddhist monastery in Carmel, New York. The group is composed of a diverse mix of students and young adults who participate in volunteer activities and social events to strengthen the practice of Buddhism. URL: http://www.baus.org/bausyg/info.htm (accessed March 2004).

Buddhist Information and Education Network. "Buddhanet is a non-sectarian organization, offering its services to all Buddhist traditions...helping make the Buddha's teachings freely available to all." URL: http://www.Bud dhanet.net (accessed March 2004).

Dharma Realm Buddhist Youth. Dharma Realm Buddhist Youth (DRBY) educates young people in the Buddhist tradition of personal growth and self-reflection. It is not a social organization but a collective group of young people who are searching for wisdom and who are committed to aiding others while advancing their own spiritual path. URL: http://www.drby.net/ about.asp (accessed March 2004).

World Fellowship of Buddhists Youth (WFBY). Founded in 1950 in Sri Lanka, the WFBY is made up of young adults representing almost every school of Buddhism. URL: http://www.wfby.org (accessed March 2004).

WORKS CONSULTED

Encyclopedia Americana, International Edition. Danbury, CT: Grolier Incorporated, 2002.

Gach, Gary. *The Complete Idiot's Guide to Understanding Buddhism.* East Rutherford, NJ: Alpha Books, Penguin Putnam, 2001.

Hata, Peter, ed. , Living Dharma Web site of the West Covina Buddhist Temple, West Covina, CA. E-mail interview, January 2003.

Magida, Arthur J. and Stuart M. Matlins, eds. *How to Be a Perfect Stranger,* v. 1. Woodstock, VT: Skylight Paths Publishing, 1999.

Seager, Richard. *Buddhists in America.* Irvington, NY: Columbia University Press, 1999.

Some Common Misconceptions about Buddhism in America. URL: http://www.livingdharma.org/Misconceptions.html (accessed March 2004).

Toropov, Brandon and Father Luke Buckles. *The Complete Idiot's Guide to the World's Religions.* New York, NY: Alpha Books, 1997.

Wangu, Madhu Bazaz. *Buddhism* (*World Religions* series). New York, NY: Facts on File, 2002.

What Is Buddhism? URL: http://teenoutreach.com/beliefs/buddhism (accessed March 2004).

10

HINDUISM

Sue Plaisance

Hinduism—major religion of India.

Beginnings:

No acknowledged founder. Believers maintain that Hinduism has existed for all time and was established by God Himself. Scholars say Hinduism arose 3,500 years ago in the Indus River Valley.

Beliefs and practices:

Belief in one Supreme Being manifest in many different deities. Principal deities—Brahma (the Creator), Shiva (the Destroyer), Vishnu (the Preserver).

No one source of doctrines and beliefs.

Oldest Hindu scriptures are the Vedas, composed over a thousand-year period beginning about 1400 B.C.E. Other important texts include the *Bhagavadgītā* (Song of God), part of the Mahabharata, a great epic poem from India.

Many devout Hindus are vegetarians as a result of their belief in not doing harm to other living things.

(continued)

(continued)
Demographics:

Current number of members in the United States is about 1.3 million.
Followed by about seventy percent of the one billion people of India—
great influence on culture of India.

Information points:

Hindu Links. URL: http://www.hindulinks.org/ (accessed March 2004).
Hindu Universe. URL: http://www.hindunet.org/home.shtml (accessed
March 2004).

Hinduism is a flexible, ever-evolving faith that stresses convergence, or
incorporation, rather than suppression of other faiths. It encourages the
reconciliation of tensions and differences between religious beliefs. The
adherents of Hinduism worship one God who has many manifestations.
Brahma, Vishnu, and Shiva are the three primary manifestations but there
are numerous other deities, all of whom are considered holy. Animals
such as cattle and peacocks are also worshipped because deities are
depicted in religious art as riding on them.

Hinduism has no specific founder. It is thought to have emerged about
3,500 years ago when Aryan invaders from Persia overran the Indus River
Valley civilization (located in modern-day Pakistan) and melded Aryan
beliefs with the beliefs of the Indus River Valley peoples.

A BRIEF HISTORY AND CORE BELIEFS AND VALUES

Hinduism is one of the world's oldest religions, having been practiced
for over 3,500 years. It emerged from a melding of beliefs and schools of
philosophy practiced in the Indus Valley region of what is now India.
Through the centuries Hinduism has also incorporated some of the beliefs
of the various invaders of that region. Religious texts were written that
have become sacred to the Hindus and form a foundation for the study of
the religion.

Hinduism, called *Sanatana Dharma* by Hindus, is a way of living rather
than a doctrine. It is a mystical, metaphysical faith in which the individual
works to personally experience the truth within, striving to reach a higher
consciousness in which man and God become one. Hinduism recognizes
a Supreme Being composed of three parts: Brahma, the creator; Vishnu,
the sustainer; and Shiva, the destroyer. There are also many minor gods

and goddesses, all of whom are considered to be reincarnations of the Supreme Being. It is felt that there is God in every human being, that we are all reincarnations of the Supreme Being.

Hindus view creation and time as cyclical—the universe is created, moves through various forms, is destroyed, and then recreated.

Reincarnation, the Hindu concept of life after death, involves the uniting of the individual soul with the Supreme Being through a series of rebirths. Hindus believe in "karma," the law of cause and effect, by which each person "creates his own destiny, through thoughts, words, and deeds" (Himalayan Academy, http://www.himalayanacademy.com, accessed March 2004).

A large body of Hindu sacred literature has been written over the last 4,000 years. *Shruti*, the texts that are to be heard, are the oldest of the writings and include the Vedas, the Brahmanas, the Aranyakas, and the Upanishads. The *smriti* writings that are tradition, or that which is to be remembered, include two great epics, the Mahabharata and the Ramayana. According to the Reverend Pandurang Shastri Athavale of Bombay, India, the *Bhagavadgītā,* an episode from the Mahabharata, is not actually a sacred scripture but more of a philosophical work intended not just for Hindus but for everyone. It is considered a divine book of radiant and powerful thoughts, meant to inspire mankind for all time to come.

Rather than having a set of specific, universally held beliefs, Hinduism is comprised of a series of loosely connected beliefs. The study of sacred writings and the practice of techniques for personal spiritual development are the methods used in an individual's search for enlightenment and ultimate goal of uniting with the Supreme Being.

Many Hindus follow the teachings of gurus, spiritual teachers who have gained enlightenment through knowledge and practice. This is very much an individual choice on the part of each person, and there are many gurus from which to choose.

Because Hindus believe that all types of life are sacred, they practice *ahimsa*, which loosely translates as non-injury and non-violence. Vegetarianism is an outcome of this belief.

Hinduism is one of the most tolerant of religions since Hindus believe that no one religion teaches the only way to salvation, and that all sincere faiths merit understanding.

Early in its history, Hindu society was divided into a caste system based on occupation. Hindu religious laws of duty taught that each caste had certain duties that must be performed to maintain society's balance and peace. Today the religious laws obligating people to respect the caste system have loosened. Modern dharma, or religious law, concentrates more on family than societal duties. Today "the family unit is considered especially sacred, and the fulfillment of obligations to the family is a religious duty" (Wangu, p. 12).

FORMATIVE EXPERIENCES

Hinduism has a few *samskaras*, or rites of passage, almost all of which are for male children only.

Originally, the sacred thread ceremony was the primary rite of passage in adolescence for males who were part of the three upper castes. In modern times this ceremony has lost much of its meaning and has become more of a formality. The ceremony took place when the male child was between eight and twelve years of age. It was intended to be a time when he was given the understanding of the rituals he was expected to follow in his daily life. Once the child had completed this ceremony, he was thought to have had a second, or spiritual, birth.

Male Hindus are thought to have four stages of life—*brahmachari* (student), *grahasthin* (married householder), *vanaprasthin* (forest dweller), and *sanyasin* (ascetic). In modern times, the first two stages are more commonly practiced than the last two.

For the student who has recently completed his studies of the sacred traditions and literature, there is another ritual that welcomes him into society. It involves a ceremonial bath, and once it is completed the former student becomes an adult member of society and is considered ready for marriage.

Female children are taught the rituals for a Hindu life at home by their parents. There are no formal or public ceremonies for them to complete.

Marriage is probably the major rite of passage through adolescence for both men and women, and the marriage ceremony marks the end of adolescence and the couple's entry into society.

MISCONCEPTIONS AND STEREOTYPES

Some people assume that all East Indians are Hindus. This is not true. Not all East Indians are practitioners of Hinduism, but they are part of the Hindu culture.

In 1990 a group of teens from the Hindu Temple of Greater Chicago in Lemont, Illinois, asked the Himalayan Academy for help in answering several questions that they were frequently asked about Hinduism. The teens received two sets of answers to their questions, a brief set of answers for those who were satisfied with a short, concise response, and a set of more extensive answers for those who wanted further explanation. Both sets of answers may be found at www.himalayanacademy.com/ basics/ tenq//tenq_1.html (accessed March 2004). Listed below are some of the concise answers that were provided by Palaniswami of the Himalayan Academy:

- Why does Hinduism have so many Gods? While acknowledging many Gods, all Hindus believe in a one Supreme Being who creates and sustains the universe.

- Why do Hindus believe in reincarnation? Hindus believe the soul is immortal and reenters a fleshy body time and time again in order to resolve experiences and learn all the lessons that life in the material world has to offer.

- What is karma? Karma is the universal principle of cause and effect, action and reaction, which governs all life.

- Why do Hindus regard the cow as sacred? The cow represents the giving nature of life to every Hindu. In honoring this gentle animal, who gives more than she takes, we honor all creatures.

- Do Hindus worship idols? Hindus invoke the presence of God, or the Gods, from the higher, unseen worlds, into stone images so that they can experience His divine presence, commune with Him and receive His blessings. But the stone or metal Deity images are not mere symbols of the Gods. They are the form through which their love, power and blessings flood forth into this world.

- Are Hindus forbidden to eat meat? Hindus teach vegetarianism as a way to live with a minimum of hurt to other beings. But in today's world, not all Hindus are vegetarians.

- Do Hindus have a Bible? The Hindu "Bible" could be considered the Veda. The Veda is comprised of four ancient and holy scriptures which those of the Hindu faith revere.

- Why do many Hindus wear a dot near the middle of their forehead? The dot worn on the forehead is a religious symbol representing the third eye, or divine sight and insight. For women, it is also a beauty mark.

WHAT ARE HINDU TEENS LOOKING FOR AT THE LIBRARY?

In addition to the national language of India, Hindi, most citizens are likely to speak at least one of the more than fifteen Indian languages, for example, Gujarati, Tamil, and Urdu; and many also speak English. Because Hindi is the national language of India, at some point most Hindus learn it. Many teens are actively involved in studying Hindi, so books in Hindi or bilingual books in English/Hindi are very appropriate for this age group. Subjects of interest include the epics of Hinduism (such as the Mahabharata and the Ramayana), grammar of the Hindi language, history of India, festivals of India, geography of that region of the world, and books on beauty and glamour. These last three topics can be purchased in English because they will have a wider audience. Almost all Hindu American teens speak English, but many are still learning Hindi and are not likely to be able to read it well.

When selecting materials for Hindu teens, look for works by well-known Hindu writers to be sure the material is authentic and does not contain ideas or attitudes that would be offensive to the teens. Authors such as Swami Harshananda, Bansi Pandit, Madhu Bazaz Wangu, Sri Meenal (also known as "The Mother"), Mohandas (Mahatma) K. Gandhi, and Pandurang Athaval are recommended.

BUILDING YOUR COLLECTION

Many of the books from and about India feature covers with intricate, elaborate designs of the art of the culture and will capture the attention of many teens who browse the collection. Colored illustrations or photographs included in books will also make them more attractive to teens. Graphic novels are very popular, but review the contents to make certain the illustrations are appropriate for a young adult collection. Themes of inner peace and planes of spiritual attainment are of perennial interest, and self-help books are also appealing.

Some Hindu teens indicated they would be disappointed to see a lot of pro-Pakistan material in the library, especially with regard to the Kashmir region ownership conflict. The region of Kashmir has been a hotly contested area for at least fifty years, since the region's Maharaja gave up hope for political independence and chose to accede to India. He signed over key powers to the Indian government in return for promises of aid, including military aid. Many areas of Kashmir are Muslim-dominated and the Muslim residents wish to be citizens of Muslim-dominated Pakistan rather than India. Since 1989, there has been a growing and often violent separatist movement fighting against Indian rule in Kashmir. Although this may appear to be primarily a political situation to Western sensibilities, the major religions are so thoroughly intertwined in the culture in that part of the world that political situations are very often religious situations too.

As librarians, we need to provide both pro-Pakistan materials and pro-India materials when selecting materials with Hindu teens in mind.

TYPES OF BOOKS AVAILABLE

There is a plethora of self-help books written by various Hindu gurus, several of whom are well-known in the United States. Books by Vivekananda, Swami Bhaktivedanta, and Maharishi Mahesh Yogi are very popular, but there are literally hundreds of Hindu teacher gurus in the United States today.

Many vegetarian cookbooks from the Hindu culture are available.

Quite a few scholarly translations of the sacred, ancient scriptures of Hinduism have been published for the American market. Comic books for children illustrate the Ramayana and parts of the *Bhagavadgītā*, and books of fables known as the *Panchatatra* and the *Hitopadesh*.

In the United States, Hindu young adult fiction seems to be very limited in availability.

Publishers

Following is a list of publishers in the United States and Canada who distribute books and materials on the many forms of Hinduism.

Auromere
2621 West Highway 12
Lodi, CA 95242
(800) 735–4691
URL: http://www.auromere.com/Books/F_Yoga_Home.html
(accessed March 2004)
E-mail: info@auromere.com
Books for the coming of age of Hindu boys and girls.

Bhaktivedanta Book Trust
P.O. Box 34074
Los Angeles, CA 90034
(310) 837–5283; fax (310) 837–1056
URL: http://www.webcom.com/~ara/col/books/ (accessed March 2004)
E-mail: legal@bbti.org

Far Eastern Books
P.O. Box 846, Adelaide Street Station
Toronto, ON M5C 2K1 Canada
(800) 291–8886; (905) 477–2900; fax (905) 479–2988
URL: http://www.febonline.com (accessed March 2004)
E-mail: Books@febonline.com

Lotus Light Publications
P.O. Box 325
Twin Lakes, WI 53181
(262) 889–8561; fax (262) 889–2461
URL: http://www.lotuspress.com (accessed March 2004)
E-mail: lotuspress@lotuspress.com
Lotus Press is a specialty publisher of books in the fields of alternative health, philosophy, and spirituality, and is also a distributor for Inner Worlds music label.

Multi-cultural Books & Videos
28880 Southfield Road, Suite 183
Lathrup Village, MI 48076
(248) 559–2676; (800) 567–2220; fax (248) 559–2465
URL: http://multiculturalbooksandvideos.com (accessed March 2004)
E-mail: service@multiculbv.com

Swaminarayan Publications (New York office)
Shree Swaminarayan Mandir (B.A.P.S.)
43–38 Bowne St.
Flushing, NY 11355
(718) 539–5373; fax (718) 353–3411
URL: http://www.swaminarayan.org/publications/index.htm (accessed March 2004)
E-mail: info@swaminarayan.org
A publishing house that promotes the Vedic Hindu traditions.

Vedanta Press
1946 Vedanta Place
Hollywood, CA 90068
(800) 816–2242
URL: http://www.vedanta.com (accessed March 2004)
E-mail: info@vedanta.org

LIBRARY SERVICES AND PROGRAMS
Travel Programs on India

Set up presentation graphics software in your meeting room and invite Hindu teens and adults to share their digital images of scenes from India. Have several people scheduled to bring their programs, and open the programs to the public.

Collection Development

Enhance your young adult and adult nonfiction collections by including books written by popular Hindu gurus. Also, include comics and graphic novels that illustrate various aspects of the religion.

Meeting Rooms

Make sure your local Hindu families know how to reserve the library's meeting rooms. They may be interested in using it for religious study groups or for dance troupe practice.

Dance Troupes

Invite local Hindu dance troupes to practice in the meeting room and invite them to perform for a library program. Dance troupes might be located by:

- Visiting a local Asian Indian grocery store and asking the proprietor for suggestions on how to locate local troupes. Check the store's community bulletin board for flyers about upcoming performances of Indian dance troupes. Also look for community newspapers that cater to the Asian Indian community and check their public service announcements and classified advertisements for dance lessons in Asian Indian dancing.
- Ask Asian Indian library patrons with whom you have established a relationship if they know of local dance troupes and if they would be able to provide contact information.
- Visit local bookstores that specialize in metaphysical topics. They will often post flyers and class notices of interest to the Asian Indian community.
- If your community hosts celebrations of India Republic Day on January 26 or Indian Independence Day in August, it is likely local Indian dance troupes will perform. If you can attend these celebrations, you may be able to make direct contact with several dance troupes.
- Check the telephone directory yellow pages under "Religious Organizations" and "Yoga Instruction" for contacts in the local Asian Indian community.

Mehndi Workshops

Set up a station in the young adult area and let patrons pre-register to have their hands or ankles decorated with Mehndi. A body art form,

Mehndi is a type of temporary tattoo in which a henna paste is used to create intricate red-brown designs on the palms and other exposed parts of an individual's body. Designs can last several days to several weeks. Mehndi is an expression of the joy of life, a way of creating a sacred space with a symbol, and is part of the culture of India, Pakistan, and some Arab countries. In India, Mehndi designs are traditionally applied to a bride's hands and feet the day before her wedding. In the Portland, Oregon, area in 2002 the cost was about $45.00 per hour for the services of an accomplished Mehndi artist.

Family Storytelling Festival

Invite all family members to participate in a family storytelling festival. At our first festival in 2002, we read aloud picture books in Hindi and English, listened to stories told in Hindi and English, and practiced saying Hindi words as part of the stories. There were crafts, and a local Indian grocery store provided refreshments. Mehndi was offered for teens during the craft time. You can focus on East Indian and Hindu stories, or you can include these stories as part of a multicultural storytelling festival.

Annotated Bibliographies

Create bibliographies of folk tales and myths from India. Since so much of Hindu philosophy is presented in story form, these lists will be of interest to all ages.

Display Ideas
Educational Displays

Design displays featuring India's national or religious celebrations—India Independence Day on August 15, India Republic Day on January 26, the fall light festival of Diwali, and other religious festivals. Remember to check your library's policy governing religious displays. Many libraries allow displays of religious materials if they are educational in nature.

New Book Displays

Display recent books on India and include newer issues of *National Geographic* or travel magazines featuring the country. Borrow posters or gift items from local gift or grocery stores that serve the Hindu community.

Display of Popular Videos

The film industry in India is huge, and entertainment videos are extremely popular with our local Hindu families. Our library was fortunate to receive a donation of almost one hundred Indian popular videos. We set up a display of them at our first Hindu Family Storytelling Festival; the videos flew out the door and continue to circulate briskly. The Multicultural Books and Video Company is a very good source of Hindi popular videos.

SELECTED TITLES

Bhaktivedanta Swami Prabhupēda, His Divine Grace A.C. *Bhagavad-Gītā As It Is.* Los Angeles, CA: Bhaktivedanta Book Trust, 1989, 1986. ISBN 089213268X. The *Bhagavadgītā* is considered one of the great philosophical and religious dialogues in history. It appears originally as an episode in the epic Sanskrit history of the ancient world, the Mahābhārata The *Bhagavadgītā* is a conversation between Lord Krsna (Krishna) and his spiritual follower and warrior, Arjuna, which takes place just before the onset of a major war between brothers. On the eve of battle, Arjuna questions the meaning of life, what happens after death, and the reasons for fighting his friends and relatives. Lord Krsna addresses Arjuna's questions and takes his friend from introspection to spiritual enlightenment. If available, the 1986 edition is recommended because it is in a large format and has sixteen full-color plates and a colorful cover.

Desai Hidier, Tanuja. *Born Confused.* New York, NY: Scholastic Press, 2002. ISBN 0439357624. Seventeen-year-old Dimple, whose family is from India, discovers that she is not Indian enough for Indian society and not American enough for the Americans. She watches her beautiful, charismatic, manipulative best friend take possession of both her heritage and the boy she likes.

Divakaruni, Chitra. *Neela: Victory Song* (*Girls of Many Lands* series). Middleton, WI: Pleasant Company Publications, 2002. ISBN 1584855975 (hardcover), ISBN 1584855215 (pbk.). In 1939 India, twelve-year-old Neela relies on a young freedom fighter to help her find her father who has gone to Calcutta to march against the British occupation.

Harshananda, Swami. *Hindu Gods and Goddesses.* Distributed in the United States by Vedanta Press, 1987, 1981. ISBN 8171201105. The gods and goddesses of the Hindu religion are considered to be the doorways leading to the one Godhead. For each god and goddess, its name, raiment, and instruments contain symbolic and psychological significance. This book describes the appearance of many of them, shares information on their ornaments and weapons, and gives a brief description of what they do and what they represent. Intricate, elaborate sketches of forty-nine gods and goddesses appear in black and white, and information on many more deities is included. The illustrations are based on images and sculptures found in well-known temples and major archeological sites. Many of the Hindu gods and goddesses appear in our Western culture on posters and tokens that are marketed to young adults and those interested in New Age religions. For teens seeking information on these images and on Hinduism, this book can be very useful in identifying major and minor gods and goddesses of the religion. This is a good book for casual browsing as well as a reliable source for more formal research.

Highwater, Jamake. *Rama: A Legend.* Bridgewater, NJ: Replica Books, 2001. ISBN 0735105030. Based on the ancient Sanskrit epic, the Ramayana, this legend introduces the reader to Prince Rama, his bride Sita, and his brother Laksmana. It is the story of Rama's love for Sita and Laksmana's dedication to both of them. Giant talking monkeys, monsters full of spiders and worms, disembodied eyeballs, the demon Ramana, and many magical creatures make this a thrilling adventure. Highwater, a winner of a Newbery Honor award, brings the ancient literary traditions of India to Western audiences.

Malladi, Amulya. *The Mango Season.* New York, NY: Random House Ballantine Publishing Group, 2003. ISBN 0345450302. Priya Rao left India for the United States seven years ago to study computer science but mostly to escape having a marriage arranged for her. Now she returns to give her family the bad news—she is engaged to an American—and she is marrying for love! And telling her family something that will break their hearts is harder than she ever imagined. But through her reasoning and explanations, the members of her family find their own truths about what they want from life.

Pandit, Bansi. *The Hindu Mind: Fundamentals of Hindu Religion and Philosophy for All Ages,* third ed. Glen Ellyn, IL: B & V Enterprises, Inc., 1998. ISBN 0963479822 (hardcover), ISBN 0963479849 (pbk.). This book includes an in-depth description of the Hindu religion, its origins, and its underlying philosophy; the symbolism behind the major Hindu deities; the Hindu epics, presenting the essence of the Ramayana and the Mahabharata; the goals, debts, and stages of Hindu life and marriage; major festivals; sacred verse-prayers known as mantras; the relationship between the Hindu religion and science; and contributions of Hindus to world culture. It provides a comprehensive look at the religion and is appropriate for older youth.

Rana, Indi. *The Roller Birds of Rampur.* New York, NY: Random House Ballantine Publishing Group, 1993. ISBN 0805026703 (hardcover), ISBN 0449704343 (pbk.). Born in India but raised in England, Sheila thinks of herself as English so she is shattered when her English boyfriend dumps her because she is too Indian. Suddenly needing to know more about her heritage, Sheila returns to her family's farm in India and rediscovers a land of amazing contrasts with a 3,500-year heritage of culture and religion. This coming-of-age story offers an extraordinary glimpse into Hindu philosophy.

Staples, Suzanne. *Shiva's Fire.* New York, NY: Farrar Straus Giroux, 2000. ISBN 0374368244 (hardcover), ISBN 0064409791 (pbk.). Parvati has been feared and shunned in her village all her life because of the circumstances of her birth. But her natural abilities in dance bring her to the attention of a great Indian dance master who invites her to study classical Indian dance at his famous academy. But is dance really her destiny?

Wangu, Madhu Bazaz. *Hinduism.* (*World Religions* series) New York, NY: Facts on File, 2001. ISBN 0816044007. This volume offers a brief, concise look at the history, beliefs, rituals, and religious literature of Hinduism. The real value of this book lies in its clear text and effective organization of information.

Whelan, Gloria. *Homeless Bird*. New York, NY: Harper Collins Publishers, 2001. ISBN 0060284528 (library binding), ISBN 0064408191 (pbk.). Thirteen-year-old Koly finds herself caught in untenable circumstances. Married, then widowed almost immediately, uneducated, and without family, Koly must fend for herself in an India that has no place for widows except as beggars. With the few skills she possesses, Koly chooses to make her own life and happiness.

WEB SITES

About Hinduism. URL: http://www.hinduism.about.com (accessed March 2004).
Hindu Students Council. Primarily for Hindu high school and college students in the United States. URL: http://www.hscnet.org/ (accessed March 2004).
The Hindu Universe. URL: http://www.hindunet.org (accessed March 2004).
Hindu Youth. URL: http://www.hinduyouth.com (accessed March 2004).
Hinduism: The World's Third Largest Religion. General information about Hinduism for the Western audience. URL: http://www.religioustolerance.org/hinduism.htm (accessed March 2004).
Hinduism for Teens. Advice for Hindu teens in the United States. URL: http://www.teenadvice.about.com/cs/hinduismforteens1/ (accessed March 2004).
Hinduism Online. Web site of the Hawaii Ashram on Kauai. URL: http://www.himalayanacademy.com (accessed March 2004).
Hinduism Today. URL: http://www.hinduismtoday.com (accessed March 2004).
Mehandi.com. URL: http://www.mehandi.com (accessed March 2004).

WORKS CONSULTED

Encyclopedia Americana, International Edition. Danbury, CT: Grolier Inc., 2002.
Gupta, Sonali. Personal interview, January 30, 2003.
Hinduism Online. URL: http://www.himalayanacademy.com (accessed March 2004).
Largest Hindu Communities. URL: http://www.adherents.com/largecom/com_hindu.html (accessed March 2004).
Magida, Arthur J. and Stuart M. Matlins, eds. *How to Be the Perfect Stranger, v. 1.* Woodstock, VT: Skylight Paths Pub., 1999.
Palaniswami, Paramacharya. Editor-in-chief, *Hinduism Today,* Kapaa, Hawaii. E-mail interviews, March 2003.
Parajuli, Pramod. Associate Professor, Education, and Director, Portland International Initiative for Leadership in Ecology, Culture and Learning, Graduate School of Education, Portland State University, Portland, Oregon. E-mail correspondence, September 2003.
Soparkar, Devang. E-mail survey on Hindu teens, October 2002.
Toropov, Brandon and Father Luke Buckles. *The Complete Idiot's Guide to the World's Religions.* New York, NY: Alpha Books, 1997.
Wangu, Madhu Bazaz. *Hinduism* (*World Religions* series). New York, NY: Facts on File, 2001, 1991.

REFERENCES

About Christianity. <http://christianity.about.com> (March 2004).

Adherents.com. <http://www.adherents.com> (March 2004).

Bowker, John W. *World Religions: The Great Faiths Explored and Explained.* New York, NY: Dorling Kindersley Publisher, 1997.

Ellwood, Robert S., ed. *The Encyclopedia of World Religions.* New York, NY: Facts on File, 1998.

Internet Public Library. <http://www.ipl.org/> (March 2004).

Librarians' Index to the Internet. <http://lii.org> (March 2004).

Mead, Frank S. and Samuel S. Hill. *Handbook of Denominations in the United States.* 11th rev. ed. Craig D. Atwood, ed. Nashville, TN: Abingdon Press, 2001.

The New Encyclopaedia Britannica. 15th ed. Chicago, IL: Encyclopaedia Britannica, Inc., 2002.

Reference Desk.com. <http://www.refdesk.com/> (March 2004).

The World Almanac and Book of Facts. Mahwah, NJ: World Almanac Books, 2003.

The World Book Encyclopedia. 2003 ed. Chicago, IL: World Book, Inc., 2003.

World Religions: Selections from the Sixteen-volume MacMillan Encyclopedia of Religion. New York, NY: MacMillan Library Reference USA, 1997.

INDEX

ABOUT THE EDITORS
AND CONTRIBUTORS

Lynn Andrews (proof reader and researcher), Reference Librarian at Hillsboro (Oregon) Public Library, has worked as proof reader and assistant editor for several professional publications.

L. Kay Carman is a Youth Services Librarian at Hillsboro (Oregon) Public Library and a convert of over thirty years to The Church of Jesus Christ of Latter-day Saints. She currently serves the Church as a Stake Relief Society Education Counselor.

Elaine Daniel is a Library Assistant in the Children's Library of Multnomah County Library (Oregon). She has served as committee chair of a Judaica library and taught in a Jewish preschool.

Jenna Miller is a Youth Services Librarian with the Hennepin County Library (Minnesota). A long-time member of the Lutheran Church, Missouri Synod, she has been involved with music ministry, Sunday school, Bible study teaching, and inter-denominational Christian groups.

Stephen Miller is a librarian with the Anoka County Library system (Minnesota). He has a special interest in early church history, events leading up to the Reformation, and historical and current Christian fiction for teens.

Sue Plaisance, Youth Services Librarian with Hillsboro Public Library (Oregon), is the staff advisor to the Teen Library Council and also has a special interest in selecting materials and creating programs to serve the library's Asian populations.

Carol S. Reich is the Youth Services Manager at the Hillsboro Public Library (Oregon). Her religious training was as a Christian Fundamentalist; she is currently inactive in organized religion. Since the mid-eighties she has worked to establish and expand the fiction and non-fiction library holdings of interest to local religious groups in the Hillsboro community.

Linda Smith holds degrees in Library and Information Science and Middle Eastern History, specializing in Safavid Persia. Her historical subspecialty is the rise of monotheism and the Ancient World. She has experience in academic, art, and public libraries.

Reverend Father **Luke Uhl** is the Chancellor for the Greek Orthodox Metropolis of Denver. He holds degrees in languages, national security affairs, and theology, and has many years of experience as an Orthodox priest. He writes and lectures extensively on the Orthodox faith.

Presvytera **Ruth Uhl** is the Secretary/Registrar for the Greek Orthodox Metropolis of Denver. She holds degrees in classical archaeology and theology. She has served as a Sunday School Administrator, Book Store Director, and oversees the Home Education Institute of a community college.

Michael Wessells is Regional Library Manager for Timberland Regional Library in Hoquiam, Washington. An ordained minister, he is currently pastor of Haven of Rest Pentecostal Holiness Church in nearby Aberdeen. He has lectured widely on the topic of Fundamentalists and Intellectual Freedom.

Rosanne Zajko is a former Eucharistic Minister, catechist, and Vacation Bible School director. She recently completed a two-year church ministry program at St. Charles Seminary in the Archdiocese of Philadelphia and is currently school librarian at Ancillae Assumpta Academy in Wyncote, Pennsylvania.